PENGUIN BOOKS
UNDOCUMENTED

Rejimon Kuttappan is an independent journalist and a migrant rights defender. He was chief reporter for the *Times of Oman* until he was deported back to India in 2017, for exposing human trafficking and modern slavery in the Arab Gulf through a front-page news story.

Rejimon now writes for the Thomson Reuters Foundation (TRF), Equal Times, Migrant Rights, Middle East Eye, *The Hindu*, *Times of India*, *Caravan*, Wire, Leaflet, and various other Indian news portals.

He has done two media fellowships with the International Labour Organization (ILO) on labour migration and human trafficking, and one each with TRF and National Foundation of India (NFI) on forced labour and Gulf migration, respectively.

Rejimon is also a researcher for the Migrant Forum in Asia and has worked as a consultant for the ILO and International Trade Union Confederation (ITUC).

In 2019, he authored an anthology, *Rowing Between Rooftops: The Heroic Fishermen of Kerala Floods*, telling the stories of heroic fishermen who rescued thousands from the 2018 Kerala floods.

Rejimon belongs to the Panan Dalit community of Kerala. Historically, Panans were ballad singers who narrated the acts of the then great warriors and kings. He wishes to continue this storytelling legacy through his books and writing.

Rejimon lives in Kerala and can be followed on @rejitweets. He can be contacted at reji.news@gmail.com.

ADVANCE PRAISE FOR THE BOOK

'In *Undocumented*, Rejimon Kuttappan, a veteran campaigner for migrant rights, provides a gripping and heartbreaking account of the lives of Indian migrants in the Gulf, and the numerous personal and legal hardships they face. From visa struggles to the crushing weight of societal expectations, the suffering recounted in this book is immense, and should concern every Indian deeply.'—**Shashi Tharoor, Indian parliamentarian, writer and former UN Under-Secretary-General**

'This book is written with great clarity, taking the reader along on the many varied journeys of Keralite migrants to Oman. It shows how the marginalization of migrants is intensified by those who are undocumented, whether by design, bastardry, serendipity, or fate. Note, however, that book is more than a collection of migrant stories, which alone are fascinating, heart-rending accounts. Importantly, the book is also about migration journalism. It is also about the author as an investigative journalist, an activist journalist; a caring, humanitarian journalist committed and determined to reveal the underbelly of this migration corridor that suppresses the truth about migrant labour exploitation and tragedy. Thus, the author does not pretend to be an invisible, arm's-length narrator. Throughout the text, he explains and reflects not only upon his own actions and the help he gives to his informants as a participant activist observer, but also on the limitations and liberations of journalism in the region. The author skillfully juxtaposes the individual narratives with the political, economic, and cultural histories that have connected Kerala and Oman for millennia. Deceived and trapped by the kafala system, these are narratives of hardship, mistakes, homesickness, separated families, longing and guilt, struggle, disappointment, and family rejection. There is the gripping story of Majeed's escape, the sham and violent marriage of Jumaila, the dangerous rescue of Sushmitha. Exposing an entrenched culture of corruption, there is Appunni, who stuck to his moral principles and "lost everything". There is the trafficking and enslavement of women, the little-known Arab Spring protests in Oman and the country's long history of rebellions; the Covid-19 pandemic resulting in employer wage theft, illness and death, and forced repatriation home to unemployment and poverty.

Fraternizing with progressive Omani nationals and wending his way through local cultural mores, these are rich ethnographies like a gripping mini-series. And then there are the "monkey visas" and the wisdom to see humour in the face of tragedy that elaborates the human experience.'—**Rajai Ray Jureidini, Professor of Migration Ethics and Human Rights, Hamad Bin Khalifa University, Qatar**

'As a storyteller, Rejimon Kuttappan takes us into the world of migrant workers whose lives are turned upside down as they deal with the status of being "undocumented". He reveals throughout the book how an "undocumented status" is constructed in migration management systems that thrive on the exploitation of labour. He tells of the power of resilience of migrant workers who go through untold challenges to make a living. Artfully, he makes the reader put down the book several times and pick it up again each time while reflecting on the power dynamics, the inequalities, and the systemic and structural deficits that have plagued labour for the longest time. In the end, the story is about heroes who survive despite the odds, and in telling their stories, Rejimon Kuttappan captures the indefatigable spirit of the undocumented.'—**William Gois, Regional Coordinator, Migrant Forum in Asia**

undocumented

STORIES OF
INDIAN
MIGRANTS
IN THE ARAB
GULF

REJIMON KUTTAPPAN

PENGUIN BOOKS

An imprint of Penguin Random House

PENGUIN BOOKS

USA | Canada | UK | Ireland | Australia
New Zealand | India | South Africa | China

Penguin Books is part of the Penguin Random House group of companies
whose addresses can be found at global.penguinrandomhouse.com

Published by Penguin Random House India Pvt. Ltd
4th Floor, Capital Tower 1, MG Road,
Gurugram 122 002, Haryana, India

Penguin
Random House
India

First published in Penguin Books by Penguin Random House India 2021

ISBN 9780143451471

Typeset in Adobe Garamond Pro by Manipal Technologies Limited, Manipal
Printed at Replika Press Pvt. Ltd, India

www.penguin.co.in

MIX
Paper from
responsible sources
FSC® C016779

As you are reading this, thousands of undocumented migrant workers are trapped, enslaved and exploited in the Arab Gulf. While some yearn to return, others live a meaningless life in deserts and shanty houses, trapped without hope. This book is dedicated to them.

Contents

Introduction

In 1963, Manikuttan, a Keralite, managed to board an illegal dhow from Daman Diu heading to Iran via 'Dufai'. He was dropped off near the Muscat coast. He swam to the shore and from there, managed to board a jeep and reach 'Dufai'. He was fifteen-years-old then, and there was no United Arab Emirates. The six Emirates were headed by warring Sheikhs.

Manikuttan received his first passport in Dubai, just prior to his first journey back home, three years after his arrival in the place of his dreams. He continued to live and work in Dubai for the next twenty-five years along with many from his home state, contributing to the creation of 'Dufai'.

Six years after Manikuttan went to 'Dufai', his neighbour Altaf followed. He too managed to board an illegal dhow to 'Dufai' from Bombay. In the middle of the sea, one of their fellow voyagers died. They tied the dead man to a stone and dropped him in the sea. One early morning, Altaf was dropped near Khor Farkkan along with the others. They swam to the shore, and soon, made their way to the city of their dreams. At that time too, there was no UAE. Altaf's first passport was made there as well.

Manikuttan and Altaf are among the Gulf-migrant workers from Kerala, who managed to make a life for themselves by going to the UAE. In that era, 'Gulf' was a magic word for many from Kerala who wished to make their fortunes in the paradise which offered them work and income.

Cut to 1993. Appunni flew to Muscat from Kerala via Bombay. He was unlucky. Despite flying to his dreamland with a valid passport, life took a different turn. He became an undocumented/illegal worker and led a life fraught with danger and suffering for twenty-years, before finally returning home empty-handed through an amnesty scheme announced by Oman in 2015. After slaving for years while faithfully remitting money to his family, he returned only to find he was no longer welcome at home, as he had not made money like his neighbours who were also working in the Gulf had done. He now lives in a white Maruti 800, which he calls his 'coffin'.

If Manikuttan, Altaf and Appunni, managed to come back legally, Majeed could not. There was neither an amnesty nor enough papers to prove that he was an Indian. Finally, with the help of a few Bangladeshi and Pakistani friends, he crossed the mountains of the Oman–UAE border at night, hoodwinking the border police. He flew back to Kerala via Bombay.

If Manikuttan, Altaf, Appunni and Majeed had migrated in search of jobs, Jumaila, a Keralite, went to Oman as the wife of an Omani 'sheikh'. She gave birth to sons who were Omani citizens. But she had to leave her husband's house after years of abuse as he had started to traffic her. She was courageous enough to get a divorce from her Arab husband while working as a domestic worker, but a twist of fate left her undocumented.

Manikuttan, Altaf, Appunni, Jumaila and Majeed had not been duped when they had migrated. Sushmitha was. She was trafficked, kept in a brothel, abused, and then sold to an Arab employer who confined her within four walls and exploited her.

Prascedha had run away from her employer, lived with a friend, and given birth to a boy. Unfortunately, neither she nor her son had documents to prove that they were Indians. Then, more recently, there was Valsala who told me the story of how she was stranded on an Iranian island due to the COVID-19 outbreak in 2020.

In telling their stories, I have covered sixty years of the history of the Arab Gulf, mainly Oman. Each of their stories is just the tip of the iceberg. Each is but an example of many others, every one of them having stories to tell that were similar in some respects but ultimately unique—of leaving their homelands to seek a fortune, but life taking a turn, making some of them 'illegals' in the eyes of local governments.

These are stories that are unheard and untold. Every story has its hidden nuances and runs the gamut of emotions—from happiness to sadness, disgust, fear, surprise, anger, and anxiety.

Happy reading.

Rejimon Kuttappan

1

On a Persian Uru

It was my dream to earn Rs 5,000. I had promised my widowed mother that I would rebuild our gutted house. I was seventeen, and the fact that I was a mere boy from a tiny village in southern Kerala did not deter me.

I was a daring leader in my locality. I was ready to take on the world . . . For this, I had to leave my village and find my own way in the world.

That I had to clamber on to a Persian Uru (wooden dhow), holding on to a knotted rope to get on board at around 8 p.m. in the Daman and Diu, did not deter me. It was a craft that was returning to Iran via Dubai.

It was not the easiest thing to do. Every time I placed my feet on the wooden dhow to push myself up, I failed. But I was not ready to give in. I was well aware that this was my climb towards success. And if I fell, I was going to lose my only chance at escaping poverty.

So, I held on to the rope tightly. I felt my palms burn against the wet and slippery rope. I slipped in my first, second, and third attempts.

I remembered my mother saying that if we failed at something on the first attempt, then we would have to fail two more times—success would come only after that. But that saying did not hold for me in this scenario. I managed to climb up in the third attempt itself. When I reached the bulwark, I pushed myself into the boat.

Even though it was a short climb, I was gasping for breath. I lay down on the deck near the main mast, with my arms and legs stretched. I could see the stars glittering in the sky. They seemed to be congratulating me on my success.

I was neither aware of the time, nor did I bother to check it. I was Aladdin, already on my magic carpet, and it was going to take me to Dubai.

These were the words of seventy-three-year-old Manikuttan, one of the first south Keralites who dared to migrate to the Arab Gulf in 1963, at a time when his neighbours had not even thought of it.

While talking to me at his home in Panenkettu, a backwater village near Attingal in Kerala, Manikuttan was visibly excited as he recalled his struggle and eventual success, all of which happened some fifty-six years ago.

As he narrated his story, I thought that he had proved himself to be a better storyteller than anyone I had met. Even at this age, he could list the incidents of his life chronologically, without missing out on any emotions that he felt when he had gone through those experiences.

Manikuttan is one of the few who had migrated to 'Dufai' in those days. To Keralites, Dubai is still 'Dufai', and for the Arab employers, all Keralites are 'Malabaris', even if one hails from central or south Kerala.

I am from central Travancore but when I migrated to Oman towards the end of 2006, I was also addressed as 'Malabari' by my Arab colleagues, especially by the more senior ones.

While a few see it as a disrespectful way of addressing someone, I have never felt that way. When you say that you are from India, they say, *'Masha Allah Hind!'* It is never 'Bharat' or 'India' for an Arab. It is always 'Hind'.

Malabar is the northern part of Kerala. Arabs had trade ties with people from this region, whom they called Malabaris, from the fourth century AD. Researchers say that the very name, Malabar (*mali*, mountain; *bar*, country), was given by the Arabs.

According to *Tuhfat al-Mujahidin*, a historical book written by Shaykh Zainuddin Makhdum in the sixteenth century, detailing the struggles of the Malabar Muslims against the Portuguese colonizers in India: ' . . . in the early years of Islam, some Arab dervishes bound for Ceylon lost their way and reached the coast of Malabar.'

In his book *Early Arab Contact with South Asia*, Indian historian Khaliq Ahmad Nizami, claims that the ruler of Malabar, Samri, was so deeply impressed by the Arab traders that he embraced Islam and even visited Arabia incognito. He died there, leaving instructions to his companions to work for the propagation of Islam in Malabar.

Two years later, Sharaf b. Malik and Malik b. Dinar, two Persian religious scholars, visited Malabar and built mosques at Kadamkor, Kolam, Baknor, Manjbor, Kanjarkot, Hailimarwi, Jarfatan, Darfatan, and other places in the seventh century AD itself. It was due to their efforts that the Muslims settled in Malabar and their population increased.

Historical evidence also points to a close connection between the Arabs and the Keralites over centuries.

'We took a different path. At that time, we didn't even have a passport office in Kerala. We never even thought of obtaining a passport to migrate,' said Manikuttan.

In Manikuttan's village, people had started migrating in the 1940s. Many made money and were enjoying better living standards migrating to Singapore, Brunei, Java and Malaysia.

'But the Arab Gulf was not on their minds. We can't blame them. Oil had not been found in the Arab Gulf yet; they were only traders of pearls and dates. What was the benefit in migrating there?' asked Manikuttan rather rhetorically.

By the time Manikuttan decided to migrate to the Arab Gulf, oil had been discovered with British and American help, and those countries had just started developing.

In the United Arab Emirates (UAE) and Qatar, the export of oil started in and around the 1960s. In Oman, it was in the late 1960s. Saudi Arabia, Bahrain, and Kuwait, on the other hand, had started exporting oil as early as the 1940s.

For the majority of Keralites, Arab Gulf meant Dubai, their dreamland, where they could earn Arab gold (*Arabi Ponnu*).

Interestingly, when Manikuttan went to Dubai at the end of 1963, the UAE, as we know it today, did not exist, nor did the Arab Gulf countries.

If we have to tell the history of Dubai, then we have to start from the entry of the English East India Company into Iran and the Arab Gulf at the beginning of the seventeenth century, to set up factories to ease the trade with India.[1]

According to the records from The National Archives in the UK, English traders from the East India Company set up factories for the trade of spices, tea, and linen in Jask, Bandar Abbas, Shiraz, and Ispahan—all Iranian ports and towns—from 1614 onwards, so that they could trade with India.

Interestingly, until 1684, all the factories in Iran were subordinate to Surat, where much of the East India Company's trading was centred. Later, they shifted to Bombay due to the aggression of the Marathas, who had plundered Surat twice. Bombay, however, was less easy to reach than Surat, and the factories in Iran, in practice, therefore, acquired a lot more autonomy.

By the 1720s, the English had become the dominant trading power in the Gulf. The political position in Persia, however, was unstable and the Company's trade suffered. In 1759, the factory buildings at Gombroon were destroyed by the French, and the Company moved its headquarters to Basra, where a factory had been established in 1723. To retain a foothold in Persia, a factory was established at Bushire. This replaced Gombroon as the centre of Persian trade, the factors reporting initially to Basra but, from 1778, to Bombay directly.

And in 1873, control of the Iran and Arab Gulf territories was passed from the Government of Bombay to the Government of India.

Unfortunately, Manikuttan's first attempt to reach Dubai failed. He had been fooled.

After coming to Mumbai with big dreams of reaching Dubai, he worked as an assistant to carriers smuggling liquor and other goods from Daman and Diu to Mumbai; he was waiting for a chance to get to Dubai.

'A Keralite from my village controlled the smuggling business in Mumbai. He employed me as an assistant to accompany women who were smuggling liquor and other items from Daman and Diu. The women would sneak the contraband under their sarees and bring it into Mumbai. They just needed to have "male" company,' Manikuttan told me.

According to Manikuttan, the crew in the Persian boat he was in, sold to locals illegally to earn some extra money.

'I was happy to accompany the women, despite earning a pittance from the smuggler. I completed one trip a day and could fall asleep just about anywhere. Nothing really mattered,' Manikuttan added.

By travelling to Daman and Diu frequently, Manikuttan learned how to emigrate to Dubai. One day, he found an agent who charged Rs 200—a big sum at the time—to help him travel to Dubai by boat. Manikuttan had some money, which he had brought from home and some that he had saved up from his previous job. Manikuttan paid the money. In return, he was given a handwritten receipt, which had only Manikuttan's name and a signature.

Manikuttan was told to hand it over to the person on the boat when he boarded. He felt excited, as though he had already reached Dubai. On the day of his travel, he accompanied the women carriers to Daman and Diu but did not return.

Manikuttan reached Daman and Diu at around 4 p.m. He was told by the agent that the uru would come only by 9 p.m.

'I had five hours. Every minute felt like an hour to me. Like many others there, I couldn't hold in my excitement. Finally, I saw the uru nearing the shore. But to reach the shore, we had to get into a smaller boat. I ran first. There were many others there with me. Some were speaking Malayalam and some were not, but I didn't care who they were. I didn't ask their names. I didn't smile. I was waiting to get the signal to run towards a small boat as soon as it came . . .' Manikuttan said.

According to Manikuttan, it was a rocky shore. So, it was easy for them to hide from the coastal police.

The agent had told them that a blinking torch light at around 10 p.m. would be the signal from the uru, heralding the arrival of the small boat.

'We waited anxiously. Interestingly, as none of us had a watch, we didn't know whether it was ten or past ten. However, we were hopeful . . . we trusted the agent,' Manikuttan said.

Finally, they saw a flash of a torch from afar. Under the moonlight, they saw a small boat nearing the shore.

'We ran frantically towards the boat. I expected to see about twenty people waiting to board, but to my surprise, there were at least thirty, many hiding behind the rocks on the shore . . .' Manikuttan said.

Manikuttan boarded the boat with the others. When the small boat reached the uru, Manikuttan was the first to climb the knotted rope. It took him three attempts to board the uru.

Manikuttan and the others were only given one meal a day throughout the journey.

'We got two small rotis and a glass of water. We had to adjust with the meagre meal. I was okay with that. My only aim was to reach Dubai,' Manikuttan said.

According to Manikuttan, the sea was rough. Manikuttan remembered how they worried about whether the uru would sink in the turbulent waters.

There were around forty people on that boat—many, dream-chasers from north Kerala. On the third day, Manikuttan and the others were told to jump into the water and wade ashore as they had reached Dubai.

'We were all excited. We saw the white sand, just like what we had imagined. We jumped and swam. But when we reached the shore, we realized that it was not Dubai, but the Rann of Kutch in Gujarat,' Manikuttan said.

Manikuttan had been doubtful from the very beginning, as the agent had said that it would take at least five days to reach Dubai. Since the uru was caught in heavy wind, Manikuttan presumed that they had simply reached early. Manikuttan felt as if all those stars that had congratulated him when he boarded the uru had vanished.

Manikuttan and the others were hungry. But there was no food for them. Interestingly, there were only two people from south Kerala—Manikuttan and another person who he had met in Daman and Diu. All the others were from the north of Kerala, and according to Manikuttan, they spoke a different dialect of Malayalam, which was difficult for him and his new friend to understand.

The language barrier was an issue, too. 'We realized that they wanted to leave us behind and travel to Mumbai. But my friend was a sort of gangster. He warned the others against leaving them behind. He took off his shirt, revealing a big scar on the left side of his abdomen. It looked like a scar caused by a knife injury. He declared himself a gangster and said that if they were planning to leave us behind, they would suffer,' Manikuttan said.

'They agreed to take us along. We walked for hours to reach a railway station. We somehow reached Mumbai by train, only to be left in the lurch again, struggling for even a cup of tea. We looked for an agent who could smuggle us to Dubai,' Manikuttan added.

Following the failed attempt, Manikuttan didn't have the kind of money to pay an agent. However, he was not disappointed.

'I was always looking for a chance,' Manikuttan said. And the day came soon enough.

'I was in Daman and Diu. Somebody told me that there was a new Persian dhow taking people to Dubai. Without a moment's delay, I ran to the shore. I didn't have a single penny in my trouser pocket,' Manikuttan said, adding that he was confident about finding a berth.

The dream-chasers had to board a small boat and travel for around ten minutes to reach the uru.

Manikuttan also did the same. He jumped on to a boat and begged the sailor to move closer to the big dhow. The sailor agreed.

'When I reached the dhow, I just jumped into the water and caught hold of the rope. I used all my energy to climb up. This time I was a bit faster. I reached on time and jumped on to the dhow. There were a few north Keralites on it, and the sailors were Iranians.

They asked for the slip which we get from the agent once we pay him. I had not paid any agent. Where would I get a slip from? So, I lied and said that I lost it. They were not ready to believe me. But in a few minutes, when the others said, "Let the boy continue the journey with us," they agreed,' Manikuttan added.

According to Manikuttan, they were served one roti, a glass of tea, and a tumbler of water each day.

'That's it. They wouldn't give us anything more. They didn't have large quantities of food and water in store. It would take around seven to ten days to reach the Gulf shore—maybe a few days more if the sea was rough. We had to survive all those hurdles. So, they couldn't provide more food than that,' Manikuttan said.

Those seven days were like hell according to Manikuttan.

'We would lie on board. Most of the time we would be tired. Even though we, the dream-chasers, wanted to get to know each other, we were too physically tired due to the limited food to start a conversation. None of us bothered to get to know each other,' Manikuttan said.

On the afternoon of the seventh day, the dhow reached the shores of Oman. The sailors told us that we should get down and find our own way to Dubai.

'I could see my dreamland. The land where I would work and earn Arab gold (*Arabi Ponnu*). As the dhow neared the shore, those who could swim jumped into the water and swam towards the shore. I was among the first lot. Those who didn't know how to swim would have to wait,' Manikuttan said.

When those who knew how to swim jumped first, the dhow was able to get closer to the shore, allowing those who couldn't swim to reach the land from the shallower waters.

While Manikuttan and his friends had a safe journey, many others who followed were not as lucky.

Mohammed Altaf, seventy-three, a neighbour of Manikuttan, dared to illegally emigrate to Dubai in 1969 on a dhow when he was merely seventeen.

Upon reaching Mumbai, Altaf was taken to the Rann of Kutch, a marshy land in Gujarat, from where they boarded the dhow to the Arab Gulf.

'We couldn't do it during the day, so, we had to wait till sunset. And we were told that when the dhow arrived, they would light a lamp as a signal to get into a small boat and row towards the dhow. But that night it didn't happen. I think there was police patrolling that night. So, we had to return to Mumbai,' Altaf said.

However, Altaf was not ready to give up. He tried his luck again after ten days.

There he was again, with a few others, at the Rann of Kutch. They waited for the signal from the boat from 8 p.m.

It was around 2 a.m. when they saw the signal—a light blinking in the waters far from the shore.

'We ran to the small boats in a rush to board the dhow. We boarded the dhow by climbing a knotted rope,' Altaf said, adding that they were least bothered about the facilities on the boat.

According to Altaf, they woke up only the next afternoon and were provided a roti, tea, and a tumbler of water.

'The sea was rough on the first day itself. And the uru we were travelling in was a small one. Not long after, seawater began to enter the dhow. The sailors used three motors to pump out the water. On top of this, it was raining heavily. Most of us gave in to seasickness and threw up. Soon, we were all too tired and slept on our vomit . . .'

'Three days later, the food stopped. We were surviving on a glass of water each day. Famished and nauseated, we kept throwing up. However, as a group, we learned to ignore that, too. Rainwater would wash us, then we would vomit again, and sleep there itself,' Altaf added.

Normally, in a week, a dhow from Gujarat would reach the Gulf coast. However, it took thirteen days for the dhow that Altaf was on.

'In between, the dhow's engine got damaged. And due to heavy winds, we lost our direction. One day, we were even told that we were nearing the Pakistan coast. Unfortunately, a person who was with us died due to illness. The sailors tied a stone to his body with a rope and threw it into the sea. What else could be done? We were not even in a mental state to cry. And on the morning of the thirteenth day, we were told that we had reached Khor Fakkan in Sharjah,' Altaf added.

Khor Fakkan is a city, an exclave of the Emirate of Sharjah, located on the east coast of the UAE, facing the Gulf of Oman, and geographically surrounded by the Emirate of Fujairah.

'The moment we reached our dreamland, we tried to jump, causing the boat to turn upside down. We swam with all our energy. When we reached the shore, we collapsed,' Altaf added.

According to Altaf, they reached the shore at around 6 a.m. but all of them slept there itself till the afternoon, from sheer tiredness.

'It would have been around 3 p.m., when we got up and walked some 2 kilometres to a small town. We found a small cafeteria there. They provided us with free food. A good-hearted Arab driver agreed to drop us to Dubai. We paid a sum of Rs 150 for this. During those days, the Indian rupee could be traded there. In Dubai, I got a job as a plumber on the first day itself. I worked for several companies, did some independent jobs, stayed for eighteen years, and then returned for good,' Altaf said, adding that AED 5 (now Rs 100) was his average monthly salary then.

While Altaf and his group were dropped off at Khor Fakkan, Manikuttan was not that fortunate. He and his friends were dropped on the Oman coast.

The Oman police were waiting for them. They were arrested and taken to jail.

'We were given a roti, a glass of water, and a mat to sleep on. The policemen were nice to us. But we were anxious because they were not talking about our release. None of us knew their language either, but we were lucky. The next day, we were told to board a jeep that was heading to the Oman–UAE border. At the border, they told us to get down and find our way,' Manikuttan said.

Manikuttan came across a jeep loaded with dates. When he asked for help, the Arab driver was generous enough to take them across the border. Without a second thought, Manikuttan and his group boarded the vehicle.

'I was feeling hungry. So, I stole a few dates from the jeep. I ate some and saved some in my pocket for later,' Manikuttan said.

According to Manikuttan, the Arab driver seemed to know quite clearly where to drop the Indians in Dubai, especially the Malabaris.

'In hardly an hour, we reached our dream city in our dream land—Dubai,' Manikuttan said.

They were dropped in front of a hotel named Deluxe, run by a Muslim from north Kerala.

The hotel was a haven for those who made it to Dubai. The owner would provide food and shelter, which could be reimbursed later when the men started earning.

'He was kind enough to give us food and shelter without asking for money,' Manikuttan said, adding that, unfortunately, he had forgotten that good man's name.

The very next day, Manikuttan started to look for a job. He was told that there was some construction work going on in Bur Dubai, which was around 20 km from the Deluxe Hotel. To reach there, he had to pay 0.5 dirhams. He didn't have that much money either.

However, there was a Malayali from north Kerala heading to Bur Dubai. He had 1 dirham with him. He shared his money with Manikuttan for the trip.

'Those days, everyone used to share money, food, shelter, or whatever was in need. People were not greedy like they are today,' Manikuttan added.

Reaching Bur Dubai, Manikuttan met a white man sitting in a jeep and talking to Asian workers.

'There was a long queue. I didn't wait for my turn. I just ran to the front of the queue and asked for a job. He asked for my name. I said it was Manikuttan. He called me Tony. He said his name was Edwin Charles and asked whether I knew carpentry. I said yes. He told me that I would get AED 15 per month as salary, and that I could join immediately. I didn't know anything about carpentry. But I decided to give it a go,' Manikuttan said.

After fifteen days of working as a carpenter, Manikuttan realized it was not for him. So, he approached Charles again and asked for a different job.

'Charles was a bit angry. But he listened to my request and gave me a job as his assistant. From the next day onwards, I joined him on his jeep carrying the survey equipment,' Manikuttan said, adding that his salary was cut to AED 8. However, he used to get AED 12, including overtime.

Manikuttan was involved in the work that was taking place to construct the Dubai port, tunnel, and the dry dock. He learned driving in between, became assistant foreman, then foreman, and finally retired as an officer-in-charge with a salary of AED 3500 in 1988.

Since Manikuttan was referred to as 'Tony' by his boss Elden, he gave his children English names—Don, Dolly, and Daisy.

When asked why he did so, Manikuttan said it was a way of expressing gratitude to Elden, who played a vital role in his life.

Manikuttan came home in 1966 for the first time, on a ship from Dubai.

He had successfully acquired a passport, and his company provided him with a visa as well. He returned after his first holidays on a plane.

Getting a passport was a difficult task as there were no passport offices in Kerala at the time. So, Manikuttan had to approach the Indian Embassy in Abu Dhabi and get a chit, which he mailed home to his mother, who handed it over to someone to make his application for a passport. 'In a few days, mother sent me the passport number by post. It took weeks to reach me here. When I handed over the number to the embassy, they printed me a passport. With that passport, I flew back home,' Manikuttan said.

When Manikuttan and Altaf reached the Gulf in the 1960s, the *kafala* system (or bonded labour) was the new practice.

In the early decades of the eighteenth century, the fall of the Safavid dynasty in Iran and the collapse of the Ya'ariba dynasty of Oman created disorder and a political vacuum in the Arab Gulf. Maritime Arab communities began to migrate from inner Arabia and Oman to the coast and resume their commercial activities.[2]

They established themselves on new sites that became the nucleus of the modern Arab Gulf states. The three leading political entities that emerged in southeastern Arabia in the early eighteenth century were the Bani Yas federations, Qawasim, and the Al Bu Said dynasty with Muscat as its capital. The current rulers of Abu Dhabi and Dubai belong to Bani Yas federations. The Dubai rulers from the Al Maktoum family descended from the Al Bu

Falasah (now known as Al-Falasi) section of the Bani Yas, a tribal federation.

In 1833, a large group of the Al Bu Falasah section of the Bani Yas seceded to Dubai under the leadership of Maktoum bin Butti bin Sohal, escaping the violence of Sheikh Khalifah of Abu Dhabi.

Meanwhile, the Qawasim tribe members who were ruling the area with their main base at Ras al Khaimah (now in the UAE), became successful traders and gained ascendancy among the tribes of the area as a very powerful federation.

However, when they grew stronger, they started to challenge Oman's dominance at sea and wrest from them a greater share of the Arab Gulf, and the Indian and African trade, which resulted in a struggle for pre-eminence between them and the Al Bu Said rulers in Oman.

And the English traders were in trouble, too, as the Qawasim appeared to threaten maritime peace and the sea routes in the region.

In 1806, an agreement was made between the English East Indian Company and the Qawasim rulers that there would be peace between the two sides and that they would respect each other's property and subjects.[3,4]

Despite this agreement, attacks on British shipping channels continued and gradually increased. In 1820, the English East India Company made the General Treaty of Peace with the sheikhs of the Arab coast by which the rulers agreed to a cessation of disturbances at sea forever.

Although some positive effects were demonstrated after 1820 by a boom in the pearl trade and the absence of attacks on foreign shipping, the treaty did not, in practice, prevent complete warfare at sea between the Arab tribes.

Therefore, the British persuaded the rulers of Abu Dhabi, Dubai, Sharjah, and Ajman to sign a Maritime Truce in 1835, banning all hostilities and acts of war at sea during the pearling season. Because of this truce, the area became known in British political documents as the Trucial Coast, sometimes referred to as 'Trucial Oman'.

Slowly, the years between the two World Wars witnessed increased British involvement in the internal affairs of the Trucial States.

After the Second World War, Britain began to play an even more active internal role with the introduction of a Political Agency in Sharjah that was later transferred to Dubai in 1953. As the production and the export of oil started in the early sixties, the importance of the Trucial States in the British strategy underwent a dramatic transformation.

Although the British left India in 1947, the Trucial States remained vital to British imperial interests in their own right. This in turn led to a fundamental change in the traditional British policy of non-interference to one of active involvement in local affairs.

In 1952, the Trucial States Council, a consultative and advisory body of the rulers of the then seven Emirates, was formed under the chairmanship of the British Political Agent to promote the idea of a union among them. And in 1965, it was taken over by the seven Emirate rulers themselves, giving rise to the Trucial States Development Council. The British Political Agent stepped down in 1966.

The Council extended its activities to internal welfare and accelerated the area's development. In the course of its numerous meetings, the sheikhs were able to create a common cause that paved the way for the subsequent emergence of the UAE in 1971.

The production of oil in Abu Dhabi in 1962, and later in Dubai and Sharjah, placed the area in a prominent position in world economic and political affairs.

The kafala system took form in the 1950s to regulate the relationship between employers and the migrant workers in many countries in the Arab Gulf.

It remains the routine practice in Bahrain, Kuwait, Oman, Qatar, Saudi Arabia, and the UAE, and also in the Arab states of Jordan and Lebanon.

The sponsorship system's economic objective was to provide temporary, rotating labour that could be rapidly brought into the country in times of economic boom and let go during the less-affluent periods.

Under the kafala system, a migrant worker's immigration status is legally bound to an individual employer or sponsor (*kafeel*) throughout their contract period.

The migrant worker cannot enter the country, transfer employment, nor leave the country for any reason, without first obtaining an explicit written permission from the kafeel.

Throughout his stay, the worker remains tied to the kafeel who sponsored his trip to the country. The kafeel must report to the immigration authorities if the migrant worker leaves his employment and must also ensure that the worker is sent back home after the contract period ends. Even the flight back home is sponsored by the kafeel.

Often, the kafeel exerts further control over the migrant workers by confiscating their passports and travel documents, despite legislation in some countries declaring this practice illegal, as this creates a situation where the migrant worker is completely dependent upon his kafeel for livelihood and residency. The power that the kafala system delegates to the sponsor over the migrant worker, has been likened to a contemporary form of slavery. The kafeel meets their labour needs in the context of immense control and unchecked leverage over workers, creating an environment ripe with human rights violations and erosion of labour standards.

Inherent in the kafala system is the assumption that workers are considered temporary contract labour, as reflected in the Gulf Cooperation Council's (GCC) official use of 'guest workers' and 'expatriate manpower' to refer to migrant workers. The kafala system serves a social purpose by emphasizing the temporary nature of a migrant worker's presence in the country, so that even if the worker is present for a long time, he/she doesn't acquire the rights of citizenship, with its alleged negative impact on social cohesiveness, etc.

The restrictive immigration policies of the Kafala System Act in theory is to limit the stay of overseas workers to the duration of their contract. Non-compliance by both employers and migrant workers in response to demand for labour has led to a significant minority of long-term or permanent residents, along with a number of second-generation migrants and the development of irregular employment.

Thus, in reality, migrant workers may remain for years—vulnerable in this situation—living with the threat of unpaid wages, arrest, detention, and ultimate deportation, should they complain or leave.

If the migrant worker decides to leave the workplace without the employer's written consent, he may be charged with 'absconding', which is a criminal offence. Even if a worker leaves in response to abuse, he remains at risk of being treated as a criminal rather than receiving appropriate victim support. The migrant worker is unable to leave the country as this would require the employer's consent and the possession of a passport.

The migrant worker is constrained further by the structure of the kafala system to make a complaint or seek protection.

In all GCC countries and Lebanon, the Ministry of Interiors rather than the Ministry of Labour is responsible for managing employment, along with the sponsor. This structure contributes to the securitization of migration, and denies migrant workers the cover afforded by protections of domestic labour laws, and the opportunity of entering a labour dispute process to address their complaints. The destination countries' governments' focus is on the costly, bureaucratic, and flawed restrictive immigration regulations, rather than on the plight of the migrant workers tied to a sponsor.

Altaf worked for seven years continuously and returned only in 1976 after organizing a passport through his relatives in Kerala. He continued to be in touch with all those who were on that dhow and according to him, only he remains alive now.

'The rest have passed away. We went to the Gulf when those countries were in their nascent stages of growth. And interestingly, we returned when the others started to arrive there. But I have no regrets. We are always thankful to the Arab Gulf for providing us with an opportunity to work there and make a better living,' Altaf added.

Altaf is married and has three children. He runs a hollow bricks workshop near his home and is happy with his life even though illness is creeping upon him.

Manikuttan is also doing well financially. He runs a cement retail shop in his village and owns some land as well.

Only a few like Altaf remain in Kerala, who hail from those days to tell their stories of how they migrated on dhows to the Arab Gulf in the 1960s.

If Manikuttan and Altaf were lucky not to be trapped in the kafala system in its premature state, many who have gone after them have suffered by being caught within the confines of the kafala system.

Many rush to the Gulf to make money. But only a few make it. The majority return empty-handed and shattered, with scars on their minds and bodies.

2

This White Car Will Be
My Coffin . . .

If Manikuttan and Altaf migrated to the Arab Gulf and
returned to Kerala before residency and work permit laws
became strict, Appunni was a 'loser' who got trapped in the
document/no document difficulty for about twenty-two years.

When I met Appunni in front of a government hospital
in a village near Kollam, Kerala, in June 2018, he looked
weary.

His shirt was crumpled, and his white dhoti was yellowish,
as if it had not been washed properly. He had a thin, patchy
beard. His eyes looked dull.

However, Appunni was looking smarter than he did
when I met him last in Oman, in 2015.

People should look healthy and happy when they are
with their dear ones at home, shouldn't they? But Appunni
didn't appear so.

I had come to Kollam on my bike on a reporting trip.
I knew Appunni's house was near Kollam.

I had not met him since 2015. But we had not lost touch. We would occasionally talk over the phone even when I was still in Oman and he had returned to Kerala.

He was always thankful to me for helping him while he was in Oman. Once in a while, he would call me and ask about my well-being.

After all the greetings, he would tell me, 'Reji, would you please help me get a job visa?' I used to ignore the question, since I didn't want him to come to Oman again. But I never wondered why he wanted to come to Oman again.

When I arrived near the hospital, I rang his number. I saw a white Maruti 800cc car coming towards me and parking. It was Appunni.

It was the car he had bought with the money I had raised for his survival. There were some scratches on the left bumper and door. The black bumper guard looked grey. The tyres were worn out.

Appunni stepped out of the car and came towards me. He hugged me. In Kerala, people don't usually hug each other, especially in public.

However, Appunni and me, having been in an Arab country for a long time, had picked up the etiquette of that country in the manner of our greeting each other.

Greetings come in all forms in the Arab world. Touching the shoulder, kissing the shoulder, shoulder to shoulder, handshaking, hugging, kissing, and then there are nose salutations, too.

Kisses are often exchanged by people who haven't seen each other for a long time.

Greetings are followed by inquiries about ones' health and family members. Getting straight to the point or getting down to business is regarded as abrupt and impolite. Interestingly, no one knows at what point in time these greetings took shape, or whether they emanated from the region or were imported from other places. But it's lovely to watch and experience.

After we exchanged greetings, I spotted a towel and a new Hamam soap, still in its wrapper, on the dashboard, while placing my backpack on the bonnet of Appunni's car. I was surprised.

I asked Appunni why he was keeping a towel and a bath soap in the car. He said, 'I don't live at home, Reji. I sleep in this car, here. This white metal box is my home. And it will be my coffin, too . . .' he said.

It was worrying for me to hear that. Being in his hometown, he was not staying in his home?

Before asking him why, the memories of Appunni talking to me when I first met him in Muscat, came to mind.

I met him for the first time on the shores of the Arabian Sea in Muscat in 2015. At that time, all he desperately wanted, was to go home.

He was wearing a white shirt with black stripes and torn, faded blue jeans. His sandals were old and didn't have buckles. I could see that he was struggling to walk with them on the sand. But he was pretending that everything was fine.

While walking, unexpectedly, he told me, 'Reji, do you know what is on the other side of this sea? It is Kollam, my home, my sweet home. Some days, I come here in the evening and sit. On the other side, there is my home. I have even thought of swimming across this sea to my home.'

He continued, 'My daughter, her child, my loving wife, my boy . . . my small home . . . it's heaven . . .'

Yes, he exhibited a desperate longing to go home. He had left his home when his daughter was ten years old. She got married off in 2005. He couldn't go to his hometown even for her wedding. He had tried. He had landed in India, too. But he was taken back, forcefully.

And now, meeting him in his hometown, Appunni is telling me that he is not living in his home.

I finally asked, why. 'Reji, I am an unwelcome guest in my own home. I stayed elsewhere for twenty-two years. It was not that I was absconding. I was earning whatever I could and remitting it home. They survived on my money. But when I came back with so much love and needing to be loved, they saw me as if I were an unwanted guest . . . so, I left . . .'

He paused, then said, 'Reji, do you remember, I asked you for a visa after I returned . . . you probably thought that I just wanted to return to live in Oman? No, it was not that at all. I wanted to die in Oman so that I could prevent my family from facing an embarrassing situation . . . I am a shame for them, Reji . . .'

In Kerala, the first question anybody would ask a migrant worker who has come on leave would be . . . '*Eppo vannu . . . eppolaanu thirichu pokunnathu* . . . (When did you come . . . when are you going back . . .?)'

If the answer had a date of return, then all would be happy. Even the near and dear ones. But if there was no date of return, then there would be long faces.

Even if a migrant worker said that he would go only after three months, it would raise eyebrows and prompt, supplementary questions would follow, 'All well there? Your job is safe? Will you be able to stay back till then without salary . . . ?'

However, what happened in Appunni's case is different. Appunni himself has the answer.

'Neighbours who had migrated to the Arab Gulf had built mansions and bought big cars. I couldn't do anything. My house is the same. Some small renovations were done. That's it. You know who can mint money in the Arab Gulf, right?' Appunni asked me.

Yes, in the Arab Gulf, a monthly wage earner will not earn much. However, those who do business, prosper. The kafala system helps businessmen to make a surplus profit by exploiting migrant workers. Additionally, even as the common man believes that Arab countries have strict criminal laws and punishments, on the ground, laws are flouted very easily. If you are a businessman with 'good' connections, you can mint money.

And if you are involved in visa trading, human trafficking—yes, human trafficking of men and women workers—or the liquor business in the Arab Gulf, in a year or two, you can build a home worth crores in Kerala and drive a luxury car.

After working as an irregular worker in Oman for some twenty-two years, Appunni was unable to earn anything substantial.

Appunni had gone to Oman in 1993 with high hopes. I asked, 'When exactly did you go?' Appunni replied, 'Reji, it was on 7 July 1993.'

Yes, Appunni was precise in telling the date of his arrival, but when I met him in Muscat, he had been uncertain about his return date.

Appunni was a driver; he got the job through his cousin brothers in an oil company in Oman.

He was not a direct employee of the petroleum company. He was employed by a single Arab employer who had a transporting contract with the petroleum company.

Like other Arab Gulf countries, Oman also practises the kafala system. Appunni had to hand over his passport to his Arab sponsor upon arrival, which eventually trapped him.

The holding back of workers' travel documents by employers is seen as an indication of forced labour by the International Labour Organisation (ILO) Convention, 1930 (No. 29).

Forced labour is 'all work or service which is exacted from any person under the threat of a penalty and for which the person has not offered himself or herself voluntarily.'[1]

This definition consists of three elements. The first one is work or service and refers to all types of work occurring in any activity, industry, or sector including in the informal economy.

The second one is the menace of penalty, which refers to a wide range of penalties used to compel someone to work.

And the third one is 'offered voluntarily' which refers to the free and informed consent of a worker to take a job and his or her freedom to leave at any time.

In Appunni's case, it was forced labour. Like any other migrant worker, as I commented earlier, Appunni was forced to hand over his passport to his sponsor, which restricted his freedom to travel.

ILO says that migrant workers may be coerced into withholding their passports or identity documents. The employer may hold the workers' identity documents for safekeeping. In such cases, the workers must have access at all times to the documents, and there should be no constraints on the ability of the worker to leave the enterprise.

In Oman, unfortunately, almost all the employers seize the passport of the worker and keep it with them as a 'guarantee' document, which will stop the worker from running away even if the employer is abusive and exploitative.

In 2006, Oman had banned employers from holding back workers' passports; however, the practice continues. If a sponsor is holding back the passport against the workers' will, the maximum a worker can do is lodge a complaint with the police, who will retrieve it from the sponsor and hand it over to the worker.[2]

Interestingly, the sponsor will not be penalized for holding back the travel and identity document.

I had witnessed those 'amicable' solutions reached in the different police stations of Oman, when I took aggrieved migrant workers there to get their passports back.

Appunni's sponsor was not his employer. Appunni was on a free visa. In reality, there is no such visa in any Arab country. But you can call a visa a free visa if the sponsor allows you to work for anyone.

Free visa is the visa issued by paying a huge amount to an agent; with this, the employee need not work for a sponsor. However, the employee has to pay a certain amount monthly as a fee to the sponsor for exempting him from working exclusively under him.

Appunni had to pay OMR 20 (approx. Rs 1,800 in the 1990s. Now, with the current exchange rate, it would be around Rs 4,000 per month to his sponsor, which he could not pay as he was unemployed.

Whether you earn or not, you have to pay this monthly 'freedom fee' to the sponsor.

For many kafeels (sponsors who practise kafala) this 'freedom fee' earned through kafala itself is an income.

Being a kafeel is also a profession for many Arabs in the Arab Gulf. Interestingly, free-visa-holding migrant workers and those who hire a free visa holder are legally punishable in Oman.

Additionally, Omani labour law states that a migrant worker can be fined and deported if he works for a different sponsor, or one who has not issued a visa for him.

But nobody cares. Those who want to benefit from cheap labour will hire free visa workers. Often, raids from the Ministry of Manpower happen and arrests are recorded.

Even Indian schools in Oman hire Indian women who are on a family visa to work as teachers. And when raids happen, teachers run out of schools to evade arrests.

Even though raids happen often, a big raid where approximately 1,000 free visa workers were arrested happened in 2015.[3]

More than 1,000 undocumented/irregular/free visa migrants were arrested for working at the terminal building under construction at Muscat International Airport. The workers had visas issued for jobs in restaurants, barbershops, tailor shops, as housemaids, and as camel keepers. The most interesting angle was that Muscat Airport was being built by the government and the irregular/free visa workers were arrested in a police raid.

The majority of the workers were from Hamriya and were hired by sub-contractors. Hamriya is a small town in Muscat. The arrested workers were fined and deported. A lifetime ban was also imposed on them. These workers who are caught in this manner are called 'illegals', which is an inhumane word in my opinion. Even in the media, they are reported as illegals. However, whenever I report on such arrests or stories of such overstayers, I either use undocumented or irregular. I have been taught that using the word 'illegal' to define an irregular, undocumented, or free visa worker, is inhumane.

In 2009, the United Nations High Commissioner for Human Rights had declared that 'the term "illegal immigrants" should be avoided and replaced by the internationally accepted definitions of "irregular" or "undocumented" migrants, which more accurately describes the situation.'[4]

The same year, the European Parliament called on the European Union's institutions and its member states to stop them from using the term 'illegal immigrant', which has negative connotations, and instead use 'irregular/undocumented workers/migrants'.[5]

Taking a cue from such advisories, several international media outlets stopped referring to them as 'illegal migrants' in 2013, including the news agency, Associated Press.

The agency's stylebook states that it won't sanction the term 'illegal immigrant', or the use of the word 'illegal' to describe any person. Save for indirect quotes, when it is essential to the story, the word illegal should only refer to an action, not a person: for e.g. 'illegal immigration' but not 'illegal immigrant'.

The *New York Times* stylebook too discourages the term 'illegal immigrant', while cautioning against the potentially euphemistic 'undocumented' and 'unauthorized'.

According to François Crépeau, the UN Special Rapporteur on the human rights of migrants, 'Migrants may be irregular or in an irregular situation, but they are not "illegal".'

'Incorrect terminology contributes to negative discourses on migration, reinforces negative stereotypes against migrants, and legitimates a discourse on the criminalization of migration, which in turn contributes to further alienation, marginalization, discrimination, and violence against migrants,' Crépeau argues.[6]

According to the International Organization of Migration, an irregular migrant is a 'person who, owing to unauthorized entry, breach of a condition of entry, or expiry of his or her visa, lacks legal status in a transit or host country.[7] The definition covers inter alia those persons who have entered a transit or host country lawfully but have stayed for a longer period than authorized or subsequently taken up unauthorized employment'.

I strongly believe and endorse that the term 'irregular' is preferable to 'illegal', because the latter carries a criminal connotation, and is seen as denying the migrant's 'humanity'.

From the host nation's perspective, 'entry, stay, or work without the necessary authorization or documents required under immigration regulations' is what defines this individual.

From the perspective of the migrant's home country, the irregularity is, for example, seen in cases where they cross an international boundary without a valid passport or travel document, or do not fulfil the administrative requirements for leaving the country.

In the main, this concept originates from the United Nations General Assembly Resolution 3449 on 'measures to ensure the human rights and dignity of all migrant workers', passed in December 1975.

The General Assembly had requested the United Nations organs and specialized agencies concerned, to utilize, in all official documents, the term 'non-documented or irregular migrant workers to define those workers that illegally and/or surreptitiously enter another country to obtain work'.

And according to the Platform for International Cooperation on Undocumented Migrants, calling a certain group of people 'illegal' denies them their humanity.

'There is no such thing as an "illegal" person. "Illegality" as a form of status has been deliberately assigned to undocumented migrants to justify a category of people who are undeserving of rights,' it says.

But in Gulf countries, the workers who don't have valid resident cards or are overstayers are always termed illegal. The media often uses the word 'illegal' only, citing space constraints and understandability concerns.

How is the free visa system enabled in any Arab country? An Arab parliamentarian, who had once been a source for me in Oman, had told me, 'Reji, it's a fact that all Arabs are not oil well owners. Many run grocery shops and drive taxis as well. Those people would approach the government for visas showing fake projects. When the government officials come under pressure, then the visas will be granted.'

When such visas are possessed, then the middlemen, most often the Keralites, would purchase those visas, looking for a potential migrant from Kerala or other south Indian states to fit the bill. When a potential migrant is found, then the agent would give him false promises, take the money, and bring him to the Arab Gulf.

A job visa would cost around Rs 60,000. When it goes through agents at different levels, then a potential migrant would pay about Rs 1,20,000 for a free visa.

In 1993, Appunni had paid about Rs 75,000 to get his free visa.

Upon arrival, Appunni needed to possess an Omani driving licence. He had an Indian driving licence. To obtain an Omani driving licence, you have to sit for a written test and attend a road test.

Getting a driving licence is quite difficult in any Arab Gulf country. I had friends who had tried perhaps ten times to get the licence. Every test would cost you around OMR 25 (Rs 2,000 then). So, when taking ten tests, you have shelled out approximately Rs 20,000.

Appunni got his licence only after the sixth test. So, he had spent close to Rs 12,000.

'Without a job, I had to take loans from my friends to pay the driving school fees and tests. I got my driving licence only in the fourth month of my arrival. Till then, I was unemployed, surviving on loans. I was not paying the freedom fee either. Eventually, the loan I had to pay became Rs 50,000 then. Without a job, how could I pay for all this? The trouble started then,' Appunni explained.

In the fifth month of his arrival, Appunni joined the company as a driver. The salary was around OMR 130

(Rs 12,000) then. There was no accommodation or food allowance.

'I had to find money for a shared accommodation and for food too. I was trying to pay back my loans then. As there was nothing left after paying back my loans, it was impossible to pay the rent for the shared accommodation and remit some money home to pay for the loan I had taken to get the visa; eventually, I failed to pay the freedom fee as well,' Appunni said.

Like in any other case of a free visa holder, failure to pay the freedom fee trapped Appunni also.

'In six months, the amount I had to pay for the freedom fee became OM 130 (Rs 12,000). As I was not in a position to pay the money, I started to disconnect his phone calls,' Appunni said.

Eventually, Appunni didn't go back to his sponsor and couldn't renew his Bataka (a local term for the residential status card).

To renew his Bataka, a worker has to have approval from his sponsor and the passport will be under the custody of the sponsor. So, eventually, Appunni became undocumented.

The visa validity in Oman for a migrant worker is only twenty-four months, and he was granted a thirty-day grace period to renew his visa.

However, an overstaying worker has to pay two different fines at two different offices in Oman. At the Ministry of Manpower, an overstaying worker has to pay around OMR 19 and at the Immigration department, OMR 20 for every month of delay.

The fine to be paid at the ministry will be calculated every month. However, the fine to be paid at an immigration office will not be calculated after twenty-five months, or once it reaches OMR 500.

So, if an overstaying or absconding worker wishes to stay back and become a documented worker, he has to shell out thousands of rials depending on the period for which he has been an undocumented worker.

Eventually, with all the fines and loans, Appunni went into hiding. He lost the driver's job, too. As it was a state-run oil company, only workers who have a valid permit card would be allowed to enter the premises. As Appunni's work permit had expired and he didn't have money to pay the freedom fee, he didn't approach his sponsor as well. Eventually, he failed to renew his card. Appunni's passport was also with his sponsor.

'I have been a ragpicker for many years. Several times, I would go to bed without having had even one meal. Sometimes, I wished that I could get at least one cup of tea,' Appunni told me.

Appunni worked in tea shops and butchery shops for survival.

'Everywhere, whenever raids took place, I would run away. I have never been caught in twenty-two years. But sometimes, I had thought that I should give in, get arrested and deported because otherwise, there was no possibility of an exit for me . . .' Appunni told me.

Appunni tried to get arrested many a time.

'But I would be "thrown out" from lockups by police officials as they were too lazy to do the paperwork and deport me,' Appunni said.

Since you are undocumented, you won't get access to medical care or legal services.

'Many a time, when I fell sick and collapsed, I would not go to a hospital. I couldn't go there without a card. There were small clinics, which would treat people like me. I would go there and get some medicines. I didn't have money as well . . .' Appunni told me.

Even while facing all these odds, Appunni never failed to remit money home.

'I would eat only lunch. I would wash cars, wash plates in restaurants, segregate meat waste in butcher's shops, clean their floors, work as a night watchman for a villa . . . I have done all kinds of jobs . . . I have remitted those earnings . . . I have never had any luxury in my entire life . . . I don't drink, smoke, and womanize . . . see, I am like a saint . . . a hardworking saint, who eats very little . . . but I am now a failure for my family,' Appunni wept while telling me all this.

Appunni had tried to come home for his daughter's marriage. He didn't have a passport. But he managed to arrange for a fake passport. This was in 2005. Appunni was undocumented and jobless. But Appunni managed to save some money and take loans.

He paid about Rs 30,000 to get a forged passport in Muscat.

It is a joke among Indian Embassy officials that some passports are printed at 'Kasaragod Embassy'. Kasaragod is in northern Kerala, one of the major towns in the state, where every house is sure to have one Keralite migrant worker in the Arab Gulf.

As they have migrated to the Arab Gulf a long time ago, and therefore know the loopholes, they know all the shortcuts.

Eventually, a few even dare to print passports. For Rs 30,000, you can get a fake passport printed at the 'Kasaragod Embassy'.

Appunni also managed to get one.

'I was excited. I bought five sovereigns of gold. I had about Rs 20,000 in hand. All went well. I boarded the flight and landed in Mumbai. I thought I would cross the official checks without any problems. But it didn't happen as I had thought it would,' Appunni said.

When Appunni landed in Mumbai, he was detained by Indian officials for holding a fake passport.

'It was an evening flight. I landed at around 10 p.m. There was a long queue. I was anxious. I was panicking. So, it was evident on my face that I was doing something wrong. When I was told to come forward, I went and gave my passport. The official, a north Indian, asked me why I looked panicky. I said nothing. I was lying. And it was evident on my face, too . . .

'The official called his superior. He came to me, took my passport and bag. I was taken to an office room and made to sit there. They asked me in Hindi whether I was Indian or Sri Lankan. Do I look like a Sri Lankan? I told them that I am an Indian and that my house is in Kollam, Kerala. But they were not ready to listen . . .

'I gave them my neighbour's phone number to call and verify. But they were not ready to even look at that pocket diary . . .

'I went down on my knees and begged them to let me go. I told them that I have come after twelve years to attend my daughter's marriage . . .

'But they didn't listen. I was told to sit. They were doing some paperwork. After thirty minutes, I was told to follow an officer. When I asked about my bag, they said it would be brought to me.

'I was taken to the departure place. I saw people standing in a queue to board a flight.

'I asked the officer, "Why have I been brought here?" He didn't tell me anything. He went to the check-in counter and said something.

'I realized that I was being sent back. But to where? I didn't know. I was not told.

'I planned to run away. But I knew that I couldn't escape. They could even shoot me. An armed guard was standing there. I had half a mind to run for it. If I ran and they didn't shoot, I could be jailed in India. That was better than being a slave in Oman.

'But I didn't know what would happen and how it would end. I was afraid of being shot. So, I stood there without doing anything.

'In a few seconds, the officer came back to me. He handed over my passport and paper. I begged him again. I asked him whether he could send me out. I even offered the gold I bought, which I had kept in the office room I was taken to.

'He just smiled. He didn't utter a single word. I was told to follow him. I had to stand in a queue. I was taken to the flight straight away. While walking the passenger boarding bridge, through the glass, I saw that it was an Oman Air aircraft.

'Yes, I was being sent back to Oman again. It was over.

'Again, I asked whether they would bring me my bag. He said, yes. He told me that I would get it when I land. I told him that there was gold in it. He didn't seem to hear me. He talked to the cabin crew and I was guided to a window seat.

'I sat there. What else could I do? The flight took off from Mumbai in thirty minutes.

'I could see Mumbai lit up. And finally, it faded away.

'I didn't even have my phone with me. They had taken it. I had told my wife that I was coming. My daughter's wedding was in two days. I was not going to be there. I had told them that I would be reaching home a day before that. They were happy. I had even told them that I would be bringing gold.

'I had seen her as a school-going child. She had grown up. In two days, she was getting married. And I was not going to be there.

'I slept and woke up only when the flight landed in Oman. I was back in Oman. It was a failed attempt . . . I failed halfway . . . I am cursed . . .

'When the flight landed, my name was announced by the cabin crew. I was told to sit in my seat.

'The announcement was in Hindi. People sitting nearby were staring at me. They asked me why my name was announced. I didn't answer. Why should I? I didn't even smile at them. Were they going to have time to listen to my story? Even if they listened, would they sympathize with me? If so, for how long? Till they got their bags from the belt? After that, they would feign sadness and say goodbye.

'So, I didn't tell anyone anything. They understood that I was not in the mood to tell my story.

'When everybody left, an Arab police officer came into the aircraft and called out my name—"Abbu . . ." It was obvious why they called me Abbu instead of Appunni. Arabs don't have *p*, they use *b* in the place of *p*.

When I used to go to Arab offices, I would be called Kuttabban, not Kuttappan.

'I stood up. I was told to accompany him. Again, back in the Muscat Airport, I told him that I had a bag to collect. He said, "*Mafi* bag. (No bag)."

'I was about to cry. I understood that my bag hadn't come to Oman.

'The five-sovereign gold I had bought for my daughter and the new saree I had bought for my wife . . . I had lost them all. I was a loser then and now as well . . .

'I was taken to an office inside the airport. It was around 3 a.m. I was told to sit there. I obeyed. What else could I do?

At around 9 a.m., some officers arrived. They took me out from the airport to a police station near Ruwi.

'They didn't say anything to me. I was told to sit. I knew that I would be jailed. When the police officers went inside, I sneaked out. I exited the front gate calmly and got into a shared cab to Ruwi.

'I had a few friends in Ruwi. I stayed there for two days. I didn't go to my place of accommodation. I knew that the Arab police wouldn't be able to find me.

'The next day was my daughter's wedding. I called my neighbour's house from my friend's phone to speak to my family. We didn't have a phone at home then. It was my wife who took my call. She was angry with me. My daughter was weeping. I told them that I had come to Mumbai, but was caught and sent back . . .

'They didn't believe me. I can't blame them . . .'

Appunni stopped his narrative for some time, then said, 'Reji, my daughter, disconnected the phone while I was on the call with them . . . she was angry with me and didn't want to talk to me. I was a loser then, and am a loser now . . .'

Appunni hadn't told me this story of his life when we met in Oman. He told me this when I met him in Kerala, which I had mentioned at the starting of this chapter.

Back in Oman, Appunni continued what he was doing, for ten more years, till I got to him.

In between, there were three amnesties, in 2005, 2007, and 2010. He could have used those amnesties to return home.

Amnesty is a programme announced by Arab governments for overstaying/undocumented/free visa migrant workers to return home without paying penalties for violating local residency/work permit laws.

Under each of the amnesties, thousands of overstaying/ undocumented/free visa migrant workers returned home.

The Arab governments present the amnesty as being benevolent to migrant workers. But the fact is that they are cleaning up the market. They know that employers would be preying upon undocumented/free visa/overstaying migrant workers' cheap labour. Job visa fee issuance is revenue for Arab governments. Other than in Oman, the population of migrant workers in the other five Arab Gulf countries is above 50 per cent. In Oman, the migrant population is at 45 per cent.

I had gone to Oman only at the end of 2006. So, I had missed reporting on the 2005 amnesty. In 2010, too, I was not too involved in reporting migrant stories. However, I had read reports and seen pictures.

By 2015, I was the Chief Reporter of the *Times of Oman* and was doing migrant stories in full swing. I was trained by the University of New South Wales in Sydney on migration and had started attending regional meetings on migration. Additionally, I had also become an active migrant rights activist in Oman by then. So, we were eagerly awaiting an amnesty to be announced.

We were at that time, looking for a veteran overstayer. Luckily, Binil, a close Keralite friend who had spent more than thirty years in Oman, told me about Appunni.

Binil had been staying in Oman and was doing marketing for a private news channel in Kerala.

He was a resourceful person. We both did many stories. Appunni's case was given to me by Binil, who had shared Appunni's number with me.

I was not sure whether Appunni would have a tellable story. But when I met him and spoke to him, I realized that I had never heard a more heart-wrenching story.

I did Appunni's story. While talking to me for the news story, which was only about 600 words, Appunni told me that no one should become an overstayer/undocumented/free visa migrant worker.

He had told me that life as an undocumented/overstaying migrant worker is hell. That was the headline of the front-page lead story. It was published on the day when amnesty was announced. The Oman Ministry of Manpower was impressed with the story and they carried it on their website, too.

After Appunni's story was published, many kind-hearted people called me and offered to help Appunni.

In my first meeting itself, I had convinced Appunni to make use of the amnesty and return home. I processed his papers and made him apply for the amnesty.

When good stories of stranded migrant workers are published, many businessmen come forward to help. The country manager of a jewellery brand came forward and helped Appunni. I took Appunni to meet him, and the country manager bought him gifts, dresses, as well as gave him a good amount of money.

Appunni was happy. He left Oman for Kerala. On the day of his leaving the country, Binil and I went to see him off at the airport.

It was a happy leave-taking on both sides. However, none of us were to know then that Appunni was returning home only to become an unwanted guest. A home that he had lived away from for twenty-two years, and which he had missed terribly.

Remember Appunni's white Maruti car, which he had bought with the money I had raised? Yes, that was money that the country manager of the jewellery store had helped raise.

A week after Appunni returned home, he called me to help him to find a job. It was then that I asked him whether he would be open to doing a driver's job if I got him the money to buy a second-hand car. He was happy to hear that and was open to trying it.

I called the country manager of the jewellery brand and told him about Appunni's request. He said he was happy to help.

He transferred Rs 90,000 to Appunni to buy a second-hand car. Appunni bought one. He was happy. The day he bought the car, he sent me a message. He would usually send me a WhatsApp message and I would call him back.

He was happy about purchasing a car. I assumed that he was happy because he could earn something and help his family.

I didn't know then that he was happy because he got shelter, in a car.

Appunni worked for twenty-two years in Oman as an undocumented/overstaying worker and had remitted money for his family. He longed to go home. But when he returned, he became an unwelcome guest. He became an embarrassment for them.

'Reji, I didn't dare sell drugs, liquor, or women in Oman. What if I had done those things? I had many opportunities to do so. But I didn't. If I had done that, I could have regularized my work permit status in Oman. I could have earned some good money. I could have built a big house. My wife would have loved me. My children would have respected me. I stuck to morals and ethics. And I lost everything. I was a loser then and am a loser now, too . . .'

'I have your number in my diary. I have kept a good note about you. When I die in this coffin, you may get a call. Do come . . .'

I didn't ask him to show me that note. I bid goodbye. I had gone to that village by 10 a.m. When I left, it was around 3 p.m. We had six or seven teas from different shops.

Before closing this chapter, I called Appunni. The Covid-19 outbreak has affected his job, too.

'Not many are hiring cars at this moment,' he told me, 'I am here in this village. I live in the white car. I am here, Reji. As I said, this is my home and my coffin, too . . .'

3

Pakistani Bhais Smuggled Majeed
Out of Oman . . .

If Appunni was able to go back under the amnesty programme, Majeed couldn't. In my telling of Majeed's story in this chapter, I have adapted situations slightly and changed names to keep confidentiality and protect identities.

Winter is the best time to be in any Arab Gulf country. The temperatures range between 23 and 27 degrees Celsius on the plains. And both at the hilltops and in the deserts, it is much lower, sometimes even dipping to 5 degrees Celsius.

No sweat and no stickiness, it is the perfect time to walk along the lit-up streets of Muscat. The sidewalks and roundabouts are like gardens. All flowers resemble Oman's national flag's colour, red and white. The air in the streets during these days is filled with tikka kebab's spicy flavours and strawberry-flavoured sheesha smokes.

In the 2011 winter, when I was walking back home through Ruwi, I took a shortcut through the sidewalks of the

Sultan Qaboos Mosque, which would help me reach the taxi stand behind Badr Al Sama hospital in less time.

I saw a young man, looking weary, staring at me. I understood that he needed help. He was standing near a Pakistani eatery, which was famous for lamb and lentil soup.

He wore a green-striped shirt, torn on the right side, and wrinkled trousers. I identified him as a Keralite. So, I shot my question. '*Enthu Patti*? (What happened?)',—the usual question any Keralite would ask a stranger who he identifies as being from his part of the world.

While I may enquire about what his difficulty is, it may not be necessary that I help him. This is understood where I come from. I could just enquire about things and listen to his litany, but I could walk away without helping him, too. However, I don't usually do that. If I ask someone what happened, I usually try my best to help them.

Here too, I was ready to help him. When I asked again, he said he had not had any food for the last two days and was surviving on the water kept for the public near the eatery.

When he came close to me, I found that he was stinking slightly. When I told him that, he felt bad. He told me that his name is Majeed and that he had arrived in Muscat last week. He had not yet got a place to stay.

'I use the public toilet near the taxi stand. However, as they don't allow me to take a shower there, I couldn't. And even if I do so, I don't have a dress to change into. I came from a police lockup, brother . . . they released me when they realized that I would become a burden for them. During the daytime, I roam around here. I beg for food. Sometimes,

I am lucky. When night falls, I sleep here outside this mosque,'
Majeed said.

In a few sentences, Majeed shared the story of his Muscat
days. From those few lines, I realized that he had a different
story to tell compared to what the majority of stranded
workers in the Arab Gulf relate to . . .

Exploited by the employer, abused for questioning human
rights violations, and beaten up by the master . . . running
away, approaching the embassy, not getting a favourable
response . . . stranded on the streets, struggling for food, with
no way to return home . . . . A struggling family back home,
ailing parents . . . paying lakhs to get the visa after getting
cheated by the agent, pending loans . . . leading the worker to
attempt suicide . . .

This would be the story of most migrant workers in
any Arab Gulf country. Only the name, place, degree of
exploitation, and suffering changes.

Having written stranded workers' stories continuously,
I developed a bad attitude. When a worker approached me
to tell his story, I would say, ' . . . just tell me the name and
place'.

For me, only that part changed. The rest remained the
same. But I soon realized that all stories are not the same. Yes,
every person has a unique story to tell.

Here, too, I assumed Majeed's story would be somewhat
similar to what I have heard. But what he said about being
thrown out of the police station was interesting.

I wanted to listen to his story and help him. So, I took
him to the Pakistani eatery and ordered two Pakistani naans
and two chicken curries. It was only around 6 p.m., so we

were a little early for dinner. We had to wait for the food. It would give us time to talk. Additionally, I was not in a hurry to go home because my wife and son had returned to India for the delivery of our second baby.

Majeed went to the washroom. From my seat, I could see him washing his face and staring at the mirror. On the right side of the mirror, a poster of Bollywood actor Amitabh Bachchan's movie *Don* had been pasted. In the Arab Gulf, Bollywood actors and actresses are favourites for Arabs and Pakistanis. There are even Arabs who sing and enjoy Mohammed Rafi's hits. And interestingly, the Pakistani restaurant was playing some soulful Sufi songs.

Majeed returned to the seat. He picked up some tissue paper, wiped his face, crushed it into a ball, and kept it near the water jug. This always irritated me.

But I didn't express my annoyance as I didn't want him to feel distant from me. I knew that if he feels brotherhood, he will open up. Majeed started to tell his story.

He had arrived in Muscat from Salalah a week ago. He was sent by a police officer from Salalah. He had come to get assistance from the Indian Embassy in Muscat to go to India. He was undocumented and had only one photocopy of his old passport.

He didn't know anyone in Muscat nor did he have money. But in two years, Majeed had trained himself in facing uncertainties and hassles.

Majeed is an orphan from northern Kerala. He is an automobile mechanic. He married an orphan girl and migrated to Oman alone when she was five months pregnant.

He got a mechanic job visa in a workshop in Salalah. All was well for the first three years. He managed to earn the trust of the employer, learn the job, save some money, remit it to his family, and see pictures and videos of his daughter through the phone sent by his wife before he lost it.

He was planning to go home very soon. He could have gone when he had completed the second year. However, due to some visa renewal issues and as his employer wanted him to stay longer, he delayed his return.

All was well. But his innocence got him into trouble. There were two Bangladeshi co-workers who worked in the workshop since much before Majeed joined.

When the Arab employer was ready to sell off the workshop, Majeed bought it with his savings and 'hand' loans. He was struggling but confident that he would be able to repay the loans. In between, the co-workers approached him for a loan as well. The innocent Majeed introduced them to a Pakistani moneylender whom he knew.

The co-workers took some OMR 3000 (approx. Rs 4.5 lakh then) as a loan and left the country. 'I never expected them to run away. They were there before I came. As I had bought the workshop, I thought they would stay with me. But they ran away,' Majeed said. 'I had to give OMR 2,000 (Rs 3.5 lakh) to the moneylender which was taken to set up the workshop. Additionally, I had to own up to the responsibility of paying back the loan taken by my co-workers. I was shocked and clueless . . .' Majeed added.

Majeed tried to convince the moneylender about his innocence.

'But he was not ready to listen. I made my Arab employer talk with the moneylender. But it didn't help. I was literally in a fix. My employer told me that he didn't want to be entangled in the issue. And so, I was alone,' Majeed said.

Majeed was really in a fix. Moneylenders are usually merciless. He begged for time. But the moneylender didn't give in. So, Majeed decided to flee from Salalah.

'Yes, one night I fled Salalah. I moved to a smaller city near Salalah. I had a few friends there. Leaving behind the workshop I owned and the small accommodation I had taken, was a great pain. At a time when I thought that I was bettering my business and would be earning more, I lost everything. In a few weeks, I was stranded on the street. I even "lost" my phone,' Majeed said.

'When I was hungry and running short of money, I had to sell my phone. An old Samsung. That's what happened. The only thing that remained with me was a diary, where I had a few phone numbers noted down. The struggle began then,' Majeed said.

When Majeed fled from his workplace, he couldn't get his passport back from his employer. Additionally, he lost his resident card. Majeed couldn't get a job. He didn't have the skills for any job besides what he had been doing. The only thing he could do was to become a waiter in small cafeterias.

But as he looked dirty and unkempt, he didn't get those jobs either. Also, nobody would hire an undocumented person. Many days, Majeed went to sleep with hunger pangs, on the street. And in between, he would be picked up by the police, too.

Before reaching Muscat, he was picked up by the police four times.

'The reason for the arrests was that I was undocumented,' Majeed said. Whenever Majeed was taken into custody, he would tell the police officials his story.

'A few officers would try to help me by talking to my employer. But as it was a mess, they would fail. And finally, they would take a stand and ask why they should interfere. They would keep me in the police station for a few days and then throw me out when they'd realize I had become a liability,' Majeed said.

'I have never slept in a police station before that. They wouldn't lock me up. They would just tell me to sit somewhere in a corner. Yes, they would provide food and water. Interestingly, they wouldn't even register a case against me. I just had to sit idle. Many officials came and went. Many would ask me questions. But nothing changed. I would be sent out after a few days . . .' he said, adding that after the second arrest, he lost his fear of the police.

Majeed was advised to go to Muscat by the last police officer who arrested him. 'He advised me, saying staying in Salalah wouldn't help in finding a solution. So, only by going to Muscat, would I be able to go to the Indian Embassy. There would be social organizations and social workers who could help me return home,' Majeed said.

The last police officer who arrested him gave him a food packet, and OMR 10 (approx. Rs 900) as bus fare to reach Muscat . 'He was a very kind officer. He was compassionate. He was the person who advised me to go to Muscat. He gave me his phone number, handed me OMR 10 ($35), and bought me a food packet too. He dropped me at the bus station in his official vehicle. He wished me good luck,' Majeed said.

'On the way back on the bus, I could see building lights running back. It was an evening bus. I would reach only the next morning. I cursed the moment I decided to help my co-workers. But we can't control fate, can we? I am cursed to languish like this . . .' Majeed added.

Before boarding the bus, Majeed managed to inform his wife in Kerala that he was going to Muscat to settle his visa issues.

He called from the police officer's phone. He didn't tell her that he was stranded without food and shelter; he only said that there were some job issues and he was going to Muscat to seek help from the Indian Embassy.

'Why should I tell her the entire story? That would make her worry. Let her be calm and okay. I will be able to manage this. I was very hopeful while on the bus to Muscat. But after reaching there, I realized that I don't know anybody in Muscat. Even after being here for the past week, I couldn't find the Indian Embassy . . .' Majeed said.

It is a fact that many Indians don't know where the Indian Embassy is located in Muscat. They know it is in Al Khuwair, but they don't know the precise location.

I understood that Majeed needed one more naan. As per my calculations, two naans would be enough for three people. However, I ordered one more naan. It was around 7 p.m. and more and more people were coming into the restaurant. A majority of them were Pakistanis. They were dressed in

Pathani kurta-pajamas. Most of them wore blue or green. A pleasant brotherhood was visible among them. It looked like they all knew each other.

In the Arab Gulf, workers are workers. Their country of origin is not a barrier to sharing love and respect. And irrespective of nationality, everybody faces the same kind of exploitation.

In Ruwi, I had good friends in the Pakistani community. The way they address us as 'bhaijaan' holds only love, respect, and trust.

Many a time, while 'trespassing' into workers' camps to report untold stories of exploitation, it was the Pakistani workers who would come to help when I was caught by the African security guards.

Most of them are above six-feet tall and heavily built. More often than not, they don't think of consequences before they extend their help.

My plan was to buy Majeed a shirt, trousers, and a pair of shoes.

So, I told him to finish his dinner soon. After wiping the bowl clean with his fingers, he said, 'Yes, let's go,' and went to the washroom.

By the time he returned from the washroom, I had paid the bill, placing the money on the dish that held the bill and a handful of sugar-coated fennel seeds.

When we stepped out of the hotel, almost all the tables were occupied. We took a shortcut by crossing a canal to the Centrepoint Mall from the hotel. Once in a while, in June, the canal is filled with water. At other times, when the canal is dry, it is used by driving schools to conduct lessons for students. When we reached the mall, I asked him whether he has any preferences for colour.

'No, I don't. I gave up on all those privileges a long time ago. You don't have to spend money. You can buy me the cheapest one,' he said.

I picked a dark green full-sleeved shirt and a pair of blue jeans. I also picked up a pair of canvas shoes for him. All three items cost me only OMR 13 (around Rs 2,000).

After paying the bill, I called a Communist Party of India (CPM) leader in Muscat and told him that I needed shelter for a person. Yes, there are Communists in the Arab Gulf. When Indians, especially those from Kerala migrate, they carry along with them their political identity as well.

There are Gulf branches for Leftists, Rightists, and Centrists. Even though there are representatives for all Indian political parties involved in assisting Indians in the Arab Gulf, the Kerala Muslim Cultural Centre (KMCC), an organization of the Indian Union Muslim League (IUML), is the most respected and active organization in the Arab Gulf. Most of its leaders are efficient at attending to labour issues, especially when it is related to body repatriation.

If an Indian dies in the Arab Gulf, to repatriate the body, a lot of paperwork is required for which one has to run from pillar to post.

According to the Ministry of External Affairs (MEA) 'a medical report, death certificate issued from a hospital, a copy of the detailed police report (with an English translation, if the report is written in some other language) in case of accidental or unnatural death, and a consent letter from the next of kin of the deceased for local cremation/burial/

transportation of mortal remains' are required to complete the repatriation process.[1]

Apart from this, a copy of the passport and visa of the deceased, documents such as clearance and arrangements for embalming of the mortal remains, and clearance from the local immigration/customs department are also required. In cases where the deceased had an unnatural death, with causes ranging from suicide to accidents, the authorities took months before allowing the mortal remains to be repatriated. Harsh working conditions and at times, non-payment of salaries by employers led to blue-collar workers running away, or in the worst-case scenario, committing suicide.

As the Indian Embassy doesn't have enough staff to do all the procedures, some social workers conduct it on behalf of the embassy, like the KMCC leaders who conduct the body repatriation process efficiently. The social workers advance upto 1 lakh to cover repatriation costs, which they later reimburse from the embassy.

I have assisted a KMCC leader of the same age as I, in repatriating bodies in Oman. We have even bribed the police officer in the mortuary to get the Indian bodies cleared first. A juice maker is enough to bribe the police officer and jump the queue. Without understanding the reality of the situation, Indian families, especially from Kerala, pressurize us to repatriate the body within twenty-four hours of death, which is impossible.

In normal cases, it may take up to seventy-two hours to repatriate the bodies. But this happens only if there is somebody like us with an influence over the police officials. Or else, the bodies lie there for years and years till the police dispose of them while clearing the mortuary.

However, the repatriation process, though cumbersome, is not as long for the economically affluent or celebrities.

According to a parliamentary paper, 7,694 bodies of Indians were stranded in foreign countries in 2015 with 2,690 bodies in Saudi Arabia and 1,540 in the UAE.

As per information available with the Ministry of External Affairs, mortal remains of 14,312 Indian nationals from 125 countries have been brought back to India from 2016 till 31 May 2019.[2]

In some cases, financial support to families of deceased Indian nationals to airlift mortal remains is made available by Indian Missions/Posts Abroad in deserving cases on a means-tested basis under the Indian Community Welfare Fund (ICWF).

Though the KMCC could arrange a shelter for Majeed, I decided not to entrust him to them. This time, I decided to ask for help from the CPM comrades.

The moment I called a Keralite comrade in Muscat (let's call him John Mathew), he agreed to accommodate Majeed in one of their centres in Ruwi.

The place he referred to was an unusual choice for accommodating a needy, undocumented Keralite. It was a small two-bedroom flat with one kitchen and a hall. It had one toilet and a balcony. And that too for a short period of time. As there was nobody there other than a regular occupant, a documented comrade, Majeed was welcome. We walked to the club. On the way, I assured Majeed that I would try my best to send him home.

I planned to talk to other comrades, take Majeed to the embassy, and with their help, repatriate him to India. Majeed only had one old copy of his expired passport. He didn't have any other paper to prove that he is an Indian.

But I didn't expect Majeed's repatriation to be this challenging. Till we reached the Indian Embassy, I believed that the old, expired passport copy would be enough for his repatriation.

I returned home. On the way, I called Comrade John and gave him details about Majeed. I told him the entire story as Majeed had told me. We decided that we would take Majeed to the Indian Embassy the next day.

The next morning, I texted my editor telling him that I would be late. In the same message, I hinted that I have a lead story ready in the folder, which would be shared when I came to the office.

The next call I made was to the comrade at Majeed's stay. When he handed the phone over to Majeed, I told him to be ready by 10 a.m. and come to a cafeteria near the police station.

I planned to get breakfast for Majeed before taking him to the embassy.

Majeed was already at the cafeteria, wearing his new clothes, by the time I reached.

When I told him that he looked great in the new clothes, he smiled and confessed that he was not wearing any briefs since we had forgotten to buy them.

I felt embarrassed. I assured him that we would buy them today. We ordered two plates of dosas and two teas.

While having breakfast, I taught him how to behave in the embassy. 'You should cry. You should tell them about your family. You should be able to convince them that you need help,' I told him.

He looked at me and said, 'Reji, I don't have to pretend to cry. I will cry when I think of my loving wife and my daughter . . .'

His wife and daughter were his only family. A hard worker, he was able to save some money and buy a small house. He was running a workshop in his hometown when he got the chance to migrate to Oman. He had migrated with high hopes like any other Keralite.

His wife was five months pregnant when he migrated to Oman. Majeed missed his baby girl's (who is now three years old) birth. 'When I had a phone, I could at least hear my baby's giggling. After I sold the phone, I lost that happiness, too. Do you think I'll be able to tell my story without any emotions? I will cry. It will happen,' Majeed told me. I too felt like crying when Majeed spoke about his little daughter.

'Don't worry, you will be going home soon,' I comforted him.

This was in 2011. Even though I was familiar with the Indian Embassy, an experienced social worker would always accompany me.

This was the first time I was taking a grieved worker to the Indian Embassy on my own. I was a bit tense. However, the comrades told me not to worry; they would talk to the embassy officials about the case. I just had to take him to the embassy, register a plea, and return.

It took only thirty minutes to reach the Indian Embassy in a taxi from Ruwi. I paid the taxi fare. We went directly to the Community Welfare section. Since some other workers were talking to the official, we decided to wait until they left.

The official recognized me when we entered. He even greeted me, calling out my name. It was a surprise for me.

'*Bathayayiye Reji Saab . . . hum kya kar sakte he aaapko . . .*'
the officer asked me. I looked at Majeed, and said, 'Sir, this is
Majeed . . . he needs help . . . he will tell you his story.'

Majeed started to speak in Hindi, with the little he knew.
I had to fill in the missing points. In some five minutes,
Majeed was crying. He was not bothered by the other workers
and officers in the room. He desperately wanted to convince
the officer and go home to his daughter and wife.

After hearing the story, the officer looked at me and said
they would work on it. 'We will talk to his employer, we
will check whether Majeed has been indicted in any cases,
we will find a way to send him home. We will try our best,'
he said.

Majeed and I felt relieved. When the officer asked
Majeed to provide the employer's number, he took out his
torn pocket diary and read out the phone number. The
officer then said, 'Give us a few days . . . we will find a
solution.'

I thanked the officer. We left the Community Welfare
room. We went to the café and got two samosas and two teas.
Holding the tea on one hand, I stepped out on to the lawn
to smoke. Lighting the cigarette, I told Majeed, 'Let us be
positive. I know these officers. They won't give up. Let's give
them a little time.'

Majeed said yes. 'I feel hopeful. I should have met you
and come here earlier . . .'

After finishing the tea and the cigarettes, we walked
towards the exit. From the road, we got into a taxi that
brought some workers from Sur—a small town, 161 km from
Muscat—who had come to complain about their employer.

Before entering the taxi, I collected one of those workers' phone numbers in the hope of getting a story.

On the way back, Majeed asked about my family and my life in Oman.

I am a chatty person. I like talking to strangers. But when I talk, I'm unable to hold back my secrets. My mother had always warned me about my habit of disclosing information about my personal life.

What is there to hide? If there is mutual trust and sincerity, what's the harm in opening up to a monthly wage earner who has nothing to lose?

When we reached Ruwi, I bid goodbye to Majeed, told him to stay in his room, and walked towards my office. While walking, I called Comrade John and updated him about what happened in the embassy. He assured me that he would talk to the officer and update me. Reaching the office, I went about my work, preparing lists, making a few calls, and filing a few stories.

That day, as I had punched in a little late, I stayed back for additional hours. At around 8 p.m., I left the office. On the way back home, I went to the Ruwi Hotel, drank a chilled Amstel, and walked back to my flat. I stopped to buy some chicken tikka and Arab bread for dinner.

The next day was quiet and uneventful. I was busy collating fresh stories. In the evening, I got a call from the reception telling me that somebody is waiting to see me. I went downstairs and found Majeed. I had not told him where my office was, but he found it. He told me that he was getting bored sitting at home and ended up at my office while taking a stroll outside. I told him to come back at around 7 p.m. as I had to complete a few more stories and do a local page, too.

Once in a while, I had to do some editing and page making as there was a staff shortage in the office. Luckily, that day, some 70 per cent of the page I had to work on was blocked by advertisements. Yes, it rains advertisements during the winter. On 18 November, Oman marks the 'National Day' to celebrate the birthday of Sultan Qaboos-bin-Said-al-Said, who reigned from 1970 to 2020.

So, the pages are filled with greetings expressing their gratitude to the ruler Sultan Qaboos-bin-Said, from both the public and private sectors. Sometimes, we even counted upto 48 pictures of the Sultan printed in separate advertisements on a single-day-42-page edition. Additionally, there would be winter sale advertisements from small to big malls.

I had to place only one lead story with around 450 words.

There was a copy of the local protocol in the official news agency. It was about new investment plans from Oman's Ministry of Commerce. I took out the copy, edited it, took down some bullet points, pasted the story page, gave it a catchy headline, pushed in the bullet points into the blurb, and forwarded the page to the chief sub-editor.

The chief sub-editor informed me that he got the page and would check it and that I could leave if I wanted. I thanked him and rushed downstairs. It was already 7.30 p.m. Majeed was waiting for me. We had dinner at a Turkish restaurant. The evenings were becoming colder. We talked about Kerala politics, how the Congress is looting the country, why Leftists are failing at the centre, what they should do to gain more support. . . . the list of topics was endless.

Majeed was a Leftist. A majority of the people in Kerala lean to the Left. But at the same time, they are God-fearing, too. At around 9.30 p.m., Majeed bid farewell to me and returned to where he was staying. I walked back home.

A week passed without many surprises. There was no positive update from the embassy. Whenever I called, the response would be the same—they were looking into it. We were getting worried.

I decided to push Comrade John further on Majeed's issue. He was also worried about Majeed. Allowing an undocumented person into their premises was a high risk. If caught, it would expose everything.

A third Friday was coming in two days. On the afternoon of a third Friday, an Open House is conducted at the Indian Embassy.

At the Open House, the Indian ambassador, his deputies, embassy lawyers, interpreters, and the note-taker would be present from 2 p.m. onwards. Indians who had grievances could come and talk to the ambassador directly.

When a case is heard by the ambassador directly, it gets prioritized and his deputies will follow it up sincerely. So, Comrade John told me that he would take Majeed to the Open House and try to meet the ambassador.

I started attending the Open House sessions with the comrades. The Open House hall was full almost all the time. In addition to aggrieved workers, a few Congress politicians, one KMCC leader, and a dozen communists would be present there.

Interestingly, there are two factions of the CPM in Oman. In the early days, I didn't belong to either faction. But later on,

I fell into one. In Kerala, unofficially, there were two factions within the CPM. The CPM may claim that factionalism is a media narrative. But the fact is that factionalism can be felt when you understand the party structure.

In 2011, the two CPM factions in Kerala were Pinarayi and Achuthanandan. The same factions were there in Oman, too.

Achuthanandan supporters were slightly more orthodox. They were against liberalization, privatization, and globalization. Additionally, they were not ready to compromise with the bourgeoisie in Kerala and the global capitalists.

When Achuthanandan was the Chief Minister of Kerala during 2006–11, in 2008, a WikiLeaks document revealed that Pinarayi, as the CPM party secretary, was ready to welcome the capitalists. The WikiLeaks document reads that 'As Kerala's Communist Party of India (Marxist) (CPI(M)) prepare to hold its State Conference during February 11–14, insiders say that the party's conservatives, led by Chief Minister Achuthanandan, will face a major defeat in the elections to the party's state committee. State Secretary Pinarayi Vijayan's faction, which is seen to be more amenable to economic reforms, is expected to tighten its grip. But the party's opposition to the US–India Civil Nuclear Cooperation Agreement remains as strong as ever.'

The document adds that 'We spoke with CPI(M) insider John Brittas, Managing Director of Malayalam Communications, the CPI(M)-controlled TV company that runs three satellite channels, and a former New Delhi correspondent for the CPI(M) daily "Deshabhimani"'.

'Brittas is a part of the CPI(M) faction led by State Secretary Pinarayi Vijayan, which is seen to be more open to economic reform and private investment,' the document reads, adding that although the Pinarayi faction may be more receptive to economic reforms, they do not have a track record of accomplishment and many doubt their ability to deliver.

The document reveals that Brittas was sharply critical of Chief Minister Achuthanandan.[3]

'In all the other states including West Bengal, the chief ministers champion the cause of economic development and private investment while the party machinery would advise caution. Here, it is the other way round: the party is for investment and economic development while it is the chief minister who wants to go slow,' he pointed out. According to Brittas, 'Achuthanandan has a good team of ministers including Finance Minister Thomas Isaac and Education Minister M.A. Baby but the Chief Minister is such a loner and a born factionalist that he cannot lead the team and produce results.'

Brittas has said in the document that, in the ongoing CPI(M) district elections, Vijayan's group is trouncing Chief Minister Achuthanandan's group. According to Brittas, Pinarayi Vijayan will emerge as the unchallenged leader in the February 11–14 State Conference of the CPI(M).

He would not rule out the possibility of a mid-term removal of the chief minister but indicated that most likely, the party would exert more control over the chief minister. Brittas added that the constant infighting within the CPI(M) and the Left Democratic Front has rendered the government ineffective and eroded the popular goodwill that brought them to power with a massive majority in 2006.

And, in 2020, Pinarayi Vijayan has been the chief minister since 2017; Brittas is the media advisor of the chief minister with a principal secretary rank. Achuthanandan is ailing and left to his hometown Alappuzha from the capital city of Thiruvananthapuram.

Achuthanandan was the poster boy for CPM in the 2016 elections. But when the Left Democratic Front led by CPM won the elections, Pinarayi Vijayan became chief minister.

Interestingly, in its last lap, in 2020 and 2021, the Pinarayi government was hit by claims of corruption, nepotism, gold smuggling, opening up the doors for capitalists, bringing in global consultancies for aiding development . . . the list is endless. In a nutshell, Communism is 'left' only by the name of the CPM.

Somehow, I became close to a comrade in Oman who was seen as part of the Achuthanandan faction. To be specific, it was not just a 'somehow' kind of occurence. His commitment towards migrant workers and a simplistic lifestyle convinced me. Let's call him Roy Xavier.

Roy is a tailor living in Muttrah for the last forty years, and he continues to live there. Even after spending four decades in the country, he has not seen all of Oman. However, migrant workers from north to south know him well and come to his tiny shop in one of the alleys of Muttrah, with great hope, when they are stranded or have no means to get out of the country.

Roy, while travelling in his 1980s model Toyota car, used to tell me, 'Commitment to the society and compassionate to the migrant community; providing help to them is ingrained in my blood.'

He also told me, 'I believe in helping people when they are in dire need. During the last few decades, I may not have become a successful person financially, but I have no regrets. I have upheld my ethics and tried my best to become a good human being.'

Roy came to Muscat from Kerala via Mumbai in 1978. The year when I was born. Since then, he has tried his best to pursue his profession and carry out his social commitments simultaneously. During the amnesty, he would pull the shutters down on his tailoring shop and go to the embassy with his wife and younger daughter to help stranded workers.

As mentioned in Appunni's chapter, amnesty is an option announced by the Arab government to provide a free exit for undocumented and overstaying migrant workers. Thousands are ready to make use of an opportunity where they could take an exit from the Arab Gulf countries without paying a fine for overstaying.

Roy lives in a small house with his family in Muttrah, eking out a living with his daily earnings. But when it comes to attending to workers' grievances, he would never think of other things.

Till I left Oman, I was the person who would accompany him to write complaints and talk to officials in English at the embassy. Together, we have handled a total of at least 500 cases. We would travel in his 1980-model car. Its air conditioning would not work most of the time. But these inconveniences would never stop us when it came to attending workers' cases. Most of the time, we would be entering the embassy with shirts drenched in sweat. But he used to say, 'for the workers'. Yes, it was for the workers.

In a case involving an undocumented family with three small children, we gave in writing to the embassy that we had known them for a long time, and on that acknowledgement, they should be repatriated to India. We had known them for only thirty days. But Roy would stand with me, shoulder to shoulder, to take risks when it came to migrant workers' issues.

In Majeed's case, too, Roy was the person who was taking him to the embassy for follow-ups. Majeed's request was not denied, but there was no positive development on his return either.

One evening, Majeed came to meet me with updates.

'I went with Roy several times. He is a very kind person. We also talked to the embassy official several times. But it seems that I am losing hope,' Majeed said.

I called Roy. He had the same story to tell. The copy of Majeed's old passport was not enough to get an exit certificate. I called up Comrade John, who tried to get some papers from his wife in Kerala, but even that failed.

The disappointment was creeping in. But I didn't express it. By then, I had learnt that Majeed was an emotional person. So, I put up a smile so that Majeed wouldn't read my thoughts.

But as I am not a good actor, Majeed could sense that I was faking it. He didn't express any curiosity. When I completed the phone call, he said, 'Reji, shall we go for tea to the cafeteria?' There was not much work to do in the office. So, I agreed. I went upstairs, logged off the computer, and punched out. We walked down to the cafeteria. Majeed ordered two teas and moved to a vacant table. Straightaway, Majeed started the conversation.

'Reji, don't worry. If the embassy can't help, then we will find some other way. Don't get tensed. You tried your best. I will always be grateful for that,' Majeed said.

'Today, let's go for a drink. Yes, I won't be able to pay. You need to unwind. You need to relax. Let's talk about the rest there . . .' he said.

I paid for the tea. We started walking down to Ruwi. Majeed was trying to divert the issue and help me stay positive.

In fifteen minutes, we reached Ruwi. We crossed the road and walked to my favourite poolside bar at the Ruwi Hotel. We ordered two Amstel beers. By then, two bowls of popcorn were placed on our table.

When the beer came, I took the first sip. I picked my phone and dialled a social worker . . . let's call him, Chandra Babu. Chandra Babu hailed from Telangana. I wanted to meet him. I was thinking of him on my way back. Somehow, I felt that he would be able to help Majeed. Babu didn't pick my call. I placed the phone on the table. I knew that he would call me back.

Babu was not a favourite of many. But I had a good relationship with him. Other social workers alleged that he made some money through ticket purchases meant for the workers. Yes, he had done a bad thing. But these are just stories. I never asked him the true story. I always had a feeling that Babu is a rogue. He has shown indications of this trait many a time.

When Indian workers went on strike in companies, Babu would take the risk and go to the action scene to get me the workers' numbers and pictures. He also knew Arabic really well. Additionally, the Ruwi labour department officials were his close friends. He had introduced me to a few senior officials in the Ruwi labour department, which had helped me with my stories.

Majeed was telling me about his village and his wife. He grew up in an orphanage run by a local mosque. After his schooling, he joined an automobile workshop and learned to work.

I had completed my second beer by then. I was ready to go. So, I requested for the bill from the young waitress from the Philippines who attended my table. She was friendly to me since I was a regular customer. When the bill came, my phone started to ring. It was Babu.

As mentioned earlier, he was a very courteous person, at least with me. He spoke very politely and softly, too, with an 'always at your service' attitude. As I didn't want to talk to him in front of Majeed, I asked for an appointment the next day. He agreed and told me that he will come and meet me in my office. Majeed didn't ask me why I was talking to Babu. I didn't tell him either.

I paid the bill and we left the bar. It was very cold. Majeed was not wearing a jacket. I told him that I had a muffler and would bring it to him the next day. I was a bit tired. So, I bid goodbye to Majeed assuring him that I will find a solution for his return. I didn't have any plans. But I was not ready to give up.

The next day, I had to file three stories. But I didn't forget to call Babu and remind him about the meeting. He agreed to meet me at around 2 p.m. I told Majeed that I would meet him at around 7 p.m. like usual.

In the afternoon, I didn't go for lunch. I walked down to a cafeteria near my office, where there is a very nice Hyderabadi chef who prepares our orders any way we want. I had a spicy Arabic sandwich and coffee. While eating the sandwich, I was watching the headlines on the Al Jazeera channel. In Oman, either the BBC or Al Jazeera is on in almost all public television screens.

Babu came and sat in front of me. I didn't realize he had come. I was trying to unroll the paper of the sandwich while watching TV. I always fail to neatly unroll the paper from the sandwich. I somehow manage to spill the mayonnaise on my clothes.

After all the greetings, he immediately asked me, 'What happened, Reji? Do you need any help?' I said, 'Yes. I have an undocumented Indian here in Ruwi; can you help me repatriate him? Another social worker, a comrade, is trying. But if you can also take a look at this case, then it would be helpful. He won't be able to raise money. But he will coordinate with the embassy. I know that you will be able to help with the money.'

Babu agreed. He told me to send Majeed to his office. 'Let me talk to him. And I will share Rs 5,000. Let him remit that money home. As he is undocumented, he won't be able to remit it. But let him try. Or else, I will do it for him. Undocumented workers won't be able to remit money. You have to produce a valid resident card.'

At money exchanges, there would be many undocumented workers waiting and seeking the help of others to remit.

Quite often, I have remitted money for many undocumented workers by presenting my resident card. Before leaving, Babu asked me who the other Indian comrade social worker helping Majeed was. I said it's John. He said, 'I will talk to him.' He paid my bill too and bid bye. I walked back to my office.

A surprise was waiting for me. In three days, I had to fly to Iran for a five-day trip to make a report on Iran's tourism potential. The airline was launching a new flight to Tehran. And it is very common to carry the carry journalists to new destinations.

Iran and Oman enjoyed a warm relationship. Oman was the only country that had strong bonds with Iran, dating back to the 1970s.

In the 1970s, when Oman was troubled by the rebels in Dhofar, Iran's ruler at the time, Mohammed Reza Pahlavi, the last Shah of Iran, sent troops and military assistance to back the late Sultan Qaboos in Oman. And with Qaboos's victory, the modern Omani nation emerged.[4]

In recent years, Oman played a vital role for Iran in diplomatic matters. Most notably, in 2011 and 2012, the Omanis facilitated secret talks in Muscat for senior American and Iranian officials.

When Majeed was with me, it was the end of 2011. So, every day, there was something fresh on the Iran–Oman ties hitting the headlines.

Barack Obama's election as president in 2008 heralded a significant shift in the US foreign policy as Obama initiated the diplomatic outreach to Iran. Oman revived its role as an interlocutor in 2009, when Omani Foreign Minister Yusuf bin Alawi told the US Ambassador to Oman, Richard

Schmierer, 'Oman can arrange any meeting you want and provide the venue—if it is discreet.'[5]

That year, Oman established a backchannel, passing messages between Washington and Tehran.[6] Oman then went even further to bring about a nuclear deal. Seeking to foster goodwill on both sides, Sultan Qaboos' economic advisor, Salem-ben-Nasser-al-Ismaily, facilitated the return of detainees in both countries. In 2010, Ismaily negotiated the release of three American hikers who allegedly crossed illegally from Iraq into Iran; Oman paid $500,000 per hiker in ransom.

I had reported the story for the *Times of Oman*.[7] Direct talks between the US and Iranian officials began in 2012 in Muscat, and soon, included members of the P5+1 (UN Security Council's five permanent members (the P5); namely China, France, Russia, the United Kingdom, and the United States; plus Germany). They reached an interim nuclear agreement, known as the Joint Plan of Action (JPOA), in November 2013; it went into effect in January 2014. The final nuclear agreement, known as the Joint Comprehensive Plan of Action (JCPOA), was agreed upon in July 2015 and went into effect in January 2016. The deal was highly controversial, as it unlocked more than $100 billion in frozen funds, which Tehran could use to fund regional terror networks and other malign behaviour.[8]

I met the chairman's secretary, a Keralite woman. She had all the papers ready for me. I just had to fill a few papers and sign them. The office administration was coordinating everything with the tourism company. In six days, I had to fly. I was excited. It was my first time going to Iran.

A few of my friends told me that if there is an Iranian seal
in the passport, then you won't get an American visa. But that
didn't bother me. I had read that history's first superpower
had sprung from ancient Iran under the leadership of Cyrus
the Great; Persia ruled the world's first true empire, centred
in Iran and stretching from Europe to Egypt to India.

Historians say that the direct legacy of the ancient
Iranians can be found across the Middle East, the Caucasus
and Turkey, the Arabian Peninsula, Egypt, Turkmenistan,
Uzbekistan, Afghanistan, India, and Pakistan. Iran's cultural
heritage reflects the grandeur and beauty of the golden age of
the Persian empire, and I didn't want to miss the opportunity
to see them.

And, of course, I wanted to meet the feisty Iranians and enjoy
the Iranian kebabs, too. I called my wife who was in Kerala. She
was happy to hear that I had got a chance to visit Iran. The day
went as usual. In between, I had called Majeed and told him to
meet Babu with my reference. I gave him Babu's office location.
Afterwards, I told him to meet me at around 7 p.m. in our usual
spot, the cafeteria, near the money exchange house.

When I reached the cafeteria, Majeed was waiting for me.
While ordering two teas, I told him about my Iran trip. He
felt sad. But he wished me safe travel. 'You haven't seen Iran.
You are lucky. I will be here if our comrades don't find a way
out by the time you return.'

When I said, 'don't worry', he said that he had met
Babu. 'He gave me Rs 5,000. I remitted it with the help of a
customer who came to the money exchange house.'

After tea, I bid good bye to him. I told him that I won't
meet him for two days. He agreed. On the way to a taxi stand,

I called Comrade John and updated him about my Iran trip. He too expressed his happiness and told me, 'Comrade, I will follow up on Majeed's case. Don't worry.'

He was happy about Babu's involvement in the case as well. Everyone believed in teamwork because it would be inconvenient to handle such social work on your own. A team can make things happen.

I left for Iran on a Friday. Majeed came to see me off at the airport. After I checked in before crossing the security channel, I stood for a few minutes with Majeed. He was worried about my leaving him alone in Muscat.

I understood that and told him, 'Don't worry, those two social workers will take care of you. If you need money, please ask Babu. I have told him to help you.' He said yes and left.

At the boarding gate, I found an Omani reporter, an old friend. He was also picked by the airline for the trip to Iran. I was happy to see a familiar face.

We flew in the business class along with a few airline officials. We landed in Tehran in two-and-a-half hours. We didn't have to stand in an ordinary queue since we were official guests. We were escorted to the VIP lounge, and after having refreshments from there, we were taken to the capital city, Tehran.

We had rooms booked in the Esteghlal International Hotel situated in the vicinity of Alborz Mountain Ranges. In Tehran, we visited the Grand Bazaar, where you can find everything from jewellery to carpets, pots, and pans for sale; we saw the eighteenth century lavish Golestan Palace, which embodies the successful integration of the early Persian crafts and architecture with Western influences, and the Milad Tower, the sixth tallest tower in the world.

Once the official sightseeing got over by 4 p.m., I took a walk around the city, ate dinner, and did some shopping.

We also spent a day in Shemshak Skiing Mountain, a two-hour travel from Tehran. I would love to vacation with my family here.

As I was not using WhatsApp and there were no roaming facilities on my mobile carrier, I was cut off from Oman. The only connection it maintained was with my office, as I was sending in stories daily. But to talk to my family in India, I had to use the hotel phone.

So, I was unaware of the developments regarding Majeed. But I was confident that Babu, John, and Roy would take care of him.

Upon landing in Oman, the first thing I did at the Muscat airport was ring Majeed. But he was unreachable.

I was getting worried, so I rang Babu. He picked the call and welcomed me back to Oman. When I asked him about Majeed, he said, 'Let's talk in person. All is well. It has been settled.' I felt relieved but was also curious to know how it happened.

I assumed that the Indian Embassy somehow managed to make a new passport with the help of the old one to repatriate him.

The travel from the airport to my flat takes forty minutes, and I was only carrying a small duffle bag and a backpack. So, I decided to get down in Ruwi and meet Babu, to find out what happened. I called Babu and told him that I will be coming straight from the airport to meet him. He said that he has to go out but will wait for me.

I reached Ruwi in thirty minutes via taxi. I got down near his office. When I stepped in, I saw that two Keralites had come to meet him. He told me to sit. I waited for them to leave. In some ten minutes, they left.

Babu pulled his chair closer to me and said, 'Majeed has reached home. I suggest you do not ask me more.' I didn't have anything else to say to Babu. When I got up to leave, he gave me Majeed's Indian number, written on a piece of paper.

I kept it in my shirt pocket. I felt relieved, but was worried, too. I called Comrade John. He said, 'Yes, it's done. Luckily, he has reached home. Let's not talk about it any more. Let's forget about it.'

I agreed. That evening, I tried calling Majeed. He picked the call on the first ring. He was excited to talk to me. He was apologetic for leaving Oman in my absence. I told him, 'I will be home, in Thiruvananthapuram, in four months, when I get my annual leave.'

He agreed to meet me and hung up the phone. Later on, he would text me a 'good morning' and 'good night' text every day. He would call me every Friday evening as he knew that it was my day off and I would be in the bar.

Office work went on as usual without any excitement. I spent most of my time in Comrade Roy's tailoring shop and home. Loitering in and around Muttrah was my main hobby those days. I was alone. My wife had gone to India. She was carrying my second son. Even though there are good hospitals in Muscat, delivering a baby in Muscat is expensive and a risky process. The treatment cost is six times higher than in India. Nobody trusts the medics in the Arab Gulf, hence the risk factor; not to mention, post-delivery care is unavailable here. I may have to hire a domestic worker for that. In India, her mother and my mother would take care of her and the baby in the best way possible.

My wife left for India when she was four months pregnant. At the end of the eighth month, she delivered a baby boy. I received the happy news when I was working in the office. I had planned for this beforehand, getting all the necessary approvals for a leave from the office; I was ready to fly to India the day I got the news. As I had a good travel agency owner as a friend, who was also an Indian, getting the ticket was easy.

I managed to book a flight for the next night. On the third day after reaching India, I called Majeed. He was waiting for my call. He told me that he will board that night's train and reach Thiruvananthapuram, my home, the following morning. I agreed. I was also waiting to hear his story. The next day, at around 8 a.m., he reached the Central Railway Station in Thiruvananthapuram, which was a twenty-minute drive from my home.

I had told him that I will wait for him in front of the Ganapathi temple near the railway station. In thirty minutes, he came to the spot where I was standing and called me.

Three months with his family and a tension-free life made him look smarter than ever. He was wearing a nice shirt and trousers. He was holding a small bag. He placed the bag down and hugged me like the Arabs do.

'Reji, did you ever think we will meet here in Kerala?' Majeed asked me.

I said no.

'In your case, everything that happened was unexpected,' I told him.

I had gone on my motorbike to pick him up. We walked to the parking lot. Majeed was asking me about my family and children. He was telling me that his child is happy and his wife is grateful for all the help.

I could understand that he was in a rush to tell me everything. We took the motorbike from the parking lot and headed home. He was in Thiruvananthapuram for the first time, but he was more interested in talking about his Muscat days. When we were nearing my house, he started to tell me how Babu and Comrade John helped him cross the Oman–UAE border.

But I stopped him and said, 'Let's talk about that later on.' I wanted to hear the entire story in detail.

Majeed had brought a small diary for me, in which he detailed what happened during those three days when he crossed the Oman–UAE border. I said, 'Yes, I will read it. But let's have breakfast first, meet my family, and roam around in the city. We will talk about everything else later. I am happy for you. Even in my absence, you have reached safely.'

At home, he was respectful to my parents and wife. He brought northern Kerala sweets for me. After having breakfast, he wanted to talk to me outside. I said, 'Yes, we will go to a park in the city, a twenty-minute drive from my home. We can sit there and talk in detail.'

At the park, I parked my motorbike at my usual spot, behind the police station. We entered the park, found a shady area, and sat there. Majeed took a small, torn diary and gave it to me.

He said, 'This is a gift from my side for all your help.
I don't have anything else to give.'

It was a small, 2009 diary with around fifty pages. He
said, 'It was lying there in our comrades' accommodation.
I asked them whether I could take it and they said yes. I also
took a pencil from there and started writing everything.'

I opened the first page. It talked about Majeed's meeting
with two men in Babu's office in Ruwi.

*'I met Rabiul and Shariful who hailed from Bangladesh in
Babu's office. I was told that they would take me to the border and
help me cross it. I wasn't sure whether it will happen or not. But I
took the risk and now, I am in Al Ain . . . I am going to write how
I left Ruwi, stayed with others like me, walked with them . . . about
my fall, their help, fear, darkness, pain, wadi dogs, and all . . .'*

It was quite interesting to read . . . but I wanted to listen.
So, I closed the diary and listened to Majeed's story. He
smiled at me and said, 'I haven't told the entire story even to
my wife. I didn't tell the social workers about my pain. But I
will tell you . . .'

He began—

'After you left for Iran, on the second day, I got a call
from Babu in the afternoon. He wanted me to meet him in
my office after 6 p.m.

'He didn't specify why. But since you told me that
I should listen to him, I said yes and went to the office by
5.30 p.m. itself. He told me to close the door when I entered.
He asked me straight away whether I was ready to take a
risk crossing the border. I was shocked. I was unhappy. In
a second, my wife's and daughter's faces flashed across my
mind. I said, "Yes, but I have to talk to Comrade John."

'Babu said that he had already talked to him and is leaving the decision to me. Babu said that if I agree, then all is set to go.

'I said, "Yes. I am ready." Babu and I were worried because you were not there, but were sure you would agree. When I said yes, he told me to come at around 1 p.m. to his office to travel to Buraimi.

'I was briefed on the plan. Babu told me that Rabiul and Shariful know the immigration officers at the border, and that they will be bribed to allow me to cross the border. And when I cross the border, Comrade John will inform his friends in Al Ain to present me at the Indian Embassy in the UAE as a person who went to the UAE and got stranded.

'As the amnesty is on in the UAE, you will be able to fly back to India with whatever documents you have. Babu's plan sounded workable. I called Comrade John. He told me to try it out. But I was still worried about you not being there. Still, I didn't want to miss the chance, Reji; that night, I couldn't sleep. First, I thought of calling my wife. But later on, I dropped that idea. If something happens to me while crossing the border, then she would get tensed. I wanted my my arrival to be a surprise for her.

The next day, I had breakfast from the cafeteria.

'I called Comrade John to make sure that his friends in Al Ain would come to pick me up as I haven't been to the UAE before, and I don't know anyone there. He told me that everything was set. When I went to Babu's office, Rabiul and Shariful were waiting for me. They found that I was a bit worried. So, they were telling me "*Saab, fikar math karo. Hum kar dhenge. Aapka dosth safe hoga . . .*"

'I was not convinced. But I said agreed when Babu kept telling me that the Bangladeshi agents had their Omani officers on the border and they would shut their eyes when I cross. I was given a bogus SIM card by Babu.

'The SIM card would be valid but the person who bought the SIM card would not be in Oman. So, it would be difficult for the police to find who the original owner of the SIM is.

'Rabiul, Shariful, and I got into a Nissan truck. The driver was a Pakistani. When the truck left Ruwi, Rabiul told me that their plan A was to bribe the Omani officials and sneak me out. And if plan A didn't work, then plan B was to cross the border on foot through the Buraimi-Al Ain border.

'The Buraimi-Al Ain border is a mountainous region. And most of the parts are not fenced, too. So, I was told that if plan A doesn't work, then I will have to move through the unfenced part of the mountain.

'While sharing the plan with full confidence, Rabiul and Shariful would also tell us every now and then that " . . . there would be police patrols. And if caught, I could get shot down."'

'Shariful told me that we would reach the Buraimi-Al Ain area by around 6 p.m. and from there, I would cross the border and nothing would go wrong. I asked Rabiul, "If we failed to cross the border, would I be brought back or is there a plan C?"

'He smiled at me and said, "*Us samay dekh lenge* . . . (We will see that at that time . . .)"'

'I had no other option but to agree with him. Before leaving Ruwi, I told Comrade John and Babu that I will keep them posted. They told me that they will check on me regularly. At around 10 p.m., I reached the official border. Our truck was parked near a teashop and Rabiul went on foot to the checkpoint. In twenty minutes, he came back with bad news. The Arab officer—Rabiul's friend—who was supposed to be on duty, had not arrived yet.

'He told us to wait. A few minutes later, six Pakistanis joined us. They spoke in Hindi. I understood that they were all planning to cross the border by bribing the officer through Rabiul and Shariful.

'We spent two more hours there. We could see vehicles entering and leaving Oman. Finally, at around 1 a.m., Rabiul told me that their officers would come only the next day and till then, they would have to wait. We had no other options. We said yes. Rabiul took us all to a small house to spend the night, and on the way there, we bought food.

'I called Comrade John and Babu and informed them about our status. They told me to be careful.

'I told Comrade John to tell our comrades in Al Ain to come to the border only after they get a message that I have crossed the border safely. He said he would pass the message on to them. I didn't talk much as I was the only Indian in the group and was feeling scared.

'I didn't sleep that night as well. The next day, we had breakfast at around 10 a.m. I knew that John had given him OMR 250 as a bribe to smuggle me out of Oman. I assumed he was buying food with that money. Interestingly, we were told not to go anywhere outside. As we didn't have valid resident cards and were in the border area, the chances of getting arrested were very high.

'I understood that. So, I decided not to go out. By 2 p.m., we got lunch.

'When he brought the lunch, he told us to be ready by around 6 p.m. He told us that his officers would be in charge and that all seven of us would be able to cross the border.

'The Pakistanis bought playing cards to spend the time. I don't play cards. So, I slept. Around 5 p.m., I woke up. I saw several missed calls from Comrade John. I called him back and told him that we will leave by 6 p.m. I apologized for not picking the calls as he sounded a bit irritated. At around 6.30 p.m., Rabiul came. We went to the border again. Our truck was parked near the checkpoint. Rabiul went on foot to the checkpoint and came back in a hurry. He told us that his officers were not there, so we had two options: either we go back to Muscat or cross the border through the mountainway.

'Reji, I didn't want to go back to Muscat. You know that we tried our best to fly out of Oman with whatever papers we had, right? But it didn't happen. So, I agreed to crossing the border. One by one, all the others said yes as well. Rabiul and Shariful told us that we should start walking by 10 p.m. Rabiul told us that it would be a six-hour walk through the mountains. We were eight, with the Pakistanis, including the driver, who was also the guide, and myself.

'Though I was the only Indian, my companions were like brothers to me. They were encouraging me to be confident. I called Comrade John and Babu to tell them about the new plan.

'Comrade John wanted me to come back to Muscat. But Babu told me to try my luck.

'After I convinced him with my plan, Comrade John said that he will tell his friends in Al Ain to wait for me the next morning. We started walking.

'It was not very dark because of the moonlight. As we were walking through a valley, one of the men told me that there would be snakes and wild dogs. We walked for around thirty minutes. Again, one of them told me that we may have to walk for three hours continuously through the valley, and then climb the mountain and continue for some three more hours . . . At that point, I was doubtful whether we would make it . . .

'At around 2 p.m., we started to climb the mountain. There was no light. Only the Pakistani driver knew the route. He was walking in front of us. I was slowing down. While walking through the valley, I got a serious cut on the sole of my right foot.

'I had stepped on a broken glass bottle. The glass pierced through my slippers. The cut was deep.

'I cried in pain and fell to the ground. All the men ran towards me. One of them helped me sit up. Another who switched on his mobile torch found that I had stepped on glass.

'My foot was bleeding. I had a bottle of drinking water. One of the men took it from me, opened the lid, and poured a little water over it. After washing the wound, they pulled out a glass piece from the cut. It was painful. I wanted to scream. But they told me not to because it would draw the attention of the people and also the valley dogs.

'The Oman valley dogs are ferocious. They will attack anyone.

'So, my companions told me to bear with the pain and not scream. It was horrible. Even though we were able to take out a big piece, there were still a few in the wound. We were not able to spot them with the mobile torchlight. But I could feel that there were small pieces still inside my foot.

'We had to wrap the wound tightly. But we didn't have any cloth. I realized that I was wearing a vest, too. So, I took off the shirt, removed the vest, and tore it into long pieces. One of the men wrapped one of the pieces on the wound and tied another on my calf. They helped me stand up. It was painful. My injured leg was shivering. Could I walk? Could I climb the mountain? I was doubtful.

'Going back was not an option. We had crossed halfway already. And even if I wanted to return, I couldn't do it alone. I am afraid of the darkness. I don't know the route. Who would accompany me? All the others have to cross the border. Either I had to wait till daylight breaks and walk back, or I had to continue on the journey. I decided to continue. It was the best option.

'With the help of my companions, I wore my shirt and stood up. I was limping while holding on to them for support. I knew that I had become a burden, and yet, they were not ready to leave me.

'They were telling me . . . "*Bhaii . . . hum to hain . . .*" I only knew the driver's name. His name was Musafar. He told me that while we were in the truck. I didn't know anyone else's name. They were all calling each other *Bhaii* . . . I was also addressed as *Bhai* by them.

'Without them, I could not have crossed the border, Reji . . . . Even though my companions helped me walk after the injury, I slipped and fell several times, slipping on loose stones. In addition to the cut, I suffered a few bruises on my left hand and lower jaw. Even though there was no bleeding there was swelling. I had also bit my tongue when I fell so it was difficult to speak. I was held up by one of the bhais. But I stepped on a loose stone and slipped. As I had bit my tongue, I couldn't talk properly too.

'The bhais decided to rest for a few minutes for me. Musafar told me that we would be entering Al Ain soon and that it was the last point where we could make a phone call. I called Comrade John. He was waiting for my call. I didn't tell him about the injuries. I just told him that, so far, all was well.

'From there, again, it was a three-hour journey. Everything looked grey under the moonlight. We had to walk together through an area filled with shrubs that hid venomous snakes. Musafar told us to be cautious. If a snake bit us, we won't be able to do anything. The only thing we had was a knife to cut the wound and a piece of cloth to tie above it. And the chances of crossing the border after a snake bite were very low.

'We hurried to cross the border before the daylight broke to avoid getting caught by the police.

'It was around 4 a.m. then. We only had three more hours at most. By then, daylight would break. Luckily, the nights were longer. But more delays would put us in trouble. At around 8.30 am, we reached the Al Ain side.

'Musafar had a UAE SIM. Comrade John had shared the Al Ain comrade's number with me. So, when I rang that number, they were able to locate our position. They told us to wait there. In twenty minutes, two Keralite comrades came to our side and one of them called my name out.

'I felt relieved, Reji. I was about to fall. I was tired. My legs were swelling and bleeding. The comrades moved me to their car immediately. We reached their accommodation at around 10 a.m. It was a good flat. I was given a new shirt and trousers. They had breakfast ready for me, too. They didn't enquire about my story. When I started to tell them, they told me that Comrade John had already told them everything.

'At around 1 p.m., I was taken to a small clinic. After taking out three small glass pieces, the doctor dressed my wounds and gave me some painkillers. We reached the accommodation that evening after spending some time in Al Ain town. The next day, they took me to the Indian Embassy in Abu Dhabi. I told the officials that I had come to Dubai for work and was laid off by my employer.

Like I mentioned before, the provision for amnesty was on. So, I applied. I had to wait for five days to get the flight ticket. And finally, on the seventh day of my arrival in Al Ain, I flew to India.'

Majeed added that if he had to thank somebody for helping him cross the border with an injured leg and tired body, it would be the bhais. 'If they had not helped me, I wouldn't have been here now. I would have either died in that valley or on the mountain . . .' he said.

I told Majeed, 'People who are stuck in the same situation will help each other. That's the goodness of people. You were lucky to experience that.'

While reporting migrant workers' woes in Oman and other Arab countries, I understood that workers aren't discriminated by their race, caste, and creed. A Pakistani worker or an Indian worker would face the same challenges. They will be subjected to the same kind of exploitation.

I have also found that the workers have great love for each other and camaraderie, too. Like I mentioned before, many a time, when I trespassed the camps to do workers' stories and was caught by the Omani security guards, it would be the tall and heavily built Pakistani workers who would come to my rescue.

My Pakistani sources would take great risks to get me a good story. I was also on good terms with the Pakistani social club officials and embassy officials. I had direct access to the Pakistani ambassadors, and they respected me because my stories on Pakistani migrant workers were always honest and sincere.

To them, an Indian running stories of Pakistani workers was new and appreciable. I have never categorized a worker as Pakistani or Indian. I only see them as a human being, deserving of respect and care.

I asked Majeed for more information about the bhais— where did they go, did they join him with the Al Ain comrades . . .

'No, Reji . . . after entering Al Ain, we had to walk an hour more to reach the meeting point near the official border checkpost. When the Al Ain comrades came to me, the Pakistani bhais bid goodbye. They had made their own arrangements. We cried and hugged each other. We didn't have anything to share but love.

'I would've died in that valley without them. Or I would have lost my way in the mountain and died due to hunger and thirst.

'Reji, they held me whenever I slipped. They washed my wound, gave me water, helped me stand up when I was limping . . . I will never forget them.'

Hearing his story, I also felt grateful to the bhais . . . When I asked whether he had collected their numbers, he said no. 'I asked, but they didn't want to share. Musafar told me that it was over. The Almighty helped them reach their destination. Although we won't see each other again, I will never forget them,' he told me.

When Majeed completed the story, it was around 2 p.m. By then, we had tea from the teashop behind the police station.

After which we got back home and had our lunch. He slept for a few hours, till 6 p.m.

I didn't. Later in the evening, we went outside. This time, to a nearby bar to have a beer. Majeed doesn't drink, but he was good company. Before entering the bar, I told him not to talk about Muscat. So, he didn't. We talked about Kerala, politics, religion, and everything else.

That night he stayed at my house, and the next morning I dropped him at the railway station. He assured me that he will call me and my parents soon. This was in the middle of 2012. I had a landline telephone connection at home. My mother had noted down Majeed's number in her diary. Years later, we disconnected the landline connection. Majeed may have changed his number, because we were no longer in touch with each other.

I am sure that Majeed thinks about me once in a while, just as I do about him. When I think about Majeed, I picture him wearing a green-striped shirt, torn on the right side, and wrinkled trousers, standing near the alley of Sultan Qaboos Mosque in Ruwi. Majeed must be happy now, because if he had any trouble, he would have contacted me. And he knows how to do it . . .[9,10]

4

My Son Is My Arabab

In March 2011, a Keralite woman came to meet a reporter with the *Times of Oman* with great hope that he would share her story.

She was undocumented and stranded on the streets of Oman. She had no work visa, no job, and no food. The return to India was easy. And the Indian embassy would manage to make it happen in a few days if she wanted. But she had a compelling reason to stay back in Oman, till she died.

However, the journalist, who was a business reporter, was neither impressed with her story nor daring enough to share the truth, which is not surprising. A majority of journalists, especially the migrant worker issues reporters in the Arab Gulf countries are afraid to tell the real stories of struggling and stranded migrant workers.

Here's their justification, which I hear time and again: 'We have come here to earn money. Who cares about journalism? Let's appreciate this government, praise the ruler and his deputies, and earn rials and dinars. And if migrant workers are getting stranded here, it is their country's fault. Why do they allow people to migrate? Why can't they provide them with jobs? This is a foreign land; we have to adjust. Let's focus on remitting money every month . . . don't try to be a journalist here.'

In the Arab Gulf, every English newspaper has Indian journalists. '*Kullu Thamaam* (All is Well)' is the default tagline of any Arab country, even if there are unrests, protests, and riots on the streets. 'All is well' is also the motto of the journalists in an Arab Gulf country.

Now, what are these 'real' stories in the Arab Gulf? That's a riddle for a newcomer, but an easy question for someone with experience.

An Arab ruler issuing a royal decree is considered a 'real' story, even if it something trivial like a change in his cabinet and shuffling of diplomats. However, once in a while, there will be decrees important for the common man, like strengthening of the Consumer Act, building a new hospital, and so on.

An Arab ruler sending a maximum 150-word greeting to his neighbouring counterpart is also a 'real' story, and it should be placed on the front page without fail.

Similarly, a press release from a multi-national company head, the regular advertisement provider, makes the list.

Interestingly, the press releases can range from the opening of an Aston Martin showroom to a mango sale festival week organized in a mall. It is quite difficult to make space for stories that matter with all these 'real' stories hogging the page.

Furthermore, you will be 'crossing' the limits set and practised for decades by the government and self-censored editors and management by publishing your story. For 'crossing the line', I was summoned twice by state-owned companies, thrice by the police, once by the Intelligence, and twice by the court between 2012 and 2017. And finally, when the Oman government found that I didn't toe their line, I was deported on 15 April 2017.

My 'crime' was exposing the human trafficking of Asian domestic workers through the UAE to Oman in October 2016. 'You don't do stories. You are an activist. A migrant rights activist. Your stories are shaming us globally. We don't want you here . . .'—these were the words told to me by a senior official at the Ministry of Information who took my press card while demanding an apology.

I gave up my card but didn't apologize. This happened in 2017.

A year before, in 2016, two independent newspapers, *Azamn* and *Al-Balad*, as well as the online website *Al-Mowaten*, were forced to close or had to suspend operations as a result of political pressure.[1]

The authorities did not let *Azamn* reopen in 2017, although an appeal court ruled in late 2016 that it should be allowed to resume operations.

Even after being the most 'outspoken' newspaper in Oman, the *Times of Oman*, where I was chief reporter, didn't manage to carry even a single line on the muzzling of the press. The situation has not changed. The World Press Freedom Index from Reporters Without Borders (RSF) ranked Oman 135th out of 180 countries.

Reporters Sans Frontiers (RSF) had coloured Oman red, for 'bad', on its press freedom map, meaning that the press is only partly free, and the situation for journalists is 'difficult'. RSF notes that censorship is ubiquitous in Oman, and journalists are often arrested and sometimes held incommunicado, given long jail sentences on charges of insulting the head of state or the country's culture and customs, or of calling for unlicensed gatherings and disrupting public order.

Meanwhile, Freedom House says freedom of expression in Oman is 'limited' and criticism of the Sultan is prohibited. It notes that there are private media outlets in addition to those run by the state, but they typically accept government subsidies, practise self-censorship, and face punishment if they cross political red lines.

Freedom House adds that the Omani government's efforts to suppress critical news and commentary extends to books and social media.[2]

Unfortunately, journalists are liable to arrest and detention if they contact international media organizations.

Journalists in Oman are supposed to disclose their sources if required by the government to do so.

Article 26 of the Omani Press and Publications Law is seen by many activists, writers, journalists, and bloggers as a blatant violation of the right to freedom of opinion, expression, and publication.[3]

Article 115 (a) of the recently updated Omani Penal Code can be viewed as threatening to any attempt at journalistic work that strays beyond the limits imposed on the rest of the press by government and security requirements.

The Omani Ministry of Information, under the direct supervision of the Omani Internal Security Service, controls the choice of correspondents by foreign news agencies, newspapers, and TV stations operating outside Oman. In a few words, freedom of the press is null and void, and the press in Oman exists only to serve the ruler and the government.

I had migrated to Oman in November 2006 after I was offered the position of sub-editor. I had not travelled abroad until then. However, I had seen the richness of Arab Gulf countries in television programmes in Kerala, and I was aware of the rial vs dollar conversion rates. When I arrived, one Omani rial was Rs 95. And I was recieving OMR 650, which was around Rs 62,000. At the Indian newspaper in Kochi where I was working, my salary was only Rs 16,000. So, the skyscrapers, the Arabs, the nightlife, and the hefty salary were the four main reasons that pushed me to migrate.

Moreover, migrating to Gulf is nothing new for a Keralite. As said in the first chapter, we Keralites are good friends of the Arabs, sharing history dating back centuries. But travelling to Oman was a disappointing experience for me. While nearing Oman, with only a few minutes to land, I peeped through the aircraft window. I could see only mountains. I couldn't see any high-rising buildings, houses, greenery . . . nothing.

I decided to return. I had a return ticket with me, which is mandatory when you are travelling on a visitor visa. Even though I was flying to Oman to take up a job, I did not have a work visa.

It is quite hard to get a work visa for a journalist in an Arab Gulf country. The newspaper which offered me the job couldn't manage one before my arrival. However, as they needed a sub-editor immediately, they issued a visitor visa and brought me in.

After only ten days of joining the firm, my visitor visa was converted into a work visa. But I was not provided with a journalist visa, instead, I used a librarian visa for four years, because of which I was unable to do any ground reporting. If you are stopped by the police and asked to show your card, then the first question they'd ask is, 'Why are you out on the field? You are a librarian. You should be there.' It is a violation of local laws to be on the action scene without a journalist visa. You can be fined and even jailed for violation of visa rules.

A long-time Keralite business editor in the Arab Gulf told me that it is common to do a job in the Arab Gulf, which is different from what is mentioned in the visa/work permit card; this is known as a 'monkey visa'. The majority of the migrants are on a 'monkey visa' in the Arab Gulf countries. There is a story behind the 'monkey visa'.

It goes like this . . .

Once a lion was brought to Dubai. The vessel was docked on the Dubai coast as the visa and immigration papers had to be cleared.

In the morning, the Lebanese manager came with a chart, checked the lion's name, and served him a banana, an apple, and oranges for breakfast. The lion assumed that in Dubai, this may be the common breakfast for all; he may even get meat for lunch. However, the Lebanese served fruits for lunch and dinner, the lion got angry.

He roared at the Lebanese manager and said, 'Do you know who I am? I am the king of the jungle! And I need meat.'

The Lebanese manager checked his papers again and then replied, 'You might be the king of the jungle, but you are here on a monkey visa. So, I will provide you with a monkey's meal . . .'

In all the Arab Gulf countries, most drivers will be on an engineering visa, and engineers on a mason visa.

In many labour cases, the 'monkey visa' has become a hurdle. For example, in cases where a company is desperately looking for a mason from India, but they only have an auto mechanic visa clearance in hand, the mason will be brought in on an auto mechanic visa and given the job of a mason.

In case the mason faces an accident at the workplace, then the company, the mason, and his family cannot claim compensation and insurance because the first report will clearly state that the person was an auto mechanic as per his visa status. And of course, the question will arise, 'What was an auto mechanic doing at a construction site?' The majority of the migrant workers don't know what work visa they have, as it is written in Arabic on their work permit cards and visa papers.

Being new to the country and journalism, I had a lot to learn and unlearn. The two good deputy editors taught me the dos and don'ts. Being there as a sub-editor helped me learn Oman and Arab journalism. Yes, there is an 'Arab' journalism. I learned to add prefixes, like His Excellencies for government officials while editing the news stories for local pages, and also re-christen a gun-toting Palestinian rebel as a fighter for international pages.

Additionally, we should be cautious to cut down or change the Jews from our stories. We aren't allowed to mention even

Kosher salt in a recipe column on the feature pages. Kosher salt was commonly used in the koshering process of removing blood from meat, following Jewish dietary laws. Anything endorsing Israel and the Jews should not be printed.

While reading about Oman, doing local pages, and learning the dos and don'ts, four years passed. And from there, I moved to the *Times of Oman*, the largest circulated English newspaper in Oman. But before moving there, I had made sure to acquire a journalist visa. Finally, I got the 'license' to do real stories.

At the *Times of Oman*, I started to tell stories of migrant workers. Most of the stories were about the challenges they faced.

I never thought of or tried to do 'success' stories of migrant entrepreneurs who were listed in the Forbes, because there were plenty of glossy coffee-table magazines to tell their stories in the market. Interestingly, all the 'success' stories had the same formula—from rags to riches.

'I started from scratch, worked hard, slept in camps, burnt the midnight oil, stood in queues. I still wake up at 3 a.m., respond personally to emails, read a lot of books, watch movies with family, and donate a lot, thanks to the benevolent ruler, stable government, friendly Arabs, great culture, good food, Arab brothers . . .'

The above-said ingredients will be added in apt quantities to make the story look fresh. Yes, to 'look' fresh.

I was looking for a story like Jumaila's, which was difficult to get. When a story comes to our office, how can I discard it? Jumaila's story was one of my first. The editor at that time, an Indian, was aware that a domestic worker had come to the office to meet our business reporter, but he was not going to do the story. So, the editor assigned me the story. I got the number from the business reporter and called Jumaila.

While dialling the number, I never expected that she would have the most interesting story I have ever heard. Jumaila was a wife of an Omani citizen for twelve years and the mother of two young Omani boys aged eleven and twelve.

But when I had called her, she was literally on the streets. She didn't know where to go or what to do. She was running in despair, from pillar to post, in the hope of getting a shelter to stay in Oman and to look after her children, Majeed and Mohammed.

In that condition, she came to our office with hopes of getting her story heard. She had to get a job in Oman for an intriguing reason.

We met at the cafeteria near my office at around 2 p.m. She was wearing a black abaya. The headscarf had some red design work. She didn't look like a Keralite woman. She had come to Oman at a very young age and had lived in an Omani house, so, she looked more like an Omani woman than a Keralite.

Jumaila was an orphan from Kozhikode, a northern Keralite coastal town, connected to Arab Gulf much more than any other district in Kerala and India. She was adopted by a physically challenged local politician from an orphanage. That's all she was ready to reveal, either because she failed to recollect those days, or she was not willing to tell me about it.

'Vaapa (father) was worried about me a lot. He was afraid that he would die soon, and I will get stranded. So, he was in a hurry to fulfil his responsibilities as a father,' Jumaila said while sipping the tea, which we had bought.

I understood that she was hungry. She might not have had her lunch. She had told me over the phone that she was struggling for daily food and shelter. When she came to meet me, she was staying with an acquaintance.

'Getting a job for an undocumented worker is quite hard in Oman. People are afraid of taking risks. So, nobody will hire an undocumented domestic worker. And it was a risk for me, too . . . . Eventually, I had no job nor money,' Jumaila said. She had been in this pathetic situation for nine months now.

While she continued to tell her story, I ordered falafels, a deep-fried ball of patty made from ground chickpeas and fava beans. We were in a Keralite cafeteria. So, we got a Keralite falafel, not the real Arabic one.

She seemed hungry. She had four falafels at one go. She didn't even bother to dip it in the yoghurt. While eating the falafel, she told me about her arrival in Oman and her life there.

She had come to Oman in 1998 when she was eighteen years old. An Arab from Oman, who claimed to be a sheikh, met her father and expressed his interest in marrying Jumaila.

'He claimed that he has a big farm and tons of money. My father was quite impressed. Hurriedly, I was married off to him and sent to Oman,' Jumaila said, cursing the moment her father took the decision.

'Why am I cursed like this? Nothing good happens in my life. Why was I given such a life, only to suffer? I am only thirty-one years old, but I have already gone through a lot of suffering.

'I was only eighteen and he was above fifty when we got married. I had become an orphan. My father believed that even if there was an age difference, I would be free from financial problems and safe in my husband's house,' Jumaila added.

It was an *Arabi Kalyanam* (*Arabi* marriage). In Kerala, Arab marriages have been, almost exclusively, a Kozhikode practice. Even centuries ago, Arab merchants used to find wives here when they had to stay for long intervals.

However, things began degenerating in the past few decades, when Kerala witnessed a Gulf boom and increased interaction with the Arab countries. More than the rich dhow-owning Arab businessmen lugging off timber and spices from these coasts, every deck-hand, *khalasi*, and menial worker in Arab gear began to find young girls here, mostly for a month or so, before their ship would weigh anchor for yet another port of call. Then the other visiting Arabs, lured by the tales, would fly in for cheap but legitimate sex.

The girls, invariably, in their teens, were available aplenty thanks to the huge dowry and other demands on their parents from local grooms. Besides, the imagined mystiques of Arabian riches were hard to resist. When the period of lust is over, the Arabs return to Arabia, offering the girls and their families some money and household items.

Unfortunately, only a few take the girls along with them. Jumaila was the lucky one who got the chance to accompany the Arab sheikh. But her luck ended on the day of arrival itself.

The day she arrived at the Arab sheikh's home, she found he had lied to her. His house was small. He was not a sheikh.

He was a security guard at a garage. He already had two wives and was the father of twelve children. The eldest one was in his thirties.

'It was a very big family and we had little money, so most days we didn't have enough food to eat. In addition to this, he used to abuse me a lot. I never complained to anybody. But I am also a human being. In 2009, I divorced him,' she said.

Usually, men divorce women. But Jumaila was courageous enough to take the first step, to divorce her abusive husband. 'The court in Oman was sympathetic to me. They heard my story and granted me a divorce,' Jumaila said.

I was a bit surprised to hear how Jumaila was bold enough to fight for justice in a foreign country. By then, she had also delivered two boys.

'I was unable to provide for their schooling, clothes, and food. I had to beg him for money. And whenever I asked for money, he would abuse me badly. He even tried to sell me. Many a time, it was sheer luck that I got away. Life was hell there. Hunger, mental abuse, physical violence, shame . . .' Jumaila said.

She then continued, 'I managed to live for ten years, somehow. But when he tried to sell me off to others for money and forced me to sleep with strangers, I left the house. I knew that the boys would not be thrown out.

'I couldn't even sleep peacefully in that house. Even during midnight, he would pull me from the bed and abuse me,' Jumaila added.

When Jumaila was telling her story, I found that the cafeteria people were also listening in even though they pretended otherwise. I told Jumaila to finish her tea, so we could go back to my office and continue the story.

In a few minutes, she was ready to go. I paid the money and walked back to my office. At the reception, there was a visitor's lounge, where reporters would sit with people who came to meet them.

It was a good, decent room. It had a coffeemaker, too. I could see that Jumaila was more comfortable in this room. She continued her narrative.

In 2009, Jumaila divorced her husband with the help of some social workers. She thought that getting a divorce would solve all her problems, but things only started to get worse after that.

After getting separated, she lost her 'family visa' status and was told to go back to India by the government officials. Jumaila wanted to stay back for her boys. So, she had to find a job.

She said, 'I have only passed Class 10. I wasn't sure I'd get a job. But I didn't give up, as I wanted to take care of my boys.'

She was staying with a friend whom she had met while at her husband's house. They worked part-time jobs in different houses.

There are many Indian women domestic workers, on a 'free visa', with experience working in the Gulf.

In Arab countries, migrant workers are allowed to work only for their employer. However, if you pay additional money to enjoy the freedom to work anywhere, then the employer will allow the same. Locally, this is called a free visa. The worker will have to pay $60 per month to be on a free visa.

If you work for a single employer, you may earn $350 per month. The kafala system keeps you bonded to your employer, making it illegal to work for anyone else who is not your visa provider. But if you manage to have a free visa, you will be able to earn some $600 with different employers.

Usually, men prefer 'free visas' but I have seen that experienced women also opt for a 'free visa'. Experienced women domestic workers work in five different houses a day and earn a decent amount. These women domestic workers start their job at 4 a.m. A few have even arranged taxis to pick them up from one house and drop them at the next. Most of them speak at least four Indian languages and Arabic, too.

These 'free visa' domestic workers are experienced enough to survive in the Arab Gulf. Most of them even carry a small knife in their bag to protect themselves from Arab and Asian employers while working during odd hours. Jumaila managed to stay with a few people whom she knew, and they also provided her with food.

Jumaila didn't have a job, money, or food. She realized that she could not continue like this for long. So, she started to look for a job. In about twenty-five days, she was able to get a job with a valid visa.

She was a domestic worker in an Indian house, working for a decent pay. 'They were a good small family. I was able to meet my boys and take care of their needs. I could also send some money for my Vappa,' Jumaila said.

'When the work visa was arranged, I went to my husband's house. In those twenty-five days, I had only seen my boys once. It was very hard to stay away from them. But I couldn't go there. He (my husband) would be there. If he sees me, he will beat me . . . I didn't want to face the embarrassment again,' Jumaila said.

Once, Jumaila met her boys in a neighbour's house. She could spend only a few minutes with them as she was afraid of her abusive husband 'catching' them. She had taken some chocolates for them, too, gifted by her roommates.

'I gave them chocolates, hugged them, and left,' Jumaila said, adding that as she had got a work visa, she would be able to come back and take care of her children in a better way.

She flew to India, stayed with her foster father, and told him everything. She was assured of his care and discussed her plans to return. 'I didn't blame him for pushing me into that hell. He thought of giving me a better life. What's the point in blaming him? I stayed for a week and then returned,' Jumaila said.

'Returning to Oman, I felt refreshed. I knew that a work visa is only for two years but was hopeful that if I worked sincerely, the employer wouldn't throw me out. The happiness of being able to meet my boys weekly, geting them books, dresses, and gifts, and sending some moncy for my father kept pushing me on,' Jumaila added.

Jumaila used to meet her boys at her friends' accommodation since she didn't want to disturb her employer. Every Friday, she would go and pick up her boys, take them to the parks, allow them to play, get them food from hotels, and spend some time at her friends' accommodation.

'On one such Friday, as usual, after spending time at the park and the hotel, we went to a place where my friends were staying. Unfortunately, there was a brothel in the same building, and we got caught up in a police raid. We were taken to the police station and questioned. I was totally broken with shame. I didn't expect my boys to be put in that kind of situation,' Jumaila said.

While telling me the police station episode, Jumaila's voice was wavering. 'It is my fault that my boys at the age of ten and eight were standing in a police station with strange women for a strange case. I should have been cautious. I pleaded with the police officers that we are innocent, but to no avail. My boys were also frightened,' Jumaila added.

Getting arrested for prostitution is a severe crime in any Arab Gulf country.

However, after reaching the police station, she was lucky. A kind officer was ready to hear her story. 'I had my bag with me. I took out my resident card and told them that I am holding a valid visa and that I am not involved in any nefarious activities. However, I didn't want the police officers to call my employer, because, whatever the truth may be, an employer getting a call from a police station saying that his or her worker has been caught for prostitution will not sound good. They would definitely see me as a bad woman thereafter,' Jumaila said.

Usually, if you are a migrant taken into custody by the police, the first thing they do is call your employer because he is the sponsor. However, most employers don't like the police calling them for this purpose, even if the worker is innocent.

Jumaila managed to tell the officer her story.

'He was affected by my story and convinced that we were innocent. Still, he asked my elder boy whether I was telling the true story. He said yes. Luckily, he was wearing a *dishdasha*, the local men's dress. So, the police officer left us. They dropped my boys back home and me at my employer's house. I was relieved and thankful to them,' Jumaila said.

In between, Jumaila managed to inform a social worker in Oman, who alerted the Indian Embassy. They both had talked to the police officials and updated them about the innocence of Jumaila. The Indian Embassy's intervention had also helped her at the police station.

'Sitting in the police vehicle with my boys, I realized they had grown up. They love me. They respect me. My efforts for them is not going to waste,' she told me.

Jumaila, later on, avoided taking her boys to anybody's house. They met in the park, ate at hotels, and returned to their respective shelters. They were happy.

But today, she had come to meet me to tell me a different story, about a challenge she was facing. Her Indian employer was not ready to renew her visa when they were planning to leave Oman. This was a shock for her.

'I never thought that my happiness would end this soon. If they are leaving, then my visa will also expire. And I will have to return. My boys will struggle; they will not be looked after by their father and stepmothers. My boys are considered disturbances there. They were not even provided proper food . . .' Jumaila told me.

With the help of the Indian Embassy, a social worker, and some good lawyers, Jumaila put up a plea at the Ministry of Interior in Oman to provide her with a permanent visa. The social workers and lawyers told her that she stood a chance to get either a citizenship or a permanent visa for her stay in Oman.

'I am a mother of two Omani boys. I strongly feel that the Omani government will not let me be stranded on the streets of Oman. I have high hopes with the government,' she told me, adding that by doing a story about her, people will talk about her; it will come to the notice of the ministers and she may be able to leverage some support for her plea.

Additionally, she also thought that after reading the story, people would come forward to provide her with a job with a valid visa, if the Ministry of Interior turns down her plea.

It was around 5 p.m. Our conversation went on for three long hours. Yes, I agreed to tell her story. Around 500 words. The story was placed well on the page. The editors on the desk who read the story were sympathetic.

The next day, people started calling. They felt sympathy for her after reading her story and were curious to know more. I thanked them.

And interestingly, many wanted her phone number to help her. But I refused to give it, because I knew they were '*Pranchis*' who would help her in a very small way, by giving her a small gift, talking to her when her plea becomes successful, and ultimately approaching us, the media, to get their help stories printed, which was their aim from the start.

The word *Pranchi* evolved from a Malayalam movie '*Pranchiettan and the Saint*', in which a south Indian star Mammootty played the lead role of a rice seller from a small town in Kerala, who tries to buy fame and awards through money.

The movie ran successfully and since then, it has become common to call people who run to media houses with pictures and press notes of the great 'help' they have done for the sufferers. Press releases will be making them 'Mother Teressas'.[4]

When the journalists find a stranded Indian, they reach out to the Pranchi. If the Pranchi is ready to help, then the reporter files the story setting a scene for the Pranchi's dramatic entrance.

And on the very next day, an impact story is printed detailing the Pranchi's intervention and benevolence, and the newspaper's commitment to telling real stories. The stranded Indian, the reporter, and the Pranchi would all be happy. Such Pranchi stories pop up on and off, making them more and more popular. That's why I don't share the contact details of the people who are featured in my stories.

The story was printed on 12 February 2011. And on the same day, her visa expired and she became undocumented. But that didn't stop her from approaching the Indian Embassy, meeting social workers, and me.

She found a new shared accommodation, stayed there, and survived on part-time jobs, mainly cooking food, cleaning rooms, and washing clothes. Every third day, she would meet her boys.

In between, she was summoned by the Ministry of Interior for the final hearing.

A day before going to the ministry, she called me. I told her, 'Don't get worried; the ministry will be sympathetic and take a favourable decision.' She said yes. But she was depressed and cynical. Meanwhile, we advised her not to go alone. We told her to take her sons with her.

In the two months that passed, nothing promising happened. As of 20 February, she became an overstayer as well, which is a punishable crime.

Not knowing what else to do, we waited. Finally, Jumaila was called to the headquarters of the Ministry of Interior on 8 May.

We were tense. If the ministry denied her plea, she would have to return, leaving behind her children.

Jumaila went with her boys to the Ministry of Interior, where she was told to say her story again. During the thirteen years living with her abusive husband, Jumaila had learnt to speak Arabic.

'When I told them my story of sorrow, my need to live in Oman and be with my children, the officers were sympathetic. But then again, they were troubled with the challenge of providing me a visa or citizenship,' Jumaila said.

While foreigners can, in theory, become Omani citizens, it is nearly impossible if they do not have a 100 per cent Omani ancestry. The only foreigners known to obtain Omani citizenship on a relatively consistent basis are the children of nationals who emigrated before 1970. They may return to Oman and apply for citizenship through the Ministry of the Interior, but are by no means guaranteed success. For this reason, the government's citizenship policy is extremely controversial. In many cases, the government will grant only a half-returning family citizenship. In others, it will not even grant some members of these families residence or work permits.

As a result, some Omanis accuse the government of retroactively punishing families who left during the country's difficult period of reform. If you have no Omani heritage, your only chance at citizenship will be through marriage to an Omani national, and even then your application will probably be denied.

In exceptional cases, Oman's ruler has the power to grant citizenship to a foreigner who has made great contributions to the state for many years, but these instances are rare. It is more common for generous employers to reward loyal workers by providing them with work and residence permits of indefinite duration. Even then, there is a good chance this support will end when those workers retire.

The government does not grant citizenship to foreign children born in Oman unless one parent happens to be an Omani citizen. Even then, children of mixed families may have different rights than their parents—this varies from case to case.

'After hearing my sordid tale, the officers paused for a moment. They turned to my boys. I was tense. What were they going to ask them? Will my boys understand their questions? Will they be able to answer? It was a crucial moment in my life. A few minutes . . . would decide whether I can be with my boys or not . . .' Jumaila said.

Luckily, all went well as she and her boys had hoped.

When the officer asked what can be done to help his mother, my eldest, who was eleven years old, said that he would sponsor me. 'I am the son of an Omani father. I am an Omani. Can I sponsor a job visa for my mother? Or can the government provide citizenship for her . . . we can't go to India. We want to live here. We want our mother with us . . . will Oman give us that?'

'The officials were surprised,' Jumaila said, adding that she could see tears rolling down her boy's cheeks when he was asking for a visa for her.

'I saw them talking to each other. They asked for a break. I was told to sit outside. In a few minutes, I was called in again. I held my boys close to me and entered the room. The officers smiled at me. I was not sure, whether that smile was a positive signal or not,' Jumaila said.

'But finally, they told me . . . I can stay in Oman. My son can sponsor me . . . paperwork will be done . . .' Jumaila said.

'I was numb for a moment. I couldn't believe that I was permitted to stay in Oman forever . . . . They might have realized that I was surprised and shocked. So, they called my name and repeated the same sentence . . .' Jumaila said.

'I cried. I thanked my boy and the government officials. I even wanted to kneel and bow. But I didn't. I had to sign some papers . . . I did that and then left,' Jumaila said.

This happened on 8 May. In the evening, at around 7 p.m., the social worker called me and updated me on the happenings at the Ministry of Interior. He said that even my story was produced as evidence to support her claim. I felt proud. I called Jumaila.

She was quite happy. She started to thank everyone. She told me that she would have never thought that her boy had grown up enough to talk to the officials.

'It was his words that helped me stay in Oman. It was his words . . . my boy had grown up. They love me. They won't discard me . . .' she said.

Before disconnecting the call, she assured me that she would meet me that week itself.

I was about to leave the office. After clearing my table, I shared the happy story with my colleague in the features edition. She reminded me that Mother's Day was coming up. This gave me an idea.

I ran to my boss's room to ask for the space to print a 450-word story on the paper. When he refused, I persevered, explaining my idea and bringing him the story published in March from the library. He got in touch with the sub-editor to run my story.

I thanked him, ran back to my desk, and typed the story in thirty minutes. I felt proud. I'll be getting a great story for Mother's Day.

The next day, when I opened the newspaper, I was impressed by the headline. 'The Best Mother's Day Gift for Jumaila: A Visa!'[5]

A week after that, when I called Jumaila, she told me that she was busy cooking biriyani for her Arabab.

I was surprised. I asked her who it was and she replied, 'Yes, sir, today my sons are coming. Have you forgotten that he is my Arabab; the one who is sponsoring me?'

I said, 'I will call you in the evening after I leave my office.'

She was happy. Later, I learnt from the social worker that she got a job in a good company as a cleaner, and was staying in a decent accommodation, taking care of her children, and sending money to her foster father. All was well.

5

We Kidnapped Sushmitha

Even after having an anti-anxiety tablet, I couldn't sleep that night. If there is something important to handle the next day, I get anxious.

I lost sleep trying to complete Thomas Piketty's *Capital in the Twenty-First Century*. Reading about inequality page after page was difficult . . . At around 10.30 p.m., I kept the book aside and tried, without any success, to sleep.

Even though I had set an alarm for 2.30 a.m., I was frequently checking the time. And as usual, before the alarm rang, I got up from bed at 2.20 a.m. I switched off the alarm and freshened up in fifteen minutes.

By then, I heard my phone ring. I knew that it would be Binil. He is a very punctual person. The previous day, we had decided to rescue Sushmitha Pandit from her abusive Arab employer.

Even if we didn't, nobody was going to take us to task about it. But somehow, the calls come to us. People, especially those who are stranded without much help, always called us.

To them, I would say in Hindi, '*Fikhar math karo. Dho dhin dhe do. Hum soch lenge aur ayenge.* (Don't worry. Give us two days. Let us think about it. And we will come.)'

While at such rescues, there is a chance that we get intercepted by Oman police and lose our jobs, we believe that we should not regret missed chances at saving a human being.

Binil is a God-fearing person and I am a rationalist. So, he would say, 'Either God or the prayers of those we have helped in the past will guide us.' Other than smiling at his statements, I wouldn't contest his theories.

Sushmitha didn't have her passport with her since it was under the custody of her employer. We just had to believe her words claiming that she was an Indian. Additionally, she told us that after she arrived in Oman, she had not gone out or been taken out of the house. This also means that the employer did not make a resident card for her—an essential document for a migrant worker. The migrant worker has to go to the Oman immigration authority to get the resident card made.

A majority of employers don't bother to make a resident card for trafficked women, which becomes a complication when they try to go back home.

Sushmitha was somewhere in Sohar, some 226 km away from Ruwi, where I lived. Yes, she was in Sohar. Why was she in Sohar? I will tell you soon.

But before that, here is some information about Sohar—northern Oman's border town—and the stories of its brave people. Oman derived its name from Sohar, or more specifically, from the settlement in an ancient town called 'Omanah' in Sohar.

Most of the people in Sohar do not have good opinions about Oman. In fact, they feel neglected by the country.

'We have to protest for access to drinking water pipes because they are first laid in Muscat,' they'd say if we asked why they were feeling agitated.

Interestingly, the people of Muscat had a different answer when they were asked why the people of Sohar are angry or upset. They would say, 'They don't know how to sit, discuss, and find a solution. They only know to protest on the streets . . . and they get more than we do.'

Like any other border town in the world, there were political tensions in Sohar. Even though I was in Oman since November 2006, I visited Sohar only in 2011, to cover the Arab Spring eruption in Sohar.

Green Marches have been taking place in Muscat for salary hikes and job security since 2018. Yes, Green Marches, not 'Red' ones. Isn't red the colour of revolution? But the Sohar comrades were different. They were brave enough to burn down a LuLu Hypermarket in Sohar, to throw stones at policemen, and to put up tents in the town centre.[1]

I travelled to Sohar without informing my office when the Arab Spring incident happened. It was not an official trip. I just didn't want to miss an opportunity to witness a protest in an Arab country.

Inspired by the Arab Springs in Egypt and Algeria, on 26 February 2011, the protest spilled over to the streets of Sohar. A common theme among the protestors was corrupt traders and their perception that a few senior ministers had pulled the wool over the sultan's eyes and were taking advantage of him for their personal gains.

The fact that the protests escalated and became more violent towards the end of February, indicated that some were dissatisfied with the government. However, the sheer diversity and volume of grievances being expressed could at times seem overwhelming.

On 23 February 2011, after the submission of a petition to the Sultan to fix these issues, it seemed as if the situation was beginning to calm down; after all, the grievances had now been aired. The petition submission failed to elicit a quick reaction from the Sultan of Oman.

Soon, the protests started to spread from Muscat. On 25 February, they reached Dhofar in the south, with a group of young protesters staging a sit-in in front of the governor's office and issuing an appeal to Qaboos labelling it as the 'call to good.'

The following day, larger protests erupted in Sohar. A protest camp was also set up at the Globe Roundabout. It seemed that the protesters were settling in for the long haul just like what happened in Tahrir Square in Egypt.

Protestors wanted development and jobs. Those who had jobs wanted salary hikes. They wanted migrant workers to be thrown out and corrupt ministers to be sacked. The demands of the Green Marches in Muscat were also somewhat the same.

But there was one crucial difference between the protests in Sohar and Muscat.

The Muscat protestors never spoke against the Oman ruler, Sultan Qaboos, unlike the Sohar protestors.

'His Majesty is a good person. He is the father of our nation. He is not at all corrupt. But his ministers are . . .'— this was the standard line from Muscat.

Muscat is the seat of Oman's ruler.

But people in Sohar had a different argument. 'How can the Sultan not be corrupt if his ministers are? Being silent about the corruption is also not fair . . . So, if his ministers are corrupt, then he is also corrupt.'

On the third day of the protest, the protesters turned violent. They burnt down the LuLu Shopping Mall in Sohar. My friends from Sohar told me that there were two reasons for this incident. One, the land on which the shopping mall was built was initially set aside for building a community centre for locals, but was given to global retailers.

The second reason was that 'non-Omanis are stealing the Omanis' opportunities.'

LuLu Mall was looted and burnt down, forcing the Sultan to deploy his black-clad forces. Tanks took over the streets. By then, the protests in Muscat were also gaining momentum.

A day before LuLu was set on fire, the protestors targeted the governor's office and a police station, setting fire to both, as well as some cars.

The police fired rubber bullets and tear gas at demonstrators gathered at the Globe Roundabout, which protesters had named 'Reform Square', leading to the death of at least two. Nobody knew their names, not even the media. We got pictures of the bullet, but not the names of the people who were shot dead.

As the protests were spreading, Sohar had its Reform Square, Salalah its Call-To-Good Square; Muscat went with People Square, and Sur, with Freedom.

However, by the end of February and the beginning of March, in a series of royal decrees, the Sultan reshuffled the cabinet of Oman. A few ministers were removed, 50,000 new jobs were created, unemployment benefits of 150 rials ($390) a month were announced, and an increase in the monthly stipend for students was declared.

Additionally, the Sultan announced the creation of a Public Authority for Consumer Protection to monitor prices, profiteering, and quality, and, in a more explicit political concession, took prosecuting powers away from the Royal Oman Police, making the Public Prosecution Department autonomous.

He also announced an inquiry into the granting of legislative powers to the *majlis*, the parliament in Oman. At the same time, though, after the burning of the Lulu and the attacks on government buildings, the protesters seemed to have realized that they had gone too far.

On 1 March, protesters in Sohar issued a public statement regretting the violence and publicly apologizing to the Sultan, which I reported on for my newspaper. They also stated, 'We have confidence in the Sultan Qaboos that he will respond to our demands.'

Indeed, the Grand Mufti, Sheikh Ahmed bin Hamad Al Khalili, denounced the protests in Sohar, but praised the actions of those in Salalah: 'The youth of Dhofar have asked for their rights without attacking anyone and have organized the protests in a civilized manner.'

The lack of further intensity in the protests suggests that the Omani public was also losing sympathy. It was perhaps this that gave the government the confidence to act. On 28 March, the army moved into the Globe Roundabout once more and cleared the twenty protestors who were still there.

The following day, reports emerged that the Public Prosecutor's Office had ordered the arrest of suspects in Sohar. By this stage, it was becoming clear just how bad things had become in the city, with reports of government branch offices besieged.

Meanwhile, local tribal elders and officials worked hard to de-escalate tensions in the country. A local leader, Khalfan Bin Saeed Bin Mohammad Al Kabbali, was arrested and accused of fomenting violence.

It was not until 9 April that the presence of the army was scaled down.

While there was a de-escalation of tension in Sohar, such a clear demonstration of force meant that protests continued elsewhere.

In 2012, the Globe Roundabout was removed. Sultan Qaboos didn't want anyone to talk about the Arab Spring when they saw the Globe Roundabout.

I had reported on the Arab Spring. I had talked to people in the Globe Roundabout. I had sat with them there. So, I had to report on the removal of the Globe Roundabout as well.

Reporting on the Arab Spring in Oman was a risky choice. I knew I could also disappear one day. But I realized that even though the Oman Arab Spring was ignored by the global media, I had to report it. What else was I supposed to do as a senior reporter in the oldest and largest-selling newspaper in Oman?

The Arab Spring in Oman got some attention only after LuLu was looted and burnt in Sohar.

I was reporting on the Green Marches but wasn't particularly interested in it. It didn't generate much excitement.

The protestors would hail the Omani ruler and rally to demand jobs. I was waiting for the 'real' protests to happen.

As I expected, some 'real' protests did take place in Sohar. They blocked trucks on the road. They sat on the roads. The numbers kept increasing.

When they started, they were only 500 in number, but the group soon grew to 2,000. I was the first reporter in Muscat to be alerted on 26 February itself.

An Indian tailor in Sohar called me on 26 February at around 2 p.m. and said that the Omanis had blocked the main road in Sohar using trucks. By doing so, they had cut the traffic from Dubai to Muscat and Sohar port.

Even though I discussed the probability of a story with my editor, truth be told, we were all clueless as to how to go about it.

Reporting a revolution is a 'big no' in any Gulf country. Do revolutions happen in Arab countries? Officially, no. The official version is that spies and terrorists funded by foreign divisive forces are disrupting the normal life. However, 'protestors are dispersed peacefully' by the Oman forces.

While this is the usual narrative, I, being a Keralite Communist who will protest over anything and everything, on hearing of rallies or protests in Oman, was very curious to learn what it was for. I wanted to know if they would be successful in shaking up Oman; would they step up for their demands and become a threat to the monarch?

No matter the outcome, I decided to visit Sohar. I landed there on the fourth day of the protest, a day after LuLu was burnt. By then, the protest was at its peak. I decided to travel by a public transport bus, to avoid being stopped and questioned at police check posts.

Even though it was my fourth year in Oman, I hadn't learnt to speak or even understand Arabic.

Still, I wasn't sure, but I thought my knowledge of Hindi could help me. Many Omani, especially taxi drivers and shop managers, could speak and understand Hindi. Additionally, they could understand Malayalam as well, because they probably had nannies who were Keralites and thus were able to interact with at least one Keralite every day.

When I reached Sohar, I didn't know where to go and what to do. I aimed to make friends with some Omanis who were protesting. I didn't want to engage with the stone-pelters and the Mullahs. I knew that neither would help me understand the situation for a possible story. The stone-pelters, in their excitement, would exaggerate all the situations, but the Mullahs would not open up at all.

I was looking for someone who would tell me the reality of events occurring there. Finally, I saw an Omani wearing a Che Guevara t-shirt and standing in the middle of a group. It is very rare to see an Omani without his national dress outside his house. If you want to see Omanis wearing trousers and t-shirts, you have to visit movie halls or malls.

In Oman, the men's national dress is the *dishdasha*, a collarless long-sleeved garment that falls in an A-line down the body to the ankles. The *wizar* (a woven hip wrap that falls to the calves) is worn underneath it, while an appropriate head covering, such as a *kumma*, an embroidered brimless cap that stands above the wearer's head, or a *massar*, an embroidered wool head wrap made of a square-shaped fabric, is fitted on the head.

The particulars of colour, cut, embellishment, and manner of wearing these pieces reveal historical connections with east Africa and the Indian subcontinent, as well as reflects Oman's own cosmopolitan history.

I was unsure whether he was an Arab or not. He was not wearing a dishdasha. He was short and didn't have the fair Arab skin. He looked like a Keralite. The only Arab thing about him was the well-trimmed and crafted beard.

He had an elegant and sharply cut beard, proving that he was careful about his appearance. A great deal of patience is required to craft a beard like that. Even though Lebanese hairstylists are experts at designing and lining such beards, a few Keralite hairstylists are also good at it. It was a skill they gained for survival. While migrating to the Arab Gulf, many Keralites would craft the Arab beard, which would not look as impressive on them. However, their love for the Arab culture makes them try it.

I gathered some courage and walked into the group, then I looked at him and said, 'Red Salute.' I was confident that a person wearing a Che t-shirt would tell me good stories.

Che is a cult figure in Oman, where revolution is taboo and the revolutionaries are disappearing. However, some cars have stickers of Che. Once, I asked an Omani taxi driver about Che, as he had a sticker on his car. He said, 'Yes. I know.' I asked him whether he had read about Che but he said he had not read much. However, he knew that Che was a Communist fighter who fought 'Amerikka' (America).

Without a pause, he shot a question at me, 'Doesn't Che look like Oman Sultan Qaboos?'

I was dumbfounded for a moment. Could a revolutionary hero, who didn't want to be in the government and ran into the jungle to do guerrilla warfare, be compared to a monarch? But before I could answer, the driver told me that there are some pictures of Sultan Qaboos in the military dress, wearing a headgear and donning a beard that make him look like Che. I finally got the answer as to why Omanis were pasting pictures of Che on mobile phone covers and cars.

They've mistaken Che for Sultan Qaboos. But the question arises: Has anyone seen Sultan Qaboos in person? Not many have seen him, except when he takes the annual tour of the villages. The common man sees him only on television, chairing the Parliament and greeting foreign dignitaries.

The Che t-shirt wearing Arab stared at me and asked, 'Hind?' I said, 'Yes, Hind.' For Arabs, all Indians are 'Hind', even if you are from south India. He greeted me, '*Lal Salaam*.'

That's it.

I was excited. That Lal Salaam instilled confidence in me. He told me that he brought the t-shirt in New Delhi, where he was studying in 2009. He was familiar with the protests in Delhi. He had read the works of many Indian writers, too. He told me that he had read Bhagat Singh's *Jail Diary and Other Writings* many times.

I was lucky to have found him. A person wearing a Che t-shirt and who has read Bhagat Singh was the perfect person to talk to at a protest.

Let's call him Muhammed, because I don't want him to disappear after this book is published. He had 'disappeared' twice during the protest, but I don't want that to happen again.

The Oman police filmed the protests. Be it the Green or the Red, they capture every moment to decide who they want to pick up later on. After we introduced ourselves to each other, he took me to the Globe Roundabout and introduced me to many elders with long beards.

Muhammed was impressed with the *Times of Oman*'s coverage of the protest. Even though the protest stories did not find space on the front page, they were reported. Three other English newspapers, *Oman Tribune*, *Oman Observer*, and *Muscat Daily* were not reporting the protest stories. *Muscat Daily* did a few. But not as much as we did.

Muhammed detailed their demands and protest plans to me.

'We are always ignored by Muscat. We have to protest on the streets to get even basic rights and help,' Muhammed said.

While I asked him about why the LuLu was burnt, he looked at me and said, 'Yes, there is a reason.'

'As the number of protestors are growing, the leaders are finding it hard to control the protesters. This incident took place on the third day of the protest. That land was meant to be given for building a community cultural centre. But as usual, corruption gave space to LuLu. This was a grievance among the locals. Additionally, they were under the presumption that jobs are given to only migrants,' Muhammed said.

According to Muhammed, jobs given to migrants are not an issue. 'And anyway, we Arabs don't want drivers, salesmen, and cleaner jobs. But LuLu getting the land which was meant for the building of a cultural centre is unforgivable. This is how land is sold by corrupt people,' Muhammed said.

Muhammed was well-connected to comrades in Salalah, Nizwa, Musandam, and Muscat. I talked to him only for forty-five minutes. But by then, he had given me a clear picture of what was happening on the ground and usable contacts all over Oman.

I had to leave the place because black-clad forces with guns standing near a tank were staring at us. I was afraid. If they shoot—and they could—what would happen? I didn't want to become a martyr in Oman. So, I bid goodbye to Muhammed and walked to the Sohar bus stand.

On my return, I was thinking of how useful the trip had been. I had even thought of the intro of the story. It was a day off for me. So, there was no rush. I was a little lazy to go back home early, too. Before reaching home, I called all the numbers given to me by Muhammed. I understood that Muhammed was a respected person amongst them. When I gave his reference, they were quite happy and started to talk to me as if I was their close friend.

They all had some good stories about their village, politics, the Oman Sultan, land grab, Dhofar revolution . . . the list of topics discussed was endless. The connections shared by Muhammed in Sohar helped me a lot in reporting the Arab Spring in Muscat.

The Sohar story didn't get published. The editor wanted to wait a little more before publishing the story. Already, the talk of the town was that we, the *Times of Oman*, were adding fuel to the fire. So, the editor wanted to withhold the story. But the day after my return from Sohar, late in the evening,

Muhammed rang me and told me that near the Muscat Airport, in front of the old parliament building, protestors were putting up tents. 'Rush, comrade . . . don't waste time,' he said.

I was excited. I ran into the editor's room and asked for permission to report on the protest. The editor called the chairman and got a green signal. But they didn't want me to go alone. They wanted me to travel in a company car for security.

When I reached the action scene, there were more police than protestors. The protestors were putting up tents. I stood there for a few minutes. I was the only one wearing trousers and a shirt, as all Omanis were wearing the dishdasha.

So, I was a little puzzled. I gathered some courage and approached a lean, short, fair-looking man with a greying beard. I greeted him. He stared at me. I told him that I was a friend of Muhammed and a reporter with the *Times of Oman*. He asked me, 'Which Muhammed?' I gave him Muhammed's full name as well as the name of the village he hailed from.

He smiled at me and said, 'Yes, come.' While entering the tent, he held my hand and told me his name. Let's call him 'Said' since he is still working in Oman and I don't want him to land in trouble. There were women protestors in abayas singing Arabic revolutionary songs. And nearby, I saw a stage being set up. There were some others, too, who were getting ready to give speeches.

Said introduced me to a few other comrades in Arabic, and they seemed to accept me as one of their own. I started to record their conversation and note down the points as well. I could hear Said saying Muhammed's name in between.

The driver who came from my office was surprised to see me getting into the tent. He was told by the chairman that I should not be heckled by anyone, and that if something like that happened, he should take me back to the office immediately.

I talked to the people in the tent for forty-five minutes, clicked a few pictures, collected a few numbers, heard the speeches for a few minutes, and then left the spot.

It was around 10 p.m. by then. I had to rush back to the office and file the story.

We reached the office at 10.30 p.m. and I filed a straight story. The protestors had shared their demands with me. I listed them, added some quotes, and provided an overall picture of the protest scene and an update from the Sohar protest.

We made it. The story got printed the next day itself. I felt proud and a bit scared as well. The front page byline for an Arab Spring story! The protestors were impressed. Nobody had done as detailed a story as we did. The next day, when the red-faced reporters from other newspapers went to the protest scene to do the story, they were denied entry.

They told the reporters that they would only talk to Kuttabin (they were trying to call me Kuttappan) from the *Times of Oman*. Even our weekly magazine editor who went there was told the same. And though I felt a little scared, I enjoyed all the attention. Muhammed, Said, and their friends helped me do some good stories. I was getting more popular and accepted by my community in Oman.

However, that spring ended soon. Many, including women protestors, had disappeared. If I called someone in the morning, I would only be able to collect his/her brother's or sister's number. I learnt that there is no guarantee that you would be able to talk to the same person again. It had happened several times. Oman is not new to the revolution. By the end of the 1950s and 60s, small revolutions and tribal clashes were happening in the border areas of Oman.

I was able to connect with them in a better way than many others from my community because I had read a few interesting stories about the Dhofar rebellion. When I migrated to Oman in November 2006, the first thing I did was read as much I could about Oman, its ruler, his family, the rebellion, and history. Yes, there had been rebellions since the 1950s in Oman. They were led by Saudi-appointed Imams and Leftists from Yemen. Russia, and even China, had backed those rebellions. The Oman Sultan Taimur couldn't suppress the growing dissidence. By the 1970s, the situation worsened in southern Oman. Finally, the British SAS stepped in. Oman's Sultan Taimur withdrew into the Salalah palace in the Dhofar region. The late Sultan's son, Qaboos, a Sandhurst-trained officer, took over power with a bloodless palace coup. He shot his father in the leg and flushed out the rebels in Dhofar with British help.[2] Following which, Qaboos 'redrew the borders' of Oman, especially the areas that shared borders with the UAE.

My Omani friends, introduced by Muhammed, mainly from Sohar, Salalah, and Musandam, and their elders in their homes, were quite open and excited about telling me stories of dissidence and how Sultan Qaboos had suppressed them.

Saleh, a friend from Musandam introduced to me by Muhammed, used to tell me about the Al Shehi tribe who were locals of that area. They spoke a local dialect named Hamriya, and refused to join the UAE and Oman. The Al Shehhi tribe populating this area lived on fishing and farming and had migrated back and forth between Musandam and the nearby Emirate of Sharjah in the past. The Al Shehi tribe was a unique challenge in Qaboos' attempt to impose state-sovereignty on the area—they were known for their opposition of both the UAE and Omani rule. Still, by a series of government orders, their land was seized very quietly.

Being a reporter in Oman who checks the Omani government news agency's feed, I was able to read all the government orders (they call it 'royal decree') that came out regarding Musandam very carefully. Stories of the Al Shehu tribe, their resistance, and different narratives of Oman overpowering them, that were told to me by a few good and powerful Omani trade union friends and progressive scholars, were always there in my mind.

The Omani version is that it is always the UAE that is instigating tensions in Sohar, by using spies from in and around Sohar and Musandam. My Omani friends have told me that this spying may take place to understand more about the Omani ruler's succession plans.

As Sultan Qaboos had no children, he did not publicly appoint a successor. But he had secretly recorded his choice in a sealed envelope addressed to the royal family council. The Sultanate law says the royal family should choose a new sultan within three days of the position falling vacant. Should they fail to reach an agreement, the nation's defence counsel, the head of the Supreme Court, and the heads of the two chambers of the Consultative Council would together open the first envelope containing Qaboos's choice and then enthrone the chosen one.

The purpose of keeping his preferred successor's name secret was to ensure the authority of the Sultan during his lifetime.

On 10 January 2020, when Sultan Qaboos, the longest-serving Arab ruler died, Oman named Haitham bin Tariq Al Said as the country's new ruler within hours. Haitham, the former minister of culture was sworn in before the ruling family council. Authorities had opened the letter left by Sultan Qaboos naming his successor, without elaborating why, before announcing Haitham bin Tariq as the new ruler.[3]

Sohar is not only known for its rebels—it is also a trafficking spot. It would take about two hours to reach Sohar. And from there, we would have to find the exact location of Sushmitha's house.

Both Binil and I had not met Sushmitha. We had not seen her picture either. She had a picture of a flower as her DP on WhatsApp. We knew her through the voice messages she'd send to Binil's and my phones for a week.

Those messages would come late at night, at around 11.30 p.m. By then, I would be asleep. So, I would listen to them the next morning. Even if I replied back, she would respond late at night as that was the only time she could send messages. She would enter the small room where she was provided with a bed after all her work for the day was done. Then she would send her messages, unless of course, she was being pulled out from that space by some abusive person in the house.

Most of her voice messages were unclear or inaudible. She wouldn't give much details in the messages either. The only thing I could understand through her weeping was that she was being mentally and physically abused, beaten up, and denied food. She wanted to be rescued.

Since I had started to get involved in such cases from 2010 onwards, I understood enough without needing more details. It was during 2017 that Sushmita started calling me.

From 2015 onwards, I had been going on rescue operations many a time without telling my family or my office. Talking about such rescue operations with my wife would scuttle the 'ops'. Like all wives, my wife would get worried and constantly check up on me. And my office would advise me not to take unnecessary risks and put the company in trouble.

So, only Binil and I would know about it, talk about it, and operate such rescues. Most of the women who sought help would be trafficked ones. The number of women trafficked was high after 2015. There was a reason for this.

After the cases of Indian domestic workers getting abused mentally and physically started to increase in the Arab Gulf countries, the Indian government made plans to safeguard Indian women. In 2015, the Indian government initiated an eMigrate system—a safe and official recruitment channel for those who wanted to migrate abroad for a job, especially to the eighteen Arab and north African countries that had signed up for the Emigration Clearance Required (ECR) system.

According to the government, all female emigrants (except nurses) emigrating on ECR passports to ECR countries, irrespective of the nature/category of employment, must be above the age of thirty years.

If the foreign employer wanted to recruit Indian female workers having ECR passports through Indian recruiting agents for overseas employment in the 18 ECR countries, they could only do so through the state-run recruiting agencies.

At present, there are nine such agencies, namely NORKA Roots and Overseas Development and Employment Promotion Consultants (ODEPC) of Kerala, Overseas Manpower Corporation Ltd. (OMCL) of Tamil Nadu, Uttar Pradesh Financial Corporation (UPFC) of Uttar Pradesh, Overseas Manpower Company Andhra Pradesh Limited (OMCAP) of Andhra Pradesh, Telangana Overseas Manpower Company Limited (TOMCOM) of Telangana, Karnataka State Unorganized Workers Social Security Board (KUWSSB), and Karnataka Vocational Training & Skill Development Corporation (KVTSDC) of Karnataka.

The foreign employer is required to deposit a bank guarantee equivalent to $2500 for recruiting a woman worker in the respective Indian Mission, in the case of direct recruitment. The embassy attestation is mandatory for direct recruitment of all ECR passport-holding women workers in all ECR countries.

In addition to this, the Indian government had also inked bilateral agreements with Gulf countries to ensure the protection of women domestic workers and nurses, who are more prone to exploitation. However, those bilateral agreements are not enough, and there is a need for more restrictions and guarantees to protect Indian immigrants.

The Arab Gulf countries and the sheikhs have long been criticized for their treatment of domestic workers and the implementation of the kafala system—the 'sponsorship system' that ties the legal residency of workers to their employers. Workers cannot quit their jobs except with the written consent of their employer. It is usually difficult for domestic workers to prove abuse. Even when they can, employers rarely face criminal charges or get indicted by the courts.

Rescued women have told me that their employers had confiscated their passports, withheld their salaries, forced them to work without rest and days-off, and in some cases, have even subjected them to psychological, physical, and sexual abuse.

Traffickers use the UAE as an entry point, as it was easy in comparison to other Gulf countries. Women can be easily made to travel to the UAE on a tourist visa and then 'sold' to employers in other countries. When the Arab provides his credentials and is eligible, he will be given clearance to provide a visa for an employee, by his government. So, when the clearance is ready, he will hand it over to his Malabari employee.

As soon as the Malabari gets the green signal and some money from his Arab employer, he will look out for women in rural areas in south India. He will alert his friends in the UAE and India. In a week or two, the Malabari agent would have lured in a poor Indian woman from Kerala or any other south Indian state.

She would be told that she can earn Rs 35,000 per month under a nice employer; she has to cook and clean in a house that will have only four people. She would be promised a separate room, and her salary would be sent to her account directly.

She would be made to feel lucky to get such a great offer. 'Just grab it . . .' the Malabari agent would say, 'you don't have to pay a single paisa, too . . .'

And to some, who are desperately looking for a job, the Malabari agent will ask for money. So, it becomes a simple business equation. When you desperately want something, then the seller will raise the demand. Some Rs 80,000 to Rs 1,20,000 would be collected from the woman who is desperate for an opportunity to migrate.

However, reality would be different. They will be trafficked and enslaved.

From my experience reporting in the field, I knew the route used to traffic south Asian women to the Arab Gulf for domestic worker jobs. Many who were rescued had told me their stories. Only the names changed. The stories were always the same. However, the degree of torture would also vary.

Janu Beevi's story, which occurred between 2015 and 2017 in Saudi Arabia, would be perfect to illustrate how Indian women were trafficked to the Arab Gulf from Kerala. Even though she was in Saudi, I was involved in her rescue. She was constantly updating me via texts. When I came to India in 2017, I had gone to meet her at her home in a rural village in Thiruvananthapuram, the capital city of Kerala.

A direct flight from Kerala to Saudi takes only six hours. But it took 336 hours —fourteen days—for Janu to reach her destination. She started her journey on 9 January 2015, from Thiruvananthapuram to Pune on a train and reached on 12 January. After a day's stay, on 13 January 2015, her agents tried to send her off from the Pune airport. But that didn't work out because the agents did not have their officials at the airport counters.

Later, she was taken to Chhatrapati Shivaji International Airport in Mumbai, where they managed to smuggle her out. As the agents couldn't get the adequate immigration clearance on the day of her arrival, she had to stay in a hotel for five days. From Mumbai, she was sent to Dubai. She stayed for a day and night in Dubai and then left for Sharjah, only to be flown to Bahrain.

From Bahrain, she was then flown to Madinah in Saudi Arabia. It took her fourteen days to reach the location. She travelled in trains, stayed in strange hotels and apartments, slept alone at airports, and reached Madinah at night on 23 January.

Did her luck change after reaching her destination? No.

After working for almost two years, she received only six months' salary. As it was quite difficult to continue there, she had to flee. She was not paid on time; she was denied food and medical treatment. She was not even given a clean space to sleep. Her employer was a police officer. She knew that justice would never be delivered.

One day, when she asked the employer to take her to the hospital, he refused. 'I was not well. I had swelling on my legs and an irritation in my throat. It got worse after I was denied medical assistance. I was afraid of dying there. I just wanted to go back home.'

But when Janu asked for help, her employer pointed a gun at her head and told her that she was not going anywhere. 'He threatened to kill me and throw me into the sea . . .'

Janu was scared for her life. She decided to run away. When the employer and his family went out, she called a social worker and fled from the house grabbing only her phone and abaya. She didn't take anything else. She knew that if she took her things, her employer would file a case of theft against her. In most cases, when a domestic worker flees from the employer's house, the employer files a case of theft to silence the abused.

Therefore, the Indian embassies advise us (those who are involved in rescue operations) to bring in the rescued domestic worker as soon as possible to the Indian Embassy. If the rescued domestic worker is admitted to the Indian Embassy shelter within twenty-four hours of the rescue, then fake theft cases won't hold in the court. If not, the employer's claim, even if it is a lie, will stand.

Janu hired a taxi to the police station where her employer worked. She was lucky that day. Her employer was not at the station so she didn't have to say she worked in an officer's house. 'I just told them that I wanted to go home and requested them to take me to the Indian Embassy in Riyadh. They frisked me. They talked to the social worker over the phone and after a few hours, dropped me at the embassy.' She had to stay in the embassy shelter for nearly two months. Life can sometimes be difficult at these shelters, where even basic amenities are not provided to the inmates.

In most of the Arab countries, the Indian embassies run a shelter home to house women who have fled from their employer. In some countries, the shelter homes are run by the Arab country itself.

Even if I am not in Oman, aggrieved workers reach out to me. They trust me even though I was made an outcast by the

Oman government. There is a reason why this happens, and I will tell you about it a little later in the book.

According to the women domestic workers who reached out to me, there were around 100 people sheltered in the two embassy-managed shelters. The situation was pathetic in both the shelters. They had told me that they were getting only limited food, once a day, and were also being denied basic amenities like a toothbrush, sleeping mats, and medicines.[4]

The women had been there since November 2019. Interestingly, the RTI reply sent to me revealed that Rs 18 lakh was spent to run the shelter in November and December in 2019 and January in 2020. On average, a sum of Rs 5.5 lakh was spent every month to run two Indian embassy shelters in Oman, where around 100 stranded women were staying between June 2019 and February 2020.[5]

'At one point, I felt that being with my abusive employer was better than this. There, at least I got food. Here, we have to beg for basic amenities.' These were the words of an Indian woman domestic worker who talked to me in January 2020, from the shelter in Oman. 'We don't have extra innerwear to change into. Whom can we tell this to?' the domestic worker asked me.

'We don't have access to the phone to call our family. Here, it's like hell,' the woman domestic worker had told me while adding that the officials from the embassy who came to meet them gave cold responses.

According to the domestic workers, the inmates of the shelter felt that the embassy officials were not bothered about their repatriation.

'When we ask for an update, they have the same answer . . . *"dekhenge* (we will see)",' one woman alleged.

Finally, I was pushed by Binil to take up the issue. Through the embassy, we provided sanitary napkins to the women in the shelter.

Janu's experience in the shelter in Saudi Arabia was not very different. She was abused by the warden there. In a few days, however, she was able to return home.

After two years of hardship in Saudi, at the beginning of 2018, Janu returned to India empty-handed.

When I met her at her house, she was surviving on what her aged parents and siblings earned. 'Sometimes, they (the family) work and bring in food. And sometimes, we all go to sleep hungry. I have lost everything . . . Before migrating to Saudi Arabia, I had a rented house and a share of my father's land. Now, there is nothing.'

She added, 'All that's left is a loan, some debt, plenty of health issues, and a daily struggle for food and medicines.'

And while coming back, Janu was diagnosed with throat cancer. She claims that if she had taken medical care at the proper time, her disease would not have worsened. 'I suffered from throat pain for nine months in Saudi. They didn't care at all . . .' She lost her share of the land as her siblings had to sell it to clear her loans.

'One of my brothers gave up his share as well. It is due to their benevolence that I have shelter and food. I need around Rs 1,000 every fifteen days for medicine alone.'

Janu added, 'The loan was around Rs 3,00,000 (USD 4800). So, when an agent approached me through a friend, I thought of accepting the offer. I was offered Rs 20,000

(USD 320) as salary. The agent said the working conditions would be good. But I was fooled.' She filed a local case against the agent.

A document tabled by the Ministry of External Affairs in 2018 in the Parliament, reveals that the Indian Missions in the Arab Gulf receive complaints from women workers, particularly female domestic sector workers, on account of the poor working conditions, non-payment or delay in payment of salaries, the denial of other benefits such as medical facilities, and the refusal of leave or denial of exit/re-entry permits for visits to India, denial of final exit visas to the workers to return to India after completion of the contract, maltreatment by the employers, etc.

'Incidents of confinement, physical abuse, and neglect have also been reported. Most of the complaints pertain to female workers, who do not have proper employment contracts as they have migrated illegally, in violation of government norms for recruitment of the "Emigration Clearance Required" workers from India,' the document adds.

In 2019, the Indian government received 610 cases against illegal agents from victims of trafficking.[6]

However, only a few traffickers were penalized. Either the police do not genuinely take up the case, or the victim lets go after becoming depressed and tired after repeated calls and summons from the police.[7]

Janu also withdrew her case in July 2017.

'I had to look for a job. Sometimes I don't have enough money to reach the station when they call me to the hearings. So, I withdrew the case,' Janu told me.

This is a common occurrence in almost all cases. Sometimes, I feel that the Indian police haven't been sensitized properly on the human trafficking law. Hubertson Tomwilson, a migrant rights lawyer in India, once told me that instead of booking the trafficker under the Indian Penal Code (IPC) 370, the police would charge them under IPC 420.[8]

Section 420 of the Indian Penal Code deals with the theft of property. But Section 370 penalizes the buying, selling, or keeping of slaves. Can a person who is trafficked and made to work for twenty hours be called a slave? Yes, definitely.

Section 370 says that whoever imports, exports, removes, buys, sells, or disposes of any person as a slave, or accepts, receives, or detains them against their will, shall be punished with either simple or rigorous imprisonment for a term extending up to seven years and shall also be liable to a fine.

'So, Section 370 involves seven years of punishment. But this is not guaranteed in Section 420,' Hubertson says.

A few police officers who are in cahoots with traffickers will get freed easily. I have seen that in all abused domestic worker cases, there is an element of human trafficking. It can involve the recruitment, transportation, transfer, harbouring, or receiving of a person (a woman, man, or a child), often over international borders but also frequently within the boundaries of a single country, for exploitation.

Although each trafficking case is unique, most identified cases follow the same or a similar pattern: a person or group of people is recruited or abducted from the country of origin, transferred through transit regions, and then exploited in a destination country.

If the exploitation is interrupted or ends at any point, the victim may be rescued and would receive support in the destination country. They may then be repatriated, relocated to a third country, or, as is too often the case, deported as irregular migrants, which frequently results in denied access to victim assistance and impunity for the perpetrators. We find a good example of this situation in Janu's case. It took fourteen days for her to reach Saudi from Kerala.

Human trafficking doesn't mean that a person has to be bundled and smuggled in a car boot. A person wearing decent clothes while crossing the immigration channels can also be considered a victim of trafficking. Subjected to fraud and deception, he won't even know that he is being trafficked.

A basic definition of human trafficking is provided in the United Nations' 'Palermo Protocol' of 2000. According to the Protocol:

'Trafficking is the recruitment, transportation, transfer, harbouring or receipt of persons, using the threat or use of force or other forms of coercion, of abduction, of fraud, of deception, of the abuse of power or of a position of vulnerability or of giving or receiving of payments or benefits to achieve the consent of a person having control over another person, for exploitation. Exploitation shall include, at a minimum, the exploitation of the prostitution of others or other forms of sexual exploitation, forced labour or services, slavery, or practices similar to slavery, servitude, or the removal of organs.'

This definition is quite complex. To summarize, in trafficking, there is an act, a means, and a purpose.

'Act' is the recruitment, transportation, transfer, harbouring, and/or receipt of a person. 'Means' includes or use of force or threat, deception, abduction, the abuse of power or a position of vulnerability, or other forms of coercion.

Finally, the 'purpose' of human trafficking is exploitation, which can include the prostitution of others, forced labour, slavery, or servitude.

In Janu's cases, all three elements were there. But she failed to get justice. She failed, just like the majority. For many, the peace and feeling of safety they get after returning home, when compared to the hell they experienced at the workplace, is akin to being in heaven.

According to the International Labour Organization, forced labour is 'all work or service, which is exacted from any person under the threat of a penalty and for which the person has not offered himself or herself voluntarily.'

In all domestic worker cases, we can see the elements of forced labour. They will be made to work for around fifteen to twenty hours, and sometimes more than that, too.

Manjusha, a domestic worker who was abused in Saudi Arabia, had told me that she was forced to work for around twenty hours every day until she collapsed. She had to eat from the garbage for survival.

There are hundreds of such cases. As I wrote earlier, only the names change. The abuse these women undergo is similar. Many go missing. Only a few are traced and rescued.

In 2016, there were eighty-six such missing cases in Saudi Arabia. All were taken to the UAE but went missing. In a coordinated effort with Rafeek, we traced about seventy-three. It took a lot of time, coordination with the Saudis, as well as pressure on the Indian Embassy and the Ministry of External Affairs.

In all these cases, we were able to track the victim to Dubai. Where they had gone or were taken after that is not known, till the women contact their families or a social worker for help.

Then, too, she won't be able to tell us the location. If lucky, she would be able to share her location through WhatsApp.

Most of the time, when families back in Kerala seek help, they tell us, 'Sir, she is in Oman.' But what they share with us would be a Kuwait number.

Even though Keralites have a long history of migrating to the Gulf, for them there are only two main places—Dubai and Muscat. Many think that rest of the countries or places are provinces of Dubai or Muscat.

In 2018, I came across a unique case of a missing person. Padma B, an Indian domestic worker from the east Godavari district in Andhra, had gone to Bahrain and Dubai with high hopes. She travelled later to Kuwait in 2009. But luck was not on her side. She was either 'dead' or 'missing' to her family.

Everything went okay for Padma for two years, till her employer died. After his death, the wife got married to another person. The new husband was quite arrogant. 'He, my late employer's wife, and her son started to abuse me physically and mentally,' Padma told me upon her arrival in Hyderabad in 2017, after her seven-year ordeal in Kuwait.

According to Padma, she was not given a phone to contact her family or her husband who was working in Dubai as a painter. She was not allowed to step out of the house or talk to any of the neighbours.

'It was a jail. A jail . . .' she reminisced.

When asked why nobody from her family had approached the Indian authorities, she said that all of them were illiterate and might have thought she had gone 'missing' or was dead.

'Only my aged in-laws are there at home. They probably didn't know what to do,' she added. Additionally, as her husband was on a work visa for his job as a painter, he was unable to travel from Dubai to Kuwait to look for her.

Gulf countries provide visitor visas depending on the nationality, job, and financial status of the foreigner. While most Gulf countries provide visas on arrival for US and EU citizens, citizens from Asian countries, including India, are not given that preferential treatment.

After seven years of 'house arrest', on 11 November 2017, Padma found the hidden location of the key. Early in the morning of 12 November, she managed to take the key discreetly, open the door, and run away.

Unfortunately, as she was unwell, she could not walk for very long. 'I fell unconscious on the road. Somebody informed the police; they took me to a hospital and I was admitted there for a week. They took a statement from me and moved me to the Indian Embassy shelter. With the embassy officials and social workers' help, I am now on my way home,' Padma told me in 2017, when she was travelling back to her home from the Hyderabad airport on a bus.

Padma was also undocumented. She didn't have a Kuwaiti resident card. However, the Indian Embassy officials managed to make an exit certificate and repatriate her to India.

Women for Sale

All we knew about the house where Sushmitha was working was that it was opposite a white mosque. To the left side of the house, there was a green garbage bin.

She sent her location through WhatsApp, so we knew that it would not be a hassle to find her. However, if she had just given the location as 'near a white mosque and a green garbage bin in Sohar', we wouldn't have been able to find her.

In an Arab country, a white mosque is a common sight. There are mosques everywhere. The green garbage bin is common too. The Arab governments give a lot of priority to cleanliness. Littering is a punishable crime, too.

When we started from Ruwi, it was around 3 a.m. Our goal was to reach Sohar before 5 a.m., so we had to rush. We had a regular halting point at a Keralite-run cafeteria near Muscat International Airport. There is a fuel station nearby, too. We could fill the tank and then stop for a black coffee at that cafeteria. At the fuel station stop, we could buy a packet of blue Dunhill cigarettes. It was our preferred brand at that time. Even though it was early in the morning, the Keralite-run cafeteria would be open.

Almost all the cafeterias in the Arab Gulf are run by Keralites, mostly by people from Nadapuram, a northern Kerala village. Every cafeteria is sure to have a tea-maker named Shameer! Interestingly, there is a saying among Keralites in the Arab Gulf. It goes like this: a cafeteria discontinued by a person from Nadapuram or a vehicle abandoned by a Pakistani are of no use.

For rescue operations, Binil would usually bring his 5.6L Nissan Armada. In fact, on the high-speed roads in Oman where 160 kmph and above is allowed, the Armada is the perfect vehicle. It would take about two-and-a-half hours to reach Sohar. When Binil added the location shared by Sushmitha in the GPS, it showed that we had to drive two hours and fifty minutes to get there.

'It is on Sohar–Buraimi road,' Binil said, adding that we would reach by 5 a.m.

This trip happened just three months after I had gone to Sohar without Binil on a sting operation to expose how Omani manpower supply agencies were selling Asian domestic workers.

With the experience of talking to trafficked women, I knew how women were sold in Oman. I must clarify, even when I say they are sold, according to the Oman government, it is just 'supplying'.

Sting Operation in Sohar

Manpower supply agents can run licensed offices. There are many in the Sohar and Buraimi areas. In certain streets in Sohar, every building has a manpower supply agency office.

Saeed Y, a Keralite and long-time resident of Sohar, knew all about the 'slave trade' there. He has been my source in Sohar since 2012 and has helped us in many rescue operations. In 2016, Saeed rescued thirteen Keralite women domestic workers. He had told me then, that if I ever visited, he would take me to places where Asian and African domestic workers were sold. He wanted to expose that trade through a story. I had been thinking of taking that risk many a time. I hadn't told my editor about making the trip to Sohar for a story. I went without informing him, on 2 October 2016, on my off-day. A junior reporter and fellow Keralite Mathew B, was with me.

Mathew was lucky to get a driving licence on the thirtieth day of his arrival. Most people have to spend years to get a driving licence in the Gulf countries.

As road accident rates are alarmingly high in Oman, the traffic laws are strict. Therefore, migrants who apply for a driving licence have to try very hard. Some even land up spending nearly Rs 1,00,000 as fees over multiple attempts.

I was Mathew's guide and reporting manager. So, when I told him that I was planning to do a sting operation in Sohar on the slave trade, he said that he would be my driver. I was happy to take him up on his offer and avoid a boring travel by bus.

I called Saeed to reconfirm our travel plans. The next morning, at around 8 a.m., Mathew was ready. I called Saeed once again and informed him that we had started our journey. As usual, we stopped at Shameer's cafeteria near Muscat airport, had our tea, and then headed to Sohar.

At around 11 a.m., we reached the Sohar roundabout where Saeed was waiting for us. Saeed took us to a small Malabari hotel and bought us breakfast. Getting Kerala food is not a problem here as the number of Keralites in Arab countries are always high and we have a centuries-old relationship with the Arabs. Along with dosa and chutney, I had a coffee, and Saeed and Mathew had tea.

While eating our dosas, Saeed gave us the details of his plan. He told us that we had to travel in his car. He would show us the manpower supply agency offices and then we had to go by ourselves and do the work. We agreed. So, Mathew parked his car and we joined Saeed. In about thirty minutes, Saeed was able to show us some eight manpower agencies that were notorious for selling women.

He knew many of them. And they knew him as well. So, he was very cautious not to be exposed. After scouting around, Saeed returned us to where our car was parked.

I didn't have any spy cameras on me. But I had a good iPhone. That day, I was wearing a shirt with a small pocket. So, by activating the spy app and putting the phone in my shirt pocket, we got good visuals. We felt confident after doing a trial run.

We stepped into one of the manpower supply agencies. Mathew was with me. He was slightly scared. I was, too. But we had travelled some 200 km to expose these traders, and I didn't want to return empty-handed. Never in my life have I stepped back without trying.

When I pushed the glass door open, I saw a fat man, who could have been from Lebanon, with his gelled hair, white shirt, blue trousers, a highly polished heavy silver bracelet, and waxed shoes that shone like a mirror. In most of the companies in a majority of the Arab countries, junior managers are always Lebanese.

The Arab world is a melange of nationalities. Let me illustrate this with the analogy of a hotel. Go to a decent hotel with a bar, and a doorman from Africa would greet you.

Stepping in, you would receive a pleasant smile from a receptionist from the Philippines. Smiling at her while looking for a vacant table, you will be guided by an African steward. Your order would be taken by another steward from either Nepal or the Philippines. The chef could be from Sri Lanka, the clerk could be a south Indian, the manager would perhaps be an Indian, and the CEO would be white.

Now, if you go to the backyard, you would meet a plumber from Bangladesh; the load lifter and truck driver may be from Pakistan. Many global migration experts have told me that migration is like a package in the Arab Gulf. They prefer certain nationalities for certain jobs.

As I entered, I said, 'Assalamualaikum.' The Lebanese manager said, 'Va Alaikum Assalam' in return. I told him that I was from Muscat, and that I was working in an automobile company. My wife was expecting to deliver a baby soon and I needed a domestic worker. A temporary one.

He was convinced by my request. He pulled out a file and placed a few CVs in front of me. All of them were Indian women. The CVs had pictures, too. I could choose anyone I wanted. The only condition was that I had to pay the sum he asked for.

He said that around Rs 2,00,000 was the price for hiring a help for two years. But as I had asked for a person for only three months, he cut down the price to Rs 1,00,000. He said that I could use—yes, 'use'—the worker for one year or longer. When I asked about the e-Migrate, the embassy permission, the visa, and the everything else, he kept his right hand on his chest and said, 'Boss, don't worry about it. You just get a visa application approved from your company; the rest I will take care.'

When I asked him how much I would have to pay as visa and agent fee, he said, 'That's up to you.'

After all the procedures were done and the payment was made, I asked when the domestic worker would arrive home, to which he simply called for his Filipina assistant and asked him to bring the women. In a few seconds, seven women—three Indians and four Africans—were made to stand in front of me.

He said I could choose any amongst the seven. And if I brought the visa approval paper and paid the money, I could take one home.

I was standing till then. But when the women came in, I pulled up a chair and sat down. I was shocked. This was 2016. Could I buy a woman? Could I choose one from those standing in front of me?

Yes, I could. When I looked at those women, I understood that they were not being properly fed. They looked tired. And a few of them had scars on their faces. All of them were wearing faded sarees. But they looked at me with hope. 'An Indian has come to purchase one of us.' An Indian employer would be better than an Arab one. At least, there would be no language barrier . . .

Meanwhile, the Lebanese manager told me that two among the seven, the women wearing the red and green sarees, were from Tamil Nadu.

'Tamil Nadu women are good. They will work hard. And as you are from Kerala, it would be nice if you pick one among them,' he said.

I just smiled at him. I was still in the shock of seeing these women displayed for sale.

All this time, my phone camera was recording everything. In about twenty minutes, I said goodbye to him, assuring that I would call him back. I collected his business card. He was confident that I would call. I understood this from his face. Meanwhile, I could see that Mathew was getting restless. He was feeling nervous. So, I decided to leave.

But before leaving, I turned to the women. I wondered what they were thinking. They were all hanging their heads down, sad and depressed. Yes, of course, they would be.

I asked the Lebanese manager whether I could talk to the Tamil women and he said no. However, I still tried. I just asked, '*Eppidi irrikkenga, ma*? (How are you?)' They didn't reply. The Lebanese manager was annoyed with me for speaking in Tamil.

After this, Mathew and I visited five more manpower supply offices. In all the agencies, the situation was the same. However, in the remaining five, women were not paraded. At around 1 p.m., we were done. So, I called Saeed again. He came to where we were waiting. He took us to a restaurant and bought us food.

Again, we had a Kerala lunch in Oman. We had some good sardine fish curry, which we call 'mathi curry' in Kerala. It is a delicious fish curry flavoured with coconut and tamarind juice. It is tasty, tangy, and spicy. In Oman, sardine is quite famous. We Keralites love sardine fish fry and curry. We get Omani sardines in Kerala as well.

Saeed grabbed the bill from the small steel plate filled with aniseed before I could. He never allows us to pay, even if we insist. In Sohar, he says he will be the host. Saeed sees it as an honour.

On our way back to Muscat, Mathew had a lot of questions on how we would do the story, what the angle should be, and what visuals should be used. I was clear on what the introduction should be like. I wanted a straight intro without any drama or sanitization. The next day, I spoke to my editor about my trip, the story, and the importance of doing the story. He checked the visuals. He was happy to see that we had a good ground report.

That day, I was excluded from handling the bureau, preparing the day list, and attending the daily meeting. I was told to work on the domestic workers' story. I called the police headquarters, the embassies, and the social workers to get comments for the story. The police, the Indian Embassy, and the Bangladesh Embassy didn't want to comment.

But the Sri Lankan Embassy was ready to give a statement. I knew the acting ambassador. The embassy didn't have an ambassador at the time. It was a young woman officer who was serving as an ambassador at that time. We had not met. But we used to often talk over the phone. She used to give me quotes on different stories. So, when I introduced the story to her, she was ready to talk.

According to her, agencies can recruit housemaids, but the job order and other papers have to be attested by the embassy here and the employment bureau in Lanka. 'Without approval from all sides, a Lankan housemaid cannot be legally hired,' she said, adding that they had come across around seventy cases of housemaids brought into Oman illegally by agents in 2016.[9]

'Worried about the trafficking, we had sought the help of the Oman government,' she told me. The official told me that earlier, housemaids could come to Oman on tourist visas and convert these into work visas. 'But it was stopped eventually, as it was being misused and put workers in a vulnerable situation,' she continued, also saying that they would approach the Oman government to stop the unfair practices happening in Oman towards domestic workers' recruitment.

That evening, I left the office in a lot of excitement. I was a bit tense, too. It was the first story on a sting operation in Oman's journalism history. Before leaving the office, I went to the visual department and checked the video footages. All was well. They had blurred the faces. So, I decided to go home. Mathew dropped me back home, where I lived alone.

Usually, I sleep early. But that night I didn't. I was awake till 11.30 p.m. to check the PDFs. Every day, PDFs of the newspaper would be emailed to me before going to print. I have to do a final round of check for errors. Other editors do the same. It is not mandatory for me to do so. However, sometimes, I would stay awake to check the pages.

That night, when the pages came, I was feeling thrilled. An error-free front page. P Sharma, the news editor, had done an excellent job. Good editing. And Santhosh V, the chief designer, had also drawn up a good and balanced design. I wrote back, 'It looks fine to me.'

My story. A story that exposes the modern-day slave trade—the first sting operation reveal in Oman's journalism history.

Buraimi, Slave Hub

It is a fact that Oman has a history of slave trade. Centuries ago, slaves were brought over from the east coast of Africa. Even then, it was Buraimi and its surrounding villages that were infamous for the slave trade. In his book, *Arabian Sands*, Wilfred Thesiger, a British military officer, explorer, and writer, reveals that the slave trade was practised in Buraimi in the 1950s.[10]

He reveals that many of the slaves sold in Hamasa, one of the two villages that made up the Buraimi Oasis, were, in fact, Baluchis, Persians, or Arabs who were kidnapped. He also adds in his book that the usual price slave traders paid for one of them was between Rs 1,000 and 1,500 and for a young African even more. 'An Arab or Persian girl was, however, more valuable than an African girl and would fetch as much as Rs 3,000,' Thesiger writes in his book.

Interestingly, Thesiger, who was visiting Zayed in Al Ain at the time, managed to persuade the Sheikh of Buraimi to release two young men from the Hadhramaut (in Yemen), whom he had bought for the absurdly low price of Rs 230.

Lord Shackleton, a British explorer and parliamentarian, said in the UK parliament in 1960 that his friend who was attached to the Trucial Oman Levies had discovered children in fetters in Buraimi.[11] The Trucial Oman Scouts was a paramilitary force that the British raised in 1951. They were initially called the Trucial Oman Levies and were to serve in the Trucial States. In 1956, the Levies were renamed the Trucial Oman Scouts.

It was the Trucial Oman Levies that captured the Buraimi Oasis from the Saudi-Arabian forces in 1955. Lord Shackleton says in his parliament speech that in one of the outlining villages of the uncertain frontier between Oman and Saudi-Arabia, his friend discovered children in fetters. Haunted by the stories told by his friend from the Levies, Shackleton had approached the Anti-Slavery Society in London.

'I met more officers from the Trucial Oman Levies; I consulted travellers, and all the sources confirmed what we have already been told—that Saudi Arabia is the main and largest market. And as wealth has increased, so has the demand for slaves, because a man is known by the number of slaves he has: it is a form of snobbery out there—like having a Cadillac. Formerly, an able-bodied slave cost £50 (Rs 4,500), whereas now he costs £150 (Rs 13,500). Similarly, an attractive girl who cost £150 (Rs 13,500), now costs anything between £400 (Rs 35,000) and £700 (Rs 66,000),' Shackleton says in his speech.

Shackleton also gives details about the two main slave routes into Saudi Arabia. According to him, the first comes from west Africa. It goes from the High Volta, through the Niger Provinces and the region of Timbuktu, across Africa to the Port of Suakin, and across the Red Sea, then by dhow to Lith, which is a port south of Djedda. The other goes from Iraq and Persia and Baluchistan across the Gulf and then, by caravans of camels, to Riyadh.

Shackleton had said in the UK parliament in 1960 that the children taken on this route are generally bought from poor parents in these countries, but quite often, are kidnapped. 'Certainly, when I crossed the frontier into Saudi Arabia with Sir John Glubb in 1943 to visit the Emir Abdul Azziz el Sidari, at Kaf, I saw no sign of ill-treatment of the slaves there,' Shackleton adds.

Shackleton adds that there are sheikhs who obtain sexual satisfaction only with very young children. 'My Lords, the children in shackles in the Buraimi Oasis were destined for Riyadh. The boys might be castrated and the girls bought by any merchant who fancied them. One of the British representatives there, in the Buraimi Oasis, noticed caravans and lorries coming into a little village called Hamassa at night, and when he tried to visit the houses, he was denied admittance. So, he began to watch the departure of Saudi airplanes. I should say that the planes were all Dakotas and, except one pilot, all the aircrews were American. Shortly before the take-off, a lorry would drive to the airstrip, and the children would be pushed and herded into the plane. My friend (I am sorry to have to keep saying "my friend" but he does not want his name used) then spoke to one of the American pilots and invited him into his house for a drink. He said to him, "Do you realize that you are carrying children into captivity?" And the man answered, "When I took on this job, I was told to keep my eyes and ears shut to what was going on around here. And that is the way it is going to be. Another seven years of flying for King Saud and I'll have earned enough money to retire for life",' Shackleton reveals in his speech, quoting his unnamed friend.

Shackleton says that the information was reported to the Foreign Office. He questions parliament why it was never used at the time of the Buraimi frontier dispute, nor after.

'Why? Because the Foreign Office does not wish to embarrass a powerful ally. Not only, I may say, is it the Foreign Office who does not want to embarrass a powerful ally because when I tried to interest various editors to this matter, some of these steely eyed despots were alarmed at what they thought might be revealed by my inquiries. However, at last, I found an editor who was prepared to back me,' Shackleton added in the Parliament.

Shackleton then found that he was not given a visa to enter any of the countries on the Trucial Coast. And since he could not get into the Coast and therefore Saudi Arabia, he decided to examine the alternative route.

In 1959, he travelled in a Land Rover from Gambia, through Senegal and Mauritania, into what was then French Sudan, and finally to the legendary city of Timbuktu, where he lived for a month making various inquiries. He then moved out into the Sahara. And there he bought a slave from his Tuareg master like one buys a piece of meat.

'His name was Ibrahim. He was twenty years old. I gave him his freedom and he now works as a free man in Timbuktu. My Lords, I bought this man and photographed the money being exchanged with the master; I took down the number of the notes and so forth, to come back with proof that slavery exists in the Sahara,' Shackleton adds,

To conclude, he says, 'My Lords, slavery exists throughout West Africa, concealed behind a legal code that asserts it has been abolished, like a cancer the doctor refuses to diagnose.'

Intimidating Phone Calls

The newspaper arrives at the Omani doorstep at around 4 a.m. itself. As I was reading the PDF late into the previous night, I was not too excited about seeing the newspaper. But then again, touching the printed paper is a different feeling. Having the first sting operation story's byline printed on the paper is a great honour, isn't it? I woke up at 4 a.m. itself. I opened the door and took the paper. I felt proud, but was also a bit afraid.

I was expecting a call from the Oman police summoning me, parliamentarians questioning my journalism, and Arab activists threatening me for tarnishing the image of Oman.

However, no one from the police called me. One of the parliamentarians called to congratulate me on the expose. However, the few calls I received from Arab activists were not encouraging. While some questioned my journalism ethics, others complained that I had ruined the reputation of Oman.

A few others told me that I would have to answer in a court of law as they were going to file a case against me. By 9 a.m., I had received around thirteen calls, out of which four were from my own community, praising my courage to conduct a sting operation in Oman.

I reached office by 10 a.m. While I was climbing up the steps to the editorial room, I met our newspaper chairman Mohammed Al Zedjali who was climbing down. He smiled at me and said, 'You are becoming famous. Keep a low profile.' At that time, I was unsure why he told me what he did. But a few days later I understood—he was also getting calls.

I got a hero's welcome at the office. The editor was singing my praises. This was my first big exposé after being promoted to the position of chief reporter a few weeks ago. That day, work went as usual. We focused on getting other stories. There were some stories already lined up for the front page. So, S (the editor) chose one among them for the next day's edition and relieved me from work for the day.

S was going on a business trip that evening, and he handed over charge to a news editor, a very senior and experienced journalist, who had joined the newspaper a few months ago. He headed the bureau meetings and guided us. He was picking up journalism in Oman faster than we, in the bureau, expected. He knew all about the work involved in getting a story done.

The next day was my day-off. But just like for any other journalist, big stories always take place on the day-offs!

The next day morning, my Gmail inbox contained alerts related to Oman. Scrolling through them while having my coffee, I saw a news item from the Sri Lankan government news portal, quoting my story and claiming that 'their women domestic workers are being sold in Oman.'

I was excited. When I searched Lankan websites with all possible SEOs, I found that a Lankan government radio news portal was carrying the story, quoting Thalaltha Athurkorla, the Lankan minister-in-charge of foreign employment at the time.

When I read the story, I started to look for her number. In an hour, I managed to get it from her Facebook account. Looking through her Facebook account, I understood that she was quite active on social media.

I called the Lankan Embassy official in Muscat to enquire if I could call the minister directly. The embassy official said that the minister would talk. So, I called the minister directly from Oman. However, I couldn't get in touch with her. I kept trying. Meanwhile, I added her on WhatsApp and sent messages as well. Finally, after an hour of desperate attempts, the minister called me back and said that I could call her after two hours.

I set an alarm. I didn't want to miss the window the minister had provided. I called the minister back at the exact time she mentioned. She heard me out and said that she had read my story. She was agitated about her fellow citizens being duped, trafficked, and abused in Oman.

'My officials will be probing into how Sri Lankan female domestic workers are travelling to the UAE on tourist visas, and crossing into Oman on work visas illegally,' she told me on record, confirming that a Sri Lankan embassy official had been sent to Colombo as a part of the probe.

This was yet another exclusive for me. Since S was on leave, I talked to the news editor, who was happy to get a solid story. The first thing he asked was whether everything was on record. I told him yes; it was all on record. He then told me to go ahead with the story. And in some thirty minutes, I filed the story on my office laptop and sent it to him along with the voice recordings of the Lankan minister.

Before sending the story, I called the Lankan embassy official and briefed her. I wanted to know whether she had anything to say that could be added to the story.

She was pleased to hear about the progress. She told me that I had done a good job and updated me on some positive developments that were happening in connection with the recruitment of domestic workers.

When I asked her about the minister's quote on an embassy official being probed for colluding with the traffickers, she said that she could not reveal much but confirmed that a probe was on.

That evening, the news editor called me and said that we would hold the story for a while as it was an exclusive, and run it on a working day.

The first story on the sale of domestic workers was printed on 25 October 2016. And the follow-up story was published only on 5 November.

By then, I was exhausted justifying my story on the slave trade to the readers. Even while appreciating my work, many were telling me that I had tarnished the image of Oman.

On most days, I would think about it. Had I tarnished the image of Oman? No, I had exposed wrongdoing. I had exposed the slave trade. I told my readers that such things are happening even in this 'all-is-well' country.

When I was feeling intimidated by the responses, the news editor told me, 'Don't worry. Your expose is an eye-opener even for the Oman government. If they act, even briefly, it would save many women from falling prey to these traffickers. Even if one woman is saved, it is from the impact of your story. What else does a journalist need in his life? Do not regret it. Don't get bogged down . . .'

I scribbled his words in my diary that day itself. I was inspired by his encouragement. I felt confident. But the follow-up story published on 5 November, with the Lankan minister's quotes, had a very negative impact. I had taken a day off on 4 November. The news editor texted me saying that the story would be carried on the front page of the 5 November edition.

I was excited. The minister's quote. An exclusive story. That night, I didn't bother to check the PDF. However, the next morning, I read the PDF email in shock.

The front page had my story alongside the headline— 'Report on Maid Sale Triggers Sri Lanka Probe'. But at the same time, it also had the pictures of the Prince of Wales and the Duchess of Cornwall who were on a royal visit to Oman. One of the pictures was of the Prince at Oman's museum, watching a ceremonial dance. The second picture was of Camilla with a child at a cancer association hostel.

I hurriedly opened the front door to pick up the newspaper. Sometimes, even after the final PDFs arrive, few changes take place before the pages go for printing. I hoped that the print copy would have a different version. Unfortunately, it didn't. It was same as the PDF! Being a journalist in Oman for almost ten years, I knew that this page would put me in trouble.

In Oman, if we have a foreign country head or a royal family member visiting, it should be the only story on the front page. If Oman's Sultan Qaboos was receiving or hosting a guest in the palace, then it needs to be the front-page story.

There should be no negative story alongside or above the picture of the Sultan. There should be no footwear or innerwear advertisements and no pictures of models, too. So, a negative story, and that too one on the illegal sale of maids, on the front page with the pictures of the Prince of Wales and the Duchess of Cornwall, was a big mistake. I knew that the Sultan would be infuriated especially since he has a close bond with the royals.

They had helped the Sultan crush the rebels in Dhofar at the end of 1960, and to remove his father from power. They had assisted him in his ascent to the throne, to find oil, sell it, and make Oman rich.

Additionally, we knew that a copy of all the newspapers printed and published would be sent to the Sultan by Oman's Ministry of Information. The Sultan reads the *Times of Oman*. My chairman had told me that the Sultan reads our newspaper. It's possible, too, as there are only four English newspapers in Oman.

So, when a newspaper carries a negative story while the Sultan's close friends are in Oman for a visit, why wouldn't he be annoyed?

I was worried. But as it is said in journalism, 'Once printed, nothing can be done.' At around 9 a.m., the news editor called me. He wanted to meet me. He told me over the phone that the editor was unhappy that the story was carried along with the Prince's pictures.

So, the news editor wanted to meet me. I went a little early to office. We met at the usual spot for meetings. The news editor looked a little stressed. He was regretting his decision to print my story that day. I understood that he was worried. So, I didn't reveal that I was tense as well.

I told him that we should forget about it, and that even if something goes wrong, I was ready to face it. S was back in the office and the news editor was briefed about the risk of publishing such stories. S was worried about losing me. This had come a week after the chairman had told me that a few people in the ministry were talking about me, which was not a good sign.

November was over, now December, too. Everything was quiet. We thought that nothing would happen. We believed that the Oman government was not going to probe us.

However, that was not the case. In March 2017, I was told by my chairman that I may get summoned by Oman's Ministry of Information. By then, I had crossed the ten-year mark of living and working in Oman. I had joined as a sub-editor, moved into the bureau, become a reporter, and got promoted to the position of chief reporter. I had earned a name and fame, faced six cases, four policemen, and two courts, all for doing stories. I had done more than 1,000 front-page stories—all exclusives. I had reported on the Arab Spring, riots, layoffs, strikes, money laundering, mysterious murders, missing children cases, poverty, corruption, exclusive bank mergers . . . the list was endless.

It was the middle of March. The chairman called me to his room. He had never done that before. We used to talk when we crossed each other in the office. He would text and email me. But I had never been invited to his room.

I knew that he liked me. His daughter who had come back from the US after her studies was appointed as an intern under me. She was told to learn from me. And she, a young and bold Arab girl, respected me a lot. She was a quick learner as well.

It was a big room. A grand one. Every item—the cosy chairs and sofas, the minimalist clock on the wall, the leather tissue paper box, a glass bowl filled with dates, the Arab coffee dallah (pot), the khanjar (Arab knife), and a few antique items on the table—had shades of brown and white.

I was told to sit. He looked very calm. After inquiring about my family, he told me that on the coming Sunday, I had to go to the Ministry of Information's office. He said that I shouldn't go alone, and that I should take Hassan Al Lawati, my younger colleague with me.

I agreed. I didn't want to ask the redundant question of why I needed to go.

I called Binil and told him about the meeting with the ministry officials. He was worried. He said we would meet me that evening at our regular bar.

After filing the stories and managing the bureau, I left a bit early from the office. At around 6 p.m., the bars open in Oman. I rushed to our meeting place, where Binil was already waiting for me. He had already opened one Corona beer, his favourite. I saw that he had ordered an Amstel for me, too. Amstel was a long-time favourite of mine.

This bar was a good place to meet, since it was a silent bar. There was no loud music and dancing. So, it was the perfect place to drink and talk. They also served large, unlimited bowls of salted popcorn.

Binil started to talk without exchanging any pleasantries. 'Why are they calling you?'

I replied, 'I don't know.'

'Son,' he said, like he usually addresses me, 'something is wrong. We should be prepared before going there. Were there any crucial stories done by you?'

I said, 'It's difficult to say. Almost all the stories were hot. Every story was crossing the "limits" set by the Oman government.'

I told him that the maximum they could do was deport me. I was ready for that eventuality. I had done all the stories I could possibly do in Oman. And the stories written by me cannot be retold by anyone.

Our discussions then moved on to other subjects. We stayed up quite late that night.

Binil dropped me at home, promising that the next day he would take me to the ministry.

I slept well that night. I was calm. I was not at all worried. The next day, I woke up a little early. My wife and family were with me in Oman during this period. I didn't tell my wife anything. At around 8 a.m., Binil picked me up. The meeting was at 9.30 a.m. We reached the ministry office by 9 a.m. itself. And when we got there, Hassan was waiting for us.

We went to the higher official's room to meet him. We were told to wait by his assistant. After a few minutes, we were called in.

Hassan and I entered the room. It was a luxurious one. Like every other office and cafeteria in Oman, this too had the Oman Sultan's portrait. A big one. A new one.

We were told to sit on the sofa. The official introduced himself. He got up from his official chair and sat opposite to us, on another sofa. He asked us to introduce ourselves. He mainly spoke to Hassan in Arabic. I could understand that Hassan was saying good things about me and that he had accompanied me because the chairman had asked him to do so.

Within five minutes of small talk, the official told me that I was giving Oman a bad reputation. Yes, those were the first words he uttered to me. I was not worried, tensed, or panicked.

When I disagreed, he continued, saying that I was writing stories only about migrants, workers, their rights, and their challenges. His list of my 'negative' reports seemed endless.

The two stories that had made the ministry angry were the one about the domestic workers on sale and the story on the Sri Lankan minister's response. These happened in 2016, in October and November. He also said that I was tweeting the stories, which was drawing unnecessary attention from global human rights bodies and activists. The official told me that I was deliberately tarnishing the image of Oman.

This was in the last week of March 2017. I had joined twitter in 2011. And in 2017, Twitter was more popular than any other social networking site. When all the news media outlets were focusing on making more money online, how could we not tweet and post stories? In this digital age, can we stop stories from crossing borders?

No, right? However, this Oman official seemed to think that if he stopped me from telling a story, then it won't be told by anyone else. Interestingly, whenever officials in Oman tell us to stop telling stories, the same stories would be told aggressively by neighbours, causing more damage to Oman.

After talking for some forty-five minutes, it was clear that the official was blaming me for damaging the image of Oman. He wanted an apology from my side. I said I couldn't apologize as I had not made any error. I also said that it would be my chairman and editors who would have the final say on whether I had to apologize or not.

It appeared that he was surprised to hear me say this. He asked me to talk to my chairman and send him a letter the next day. And that this was mandatory. He asked for my press accreditation card and took it from me. Less than ten people all over Oman, including the local press, had press accreditation.

I had got it because my chairman pursued the application with a special interest, when he realized that I needed a press card for my stories. Even during the Arab Spring, when the black-clad police used to stop me from entering tents, it was the press card that helped me continue on my job. Many local journalists were envious of me for having the press card.

I surrendered my card and walked out of the office. Hassan looked sad. He knew that I was not going to apologize and would have to leave Oman.

Binil was waiting outside. I bid goodbye to Hassan and joined Binil.

Binil asked me when I would be leaving Oman, as though he had heard everything that happened during the meeting. I replied, 'Very soon!' He replied with his typical loud laugh and asked me what happened. I told him the entire story. He asked me whether I was going to apologize.

I said, 'No. Never. Why should I? They have told me that I am writing about migrants, undocumented, workers, rights . . . What I am doing is not a crime. So, why should I? I am not going to apologize.'

Reaching the office, I called my chairman, as the editor was not in his room. He called me to his room. I briefed him on what had happened at the ministry's office. The chairman asked me whether I was going to apologize. I told him that I would write a letter detailing how the story was done, but wouldn't apologize. I emailed the letter to the editor and the chairman, both of whom 'okay-ed' the letter.

Then we took a printout, signed, and sealed it. According to the official, I had to submit it to his office the next day. The chairman and the editor decided that I could do stories, but had to avoid bylines for a few days.

The next day, Binil took me to the ministry's office again. The officer told me to hand the letter over to his subordinate and leave. He was angry because I didn't cave in to their demands.

So, I gave the letter to his subordinate and left. By then, I was mentally prepared to leave Oman.

I reached the office. All was well for a week. But at the end of March, the chairman called me from the ministry's office. He wanted to know when I will leave Oman. I understood that he was under pressure. I didn't want him to get into trouble, so, I said, 'In fifteen days.' He agreed. He said that he would tell the ministry that 15 April would be my last day in Oman.

Later on, I was told that the ministry didn't accept the fifteen-day period. They wanted me to leave Oman in a day or two. However, the chairman was not ready to accept such a short notice.

My children, who were then six and four years each, were studying in Oman. I would have to pull them out in the middle of the academic year, sell household items, clear bank loans, courier some personal items, purchase tickets, and get several other tasks done. I needed more than fifteen days for all of this. My chairman was bold enough to fight for me when Oman refused to give me that time.

I was told that the chairman was holding talks with the ministry since October 2016, after the first story was published. But he hadn't told me or anybody else in the office. He tried his best to retain me as he respected my work.

Before I left Oman, he called me to his office for the last time. He spoke for at least an hour with me, even though guests were waiting to meet him.

During that conversation, he told me, that in workplaces, there are a few people the management hopes will resign and leave. When they do, the management would be happy.

He said that there is also another kind of people; when they leave, the management would be sad. The chairman said that I belonged to the second lot. He also added that I was leaving Oman at the peak of my career and this would not be forgotten by the *Times of Oman* or Oman.

It was 2 April. There were only a few more days left for me in Oman. Tickets for my family were purchased by my office. Almost everyone helped me. We had to leave behind many household items. We couldn't carry everything back to our hometown. We gifted several items to our neighbours and the needy. Everything was done.

And on 15 April, we left Oman with our heads held high.

I had to undergo some special procedures at the immigration since I was being forcibly sent back. My chairman had sent an official from the office to assist us. When all the immigration procedures were over, this official came and hugged me.

'We have not interacted much while in office. But Allah will bless you. Don't worry. Everybody in the office has high praise for you . . . .'

I wanted to weep. But I didn't. This was the last time we'd cross the Oman immigration. My wife was worried. I didn't want to stress her further and make her cry. After the immigration procedures were done, we moved to the food court. I bought an iced coffee for my wife and two milkshakes for my boys.

And I tweeted . . . 'I was forced 2 leave #Oman 4 writing stories on #humanrights #migrantrights #workersrights.' I pinned the tweet so it would remain at the top of the page.

I migrated to Oman like any other Keralite would, to improve my life and my career. However, the ten years there had changed my life.

Unknown to me at that time, a file was being prepared at the ministry since 2015. I would be summoned one day. During January, February, and March, I was involved in domestic worker rescue ops, visiting camps, feeding hungry workers, raising money for bedridden workers, handling medical bills, helping the embassy document undocumented workers, assisting global rights activists visiting Oman, and doing more and more aggressive stories on migrants issues.

So, when Binil and I planned the rescue of Sushmitha, we didn't know that I was under the watch of the Oman government.

Sushmitha didn't come out of her house as she had agreed. We reached the location at around 4.50 a.m. We did spot the white mosque and a green garbage box as she had mentioned.

There were two huge villas. From the streetlights shining on the villas, we could make out that one was made of pure white marble, and the second one had been painted in a sandal colour. We didn't know which villa Sushmitha would come out from. So, we had to wait. But I texted her saying that we were here. As per the plan, as soon her master left for his prayers at 5 a.m., she would come out to drop the garbage in the bin and then get into our car. We had told her we would be coming in a black Armada.

She didn't turn up. It was already 5.30 a.m. Meanwhile, we saw an Omani in a dishdasha stepping out of the white marble villa. We saw him opening the big gate, coming out, and heading towards the mosque. Then we noticed many others, too, walking towards the mosque to perform Salat Al Fajr, the prayer before the sunrise.

I was aware of the prayer names in Arabic as I used to check the front pages before they went to print. I had to learn them as they get printed daily in the ear panel of the paper. Page designers at the news desk sometimes forget to change the date. Sometimes, spelling mistakes also creep in. So, I had to know their names and spellings.

We didn't see Sushmitha. We were slightly disturbed. As it was risky to send her messages repeatedly, the only thing we could do was wait for her or for her message. By 6 a.m., I got a phone message alert. It was Sushmitha. It read that she had been stopped going out to dump the garbage, so, she couldn't come out.

I texted her back, 'What should we do?' She didn't reply. We were in a fix. 'We should not leave,' Binil said. We should wait for her next message. 'We don't know when she will come out,' he added.

So, we decided to wait. At around 6.30 a.m., I got a WhatsApp voice message. '*Saabji, hum das baje ayenga.* (Sir, I will come by 10 a.m.)'

We were literally stuck in that area, and it was only 6.30 a.m. We would have to wait for nearly four hours! Binil had some work in Muscat and I had to get back to office as well. But it was impossible to miss the opportunity to rescue her, and so we decided to wait.

I texted her back, '*Jaroor aana. Hum wait karenge.* (Come, definitely. We will wait.)'

Binil and I then drove out to find a teashop or a small hotel to have breakfast. After a twenty-minute drive, we found a small restaurant. At that time, only coffee and tea were available. But they told us that by 8 a.m., breakfast would be ready.

We had coffee. As we had nothing else to do, we waited there. I felt sleepy. So, I told Binil that I would take a nap in the car. Binil was playing some old Malayalam songs in the car. They were perfect ones to sleep to. I don't know when I fell asleep, but at 9 a.m., Binil woke me up and said, 'Let's have some breakfast and move back to the location.'

In almost all the small cafeterias, the breakfast would be dosa and chutney or poratta and keema curry. Both of us had dosas, chutney, and coffee with fresh milk. At small cafeterias in Arab countries, if you don't insist on fresh milk tea or coffee, the tea-maker will add condensed milk, which spoils the taste of the tea or coffee.

By 9.30 a.m. we left the restaurant and reached the location by 9.55 a.m. I texted her one word: 'Waiting'. She replied, *'Ayenga* (will come).'

At around 10.15 a.m., we saw a tall woman in an abaya coming out with a small barrel bag. Binil started the car. She was walking towards the car in a hurry. Binil unlocked the car doors. She came near the car, looked at us, and opened the door.

She asked *'Reji Saab . . .* (Reji Sir)?' I told her *'Haan . . .* (Yes . . .),' and asked her, *'Aap Sushmitha* (Are you Sushmitha?)'

She got into the backseat of the car and pushed her bag to one side. *'Chaliya Saab . . . Jaldhi chaliye . . . Seedha muje embassy me chod dheejiya whan se hum ghar vapas jayenga.* (Let's go, sir. Let's hurry. Drop me straight away at the embassy. I will go home from there.)'

She was wearing a faded brown saree and her head was covered by a dupatta. She looked tired, and her eyes were swollen. We could tell that she had cried a lot and had not slept either. Binil started the car. He used the GPS to get out of that small town to the main road. We could see that Sushmitha was tense. She was gasping. It was winter in Oman, but she was sweating. Binil increased the AC.

In ten minutes, we entered the main road to Muscat. Binil told me to look for a new car freshener in the dashboard. I opened the dashboard and found one. I opened the pack and replaced the old one in the car. There was stale body odour in the car after Sushmitha had got in.

Binil told me that we would not stop. We were going to reach Muscat in one long drive. I agreed. Having an unknown woman in the car, and that too one with no proper documentation, was a risk. If we were stopped by the police, we would be the ones booked for human trafficking!

Sushmitha had told us earlier that she didn't have a work permit; she only had her passport with her. When we entered the main road, Sushmitha asked us when we would reach the embassy. She wondered if it would take more than an hour.

Binil replied, 'In some four hours, we will reach Muscat.'

She was surprised. 'It's that far? Is this country that big? Is it bigger than India?' Sushmitha asked.

I informed her that Oman is almost equal in size to Madhya Pradesh. She had told me earlier that she was from Bihar. So, she must know about Madhya Pradesh.

'Don't worry. We will reach soon,' I said and then told her to share her story.

'*Kahenga ji . . .*' she said.

I will be paraphrasing what she told us since she only spoke to us in Hindi.

Sushmitha was married and had two girls, aged ten and fourteen. She was from Bihar, and her husband was ill and bedridden. He was a truck driver. He met with an accident in 2015, near the Nepal–Bihar border. Since then, he hadn't been able to work or take care of his family.

Sushmitha tried many jobs for survival, but failed at them all. Additionally, her eldest daughter, aged thirteen, was frequently falling ill due to chronic breathing issues. So, whatever small amount she was making was not enough to make ends meet. Her elder daughter was not going to school and the younger one was studying in Class 4. The older one's name is Savitha and the younger one is Mitu.

She then began looking for a job abroad. She had heard from her neighbours and a few relatives in Nepal that if you migrated to the Gulf, you could earn thousands. Being there even for two years would help her settle for life.

Sushmitha belonged to a village bordering India and Nepal, in Bihar. For decades, many Nepali men and women crossed the Indian land border and migrated to the Arab Gulf, circumventing the Nepal government's initiatives to ensure safe migration.

Sushmitha knew quite a few who had done this. So, she was confident that she would get a decent job and overcome the crisis at home. She started looking for an agent who could help her to migrate to the Arab Gulf. She told her friends who visited Patna to help her. Finally, a neighbour managed to get an agent's phone number in Bihar.

She rang him.

'*Voh bola sub aasan he* . . . (He said, everything is easy . . .),' Sushmitha said.

The agent told Sushmitha that a passport could be made easily and that she could fly out of India soon; she could later work and earn in petrodollars.

Sushmitha didn't have a passport. She had to make one. The agent in Bihar told her that his friend would come to her village and help her make a passport. And for that, she had to pay Rs 5,000. Sushmitha didn't have that kind of money. But she was confident that in about 15 days, she would be able to raise it. Her salary from a farm lord was pending.

Sushmitha was a daily wage worker on a potato farm. On an average, she would get Rs 6,000 if she worked for a month. She hadn't received her pay for two months. So, she was confident that she would get that money if she asked.

Unfortunately, she got only Rs 4,000. The farm lord told her that the rest would be given in a few days. Sushmitha didn't know what to do as she needed Rs 5,000 to pay the agent to make the passport. She was short on Rs 1,000.

'I didn't know how to make that Rs 1,000. But that evening, I got an idea. There was a dairy farm nearby with 60 cows. I met the owner. I offered to clean the cowshed in the morning and evening for a month if he paid me Rs 1,000 in advance. He agreed and paid me the money,' Sushmitha said.

'So, I got Rs 5,000 in my hand. I was happy. I called the agent. He agreed to come the next evening itself. I said that I would meet him before going to the dairy farm,' Sushmitha added.

As per their plan, Sushmitha met the agent and handed over the money, the school certificate, and the Aadhar card as proof.

'He told me that it may take thirty days to get the passport. I had to sign some blank papers, too,' Sushmitha added.

Sushmitha got the passport on the twenty-second day itself. It came to her house through a courier. In between, a policeman also came for verification.

'I had to pay him Rs 100 while handing over the passport,' Sushmitha said as though it was a normal thing. 'Police means money . . .' she added.

After she got the passport, she called the agent in Patna and told him that she had got her passport. 'The agent told me that he would send somebody to collect it to process the papers. He also advised me to be ready to fly to the Gulf in a month or two,' Sushmitha said.

Sushmitha had not travelled out of her village before. She had visited only her relatives in Nepal. Other than that, she had not crossed any border.

Her husband was not happy to know that she was going to the Gulf to work. 'He was a person who felt that the women at home should not work, especially in a foreign land. So, he was not willing to send me abroad. But I somehow convinced him. I argued that by going abroad, we could come out of this poverty, find some money to get him treatment, and save some for our children,' Sushmitha said, adding that she was now back to where she had started.

'We still have to go to bed with hunger pangs and skip medical treatments,' Sushmitha said. Her voice was shaking. I understood that she was feeling distressed.

Before I could say anything, Binil told her, 'Life is like this. You thought you would die here. Now, we are heading to the embassy. Soon, you will fly home. Don't worry . . . life has a lot of surprises . . .'

Sushmitha didn't reply. She continued her story.

'One day, I got a call on my neighbour's phone telling me to call back the next day at 10 a.m. It was the agent from Patna,' Sushmitha said.

When Sushmitha called him, she was told that in ten days, she had to go to Patna, from there to Delhi, and then fly to Dubai. She got a job as a domestic worker in Dubai with a good Arab family. She was happy and surprised on hearing the news. She was also told that she didn't have to pay a single rupee for the job.

'He told me that all the formalities were being done by the agency in Delhi and the Arab employer,' she said.

On the tenth day, a Monday, she travelled to Patna with her brother. She only had a small barrel bag with her. It was the same one she was carrying with her in the car. She came with a small barrel bag and was now returning with the same one, too.

'It was very hard to convince my children and husband. Somehow, I managed to do that. My elder daughter who is thirteen, told me that she would take care of her father and younger sister. She had already been doing that when I was going to work on the farm, so I was not worried. Even though she was suffering from a breathing illness, she could take care of the family,' said Sushmitha.

Sushmitha travelled by a local bus to Patna with her brother. She had only Rs 2,000 with her. She didn't know whether that would be enough or not. But that was all she could manage to raise. When Sushmitha and her brother arrived at the Patna agent's office, they were served tea and then briefed about the travel plan. She had to board a train from Patna that evening, reach Delhi, and go the main agency office.

'The address was given to my brother. He had also never been to Delhi. But we decided to go. The agent in Patna called the agent in Delhi and briefed him about my arrival,' Sushmitha said.

They were told that a person would be waiting for them at the railway station. The agent sent a boy to accompany Sushmitha and her brother to the railway station. Sushmitha was told that all the documents will be given by the Delhi agent.

'The agent's office boy, who was also from Patna, didn't speak to us. He hired an autorickshaw and dropped us at the Patna railway station. He didn't wait or help us buy a ticket,' Sushmitha said.

Sushmitha's brother managed to get tickets for them. It cost them Rs 1,000. Her brother had carried some rotis and dal curry with him. 'He filled water from a public tap. We found the platform where the train would come. We sat on the floor of the station as all the seats were occupied,' Sushmitha said.

She and her brother had to wait four more hours, since the train would come only by 11 p.m.

'Sahab, while sitting there we were tensed. Especially me. My husband had to be fed. I didn't know whether my Savitha would be able to do that,' Sushmitha said.

Sushmitha called her neighbour from her brother's phone to update them about her recent travels. 'While eating my roti, I was thinking of Savitha and Mitu. It was difficult to adjust to those new thoughts. But I was hopeful,' Sushmitha said.

The next afternoon, they reached Delhi. A person, who introduced himself as Ram from Madhya Pradesh, was waiting to receive them.

'He was a tall person. But he was soft-spoken. The first thing he asked us was whether we had eaten breakfast. When we replied no, he told us that on the way to the office, he would get us food. And he did,' Sushmitha said.

I could tell that the only person Sushmitha liked in her entire journey of migration, was Ram.

After having breakfast, they headed to the office.

'At the office, at least a dozen women were waiting. I was told to meet Sahab . . . After an hour, I was told to meet a woman who didn't tell me her name. She gave my passport and handed a ticket for the flight to the UAE to me. I was told that I would be working in the UAE. I had to board the flight from Delhi the next day. I would be accompanied to the airport and provided accommodation for the night so that my brother could go back . . .' Sushmitha said.

It was her first night outside her home.

'I was scared, but I pretended that I was a bold woman. It was a long night. I was waiting impatiently for the morning light. At 5 a.m., I woke up and freshened up. I was told that the flight was at 10 a.m; I had to be ready by 6 a.m. I was given a cup of tea at breakfast. Then I was told to accompany another man to the airport. We went to the airport in an autorickshaw. He parked the autorickshaw outside the airport. While walking inside, he told me that he didn't want to pay the entry fee,' Sushmitha said.

'It was my first time in an airport. I was holding on to the passport and ticket so hard they got crushed. The man from the office came up to the entry gate. He told me that the policemen inside would help me,' said Sushmitha.

Sushmitha was told to lie that she was going to Dubai for two months to help her relative who had a newborn baby, as she was being sent on a tourist visa. She was not aware of this. She didn't know what kind of visa she was holding or travelling with. She was told that she would be able to work for two years in Dubai and get Rs 30,000 per month.

The man who accompanied her instructed Sushmitha on what to say if she was questioned by the immigration officials.

'Where was I going? Why was I going? I was asked many questions. I lied, as I was taught. I could figure out that he was not convinced. I knew he was not convinced, but he didn't want to waste time and quickly cleared my document examination,' Sushmitha.

Sushmitha was given a return ticket as well by the agent that morning. She had asked him why she was being given a two-month return ticket if she was going to work for two years. The agent had told her that this was a routine procedure.

'If you are travelling on a tourist visa, you need to have a double-way ticket. Or else, you will not be cleared to travel to any country by our immigration officials,' he told her.

So, Sushmitha was given a two-way ticket.

'After clearing the immigration, I didn't know what to do. I followed a queue. Interestingly, after standing there for five minutes, I found out that it was for a flight to Oman. I asked the attendant whether the flight was going to Dubai. He said no; my queue was at the gate for the flight to Muscat. He was a nice person. He took my ticket, checked my gate, and directed me there,' Sushmitha said.

She had to walk for over ten minutes to reach her gate. She didn't use the walkways or the escalator, since both were alien to her; she was afraid she would fall.

'*Ghir jayenge tho . . .?* (If I fall . . .?)' Sushmitha asked.

Everything was new for Sushmitha.

Airport, security checks, moving walkways, escalators, metal detection doors, the cabin crew, the take-off, food delivery, the landing, the airport, the exit . . .

'I was scared every moment,' Sushmitha said, adding that she was told by the agent that a person holding a placard with her name would be waiting for her on arrival.

When she arrived, she was taken by the agent in an old car to the place she was supposed to stay at.

'I could only see buildings for an hour. Then the colour of the buildings changed into the colour of mud. We were entering many small roads. I was afraid and confused—if they were planning on dropping me somewhere there, I wouldn't be able to get out,' said Sushmitha.

At that time, Sushmitha had no idea that she was already trapped and wouldn't be able to leave till she flees unseen. Women like Sushmitha see Dubai and its colourful skyscrapers only once. After which, they only get to see the mud-coloured buildings, green garbage bins, and white mosques the rest of their lives.

Sushmitha lived in a brothel for the first twenty-five days. She was made to sleep with men, although she resisted. She was beaten up and denied food.

'We used to get rice in a small bowl and some dal curry, and at night, three pieces of Arab bread (kuboos) and some sausage curry. In the morning, we had only two pieces of bread and black tea,' Sushmitha said. 'They would beat me up a lot. Once, they even burnt my left hand.' Moving her dupatta, she showed us the scars.

Though it's been two years since then, the burn scars had not faded. With little food and sleep, her skin was wrinkled, and the veins on her hands were standing out. Sushmita was only thirty-two. But she looked like a fifty-year-old woman.

Before getting into Sushmitha's case, Binil and I had dealt with Meenu's case, which was similar. Meenu was also duped by an agent in Kerala, trafficked to the UAE, smuggled to Oman, enslaved, and finally rescued and repatriated.

She was rescued by Binil and one of his friends in Sohar and taken to his office. Binil had to interview her to do a news story for an Indian news channel.

I was also called to Binil's office. When I got there, Meenu had already started to tell her story. All of a sudden, she tore her top and showed us the burn scars on her right breast.

Binil was shocked. He told his cameraman to stop rolling. Meenu told us that she was burnt by her Arab employer.

When her employer was drunk, he would drag her to the living room, make her sit down next to him, and abuse her. And when she resisted, he would stub his cigarette on her breasts.

'This would continue again if I resisted . . . so, later on, I used to "cooperate" . . .' she told us.

I remember it all—Meenu's words, her face, Binil's office room, his cameraman Siddik . . . and how we took her to the embassy . . .

Sushmitha was now moving to narrate the part of her story that was set in Sohar. I stopped her to find out more about the brothel in the UAE.

'Sushmitha, tell me more about the brothel,' I said.

'*Saab* . . . I will never forget those twenty-five days I spent there . . . It was a scary place. A mud-coloured villa in an ash-coloured gated compound. We stayed in a building that had seven rooms, two halls, and a kitchen. There was a seperate single-roomed building as well, where I often saw men wearing long pajamas and kurtas,' Sushmitha said.

'There were two white cars,' Sushmitha added.

I could feel that Sushmitha was not ready to open up about the women in the brothel as she was talking more about the flat, the men, and the cars. I had to ask her more questions about the women—how many of them were there, did she talk to them, were they being trafficked, how many of them were Indians, were there any other nationalities, etc.

She started speaking more slowly . . . in limited words.

'*Saab* . . . there were eight women, including two Africans and one Sri Lankan. There were two men and a matron, a

Keralite woman . . . the business starts by 10 in the morning. It peaks at 6 p.m. and goes on till 11 p.m . . . liquor is also served . . . there are no beds. Mattresses are laid on the floor. The only good thing in the rooms is a sandalwood air freshener . . .' Sushmitha said.

'I could see men and even boys coming in . . . As I was not ready to sleep with them even after being physically tortured, I was put in the kitchen. And from there, I could see people coming in and going out. Whenever somebody passed by the kitchen door, I would look at him and hope that he would be my saviour . . . I even had a piece of paper that said I needed help and that women are sold here, in Hindi,' Sushmitha added.

But Sushmitha was unlucky. She couldn't find anyone she could trust. She was worried. And as she continued to resist, the torture was increasing as well.

'The kitchen was my world. I had to stay there till 1 a.m. on most days, as clients would have occupied the rooms,' Sushmitha said. She also told us that even the people who entered the kitchen for water or to grab a bite would abuse her.

'Even if it was only for a second, they would try. Many times, I suffered,' Sushmitha confided.

Sushmitha managed to befriend a Keralite woman who had also been trapped by the crooked agents back home. 'She was from Kozhikode, Kerala. Her name was Geetha . . . I don't know if that was her real name . . . She had come on a tourist visa like me but got abducted. She failed to fight like me, it seems. But I never asked her about it. She was there when I was taken out of Oman . . . I don't know what happened to her,' Sushmitha sounded worried while talking about Geetha.

People working in low-income jobs may not have a good cell phone, and even if they did, would fail to share their numbers and may leave the country at any point, often unexpectedly; so, they cannot say goodbye to those they have made friends with . . .

Sushmitha didn't have a phone at that time. It was Geetha who gifted her a phone.

'Geetha had got it from a client. It was an old one. It had a broken screen and a faded cover. But it was working. Geetha gifted me a SIM card, too. She taught me how to make a call and recharge the phone,' Sushmitha said.

The first call she made from that phone was to her neighbour in Bihar to inform her family that 'she was well'.

Sushmitha made that call on the ninth day of her arrival in Dubai. Before that, she couldn't get an opportunity to make a call even though she pleaded with her bosses many a time.

'I didn't want to tell them that I was trapped. Additionally, on that first call, I didn't have much credits. So, the call had to be short. And it was quite inconvenient to give them the number, so I didn't,' Sushmitha said.

Sushmitha refused to be cowed down by anyone. Finally, on the twenty-fifth day, she was told to take her bag and join a new person who was travelling to Oman by road. She was told that she had got a job.

Sushmitha was taken to an agent's office somewhere in the Sohar–Buraimi area. Sushmitha couldn't tell us where it was. But she told me that there were twenty-one women sheltered in that small office, which had one reception, three rooms, and one kitchen. She said that it was on the outskirts of the city and she could see a saloon, laundry, and a hotel near the agency office.

'I could see those buildings through the window. They had name boards in Hindi, too,' Sushmitha said. Sushmitha was put in the agency office for two weeks. There, she was put for sale and sold after the sixth attempt.

She was bought by an Omani family. Her master wanted her to take care of his newborn baby, wife, parents, and two teenaged boys.

Sushmitha was ready to go with anyone. She was afraid of ending up in another trafficker's hands if she became an 'un-sellable' woman.

On the thirteenth day, Sushmitha was taken in a car to the employer's house. Before leaving the agency house, Sushmitha managed to get a SIM card with the help of a *dhobi* from the laundry shop.

In the Arab Gulf, a majority of the people who run laundry shops are from the Uttar Pradesh.

'The *dhobiwala* was from Lucknow. I am from Patna. But he was helpful. When I told him my story, he was compassionate,' Sushmitha said. Sushmitha met him while she was being sent by the agency office to hand over linen for washing.

Upon reaching the employer's house, Sushmitha believed that her struggle would end, and that she could work and send some money home.

But it didn't happen as she had hoped. Even though the first few days were okay, later on, the relatives of the Arabab started to make regular visits.

'On Fridays, there would be at least ten guests. They would stay back. So, including the six people at home, there would sixteen people in the house. And I was the only person to cook for everyone. I wouldn't even be able to eat the food I made. I was not supposed to. There would always be some leftover food, which I had to eat instead of the freshly-cooked food. Eating stale food every day in itself was worrying. Though we didn't have much to eat back home, we never ate stale food,' Sushmitha said.

But it was not only continuous work or the lack of food that had prompted her to seek help from us . . . it was the sexual abuse she faced in the house.

'A young boy, a relative of my employer, used to come home on Thursday evenings. He behaved well initially. But at night, when everyone was asleep, he would come to my room, a small space under the stairs, and force me to sleep with him,' Sushmitha said.

When Sushmitha resisted, the boy started to blame her unnecessarily during the day. And that created a disturbance at home. Ultimately, everyone began to blame Sushmitha. 'I became the dirtiest and the most unwanted creature there. This started to happen in the second month. I started to receive a lower salary of OMR 70 (INR 14,000) though I was initally offered OMR 100 (INR 20,000). My employer used to tell me that the rest would be paid in the coming months. I was okay with that. The money was sent to my Indian account. My family was also happy . . . but I couldn't adjust to sleeping with that boy at all,' Sushmitha said.

According to Sushmitha, she worked for eleven months like a slave while resisting rape several times but got only five months' worth of reduced salary.

By then, Sushmitha had made some friends in the neighbourhood. She learned how to avoid rape. She learned the skills needed to avoid the tension in the house. But the only thing she couldn't avoid, was the long hours—fourteen to sixteen hours of daily work.

Once in a while, she would call the neighbour in Bihar. Most of the time, it would be during the Friday afternoons.

'I would call them once a week to know whether they had got the money since it was being remitted by the Arabab . . . and if he hadn't remitted the money, I would keep begging, which would always lead to a fight,' Sushmitha added.

After six months, she decided to flee as she was unable to adjust with life in the Arabab's home.

'Yes, I decided to run away. But where or how . . . I didn't know. I had only one friend in that area. Her name was Shahina Begum. She was a domestic worker from Kerala, who lived in the opposite villa. We used to meet daily at 10 a.m. when we went to drop off the garbage. Yes, the garbage bin was our meeting point . . . and that too for a maximum of five minutes. If we exceeded that time limit, then someone would shout for us,' Sushmitha said.

After Geetha, Shahina was her second friend in the Arab Gulf.

'She could understand what I was struggling with. Some days I would have swollen eyes from crying too much. Shahina would understand that I had a bad day. Every day was bad . . . but some were worse,' Sushmitha said, adding that Shahina, in her fifties, was a veteran who had worked in different countries.

It was Shahina who advised Sushmitha to run away and seek shelter in the embassy. It was Shahina who told her to seek somebody out and to reach out to the social workers in Muscat.

'But I couldn't. I didn't know anybody other than Shahina. I was confused. I asked Shahina whether she could introduce me to somebody and she agreed. But she said it would take time,' Sushmitha said.

However, Sushmitha didn't wait for Shahina's help. She had noticed that an Indian usually walked down the lane on the left side of the villa at around 6 p.m. So, Sushmitha thought of seeking his help. Sushmitha wrote on a piece of paper, *Mujhe help chahiye . . . 9XXXXXX1 . . .'* and dropped it when the person was entering the lane.

'Usually, he would stare at me. I would smile at him, but he never smiled back. He would look down and walk away. But I was confident that he would help me . . . so, I dropped the paper . . . He took it, read it, and walked away . . . he did not even look at me . . . I was disturbed . . . but I decided to wait . . . there was nothing else I could do,' Sushmitha said.

The person who walked down the lane daily was a Keralite working in a fuel station nearby. He lived some five buildings away from where Sushmitha lived. He was a friend of a friend. A friend of mine, Vigeesh, who works in a hypermarket in Sohar, knows Suresh.

I had met Vigeesh when I went to Sohar during the Arab Spring. He was one of my sources in Sohar. Many a time, he would work for me as a local reporter. He would collect details and send them to me.

When Suresh handed over Sushmitha's SOS message to Vigeesh, he took a picture of it and WhatsApp-ed it to me. He then called me. I told Vigeesh that she would be rescued. I tried calling the number, but nobody picked up.

I knew Sushmitha would call back. At that time, I didn't know her name. So, I saved her number as 'Sohar rescue 2017 Jan'. Yes, I used the location-rescue-year-month format till I got the name to avoid any confusion.

We received such cases every month. A few would end happily but the rest would become a cause of pain for us. A pain I wished to forget sometimes.

On the same day, as I was walking back home at around 6 p.m., I got a WhatsApp message asking me who I was. It was in Hindi.

I replied in Hindi saying, 'I am Reji . . . My friend gave me your number . . . Call me when you can . . .'

Later in the night, at around 11 p.m., I got a call from the 'Sohar-rescue-2017-Jan' number.

'*Mera naam Sushmitha. Aap muje bacha sakthe he?*'

I had only one answer to that question. 'Send me your location through WhatsApp. Let me try . . .'

Sushmitha told me that she didn't know how to send her location through Whatsapp. But when I sent her a WhatsApp message with the instructions, she didn't reply back.

So, I left it there. The next morning at around 10.30 a.m., I received the location and a voice message from Sushmitha asking me when I could rescue her.

'*Soch ke bathayenge . . . messej karega,*' I replied.

That afternoon, I called Binil. I told him to check the details regarding Sushmitha's case. As we knew what the issues would be, neither he nor I needed any briefing. He agreed to call and update me.

Binil managed to talk to Sushmitha that evening. On Tuesday, he introduced himself by referring to my name. Binil told her that, after giving out a confirmation on Thursday, we would arrive early in the morning on Friday in a black car and rescue her. Friday is a perfect day for all of us.

Friday is a weekly day-off in the Arab countries. There would be fewer policemen on the roads on Fridays. That's a good thing for us because we could drive safely with an unknown and undocumented woman in our car.

Travelling with an unknown woman, that too if she is undocumented, would result in the driver being taken into custody for human trafficking. So, we always carried out our rescue operations on Friday.

On Wednesday, Binil informed the Indian Embassy to arrange a shelter for a rescued woman by Friday. The Indian Embassy had to be informed in advance the details of the case. Even though the rescue operation is done with the knowledge of the embassy, if something goes wrong, the embassy would not take responsibility. But that didn't mean that the embassy would give up. Of course, they would come to help.

The Indian Embassy has in the past issued letters to those going for such rescue operations stating that 'so-and-so was an Indian Embassy social worker'. The letter would not be of much help. But then again, it would give us a temporary feel of diplomatic immunity—a feeling that we were a part of the Indian Embassy.

On Thursday evening, I called Sushmitha to confirm our plan for the next morning. Luckily, all went well. We were able to rescue her. By the time she completed her story, we had reached Barka, a small town an hour away from Muscat.

Sushmitha watched the places pass by at a speed of 100 km/h. I was late for office. On Fridays, I was in charge of the edition. So, I had to reach the office earlier than usual. When Binil and I stopped near the airport cafeteria for tea, Shameer the cafeteria guy, greeted us, and asked us if we were returning only now . . .

Binil replied saying yes. I lit my Dunhill cigarette and grabbed a cup of tea. I saw Binil carrying tea for Sushmitha who remained in the car. She looked scruffy, but allowing her to step out of the big and luxurious car would draw unnecessary attention. We had our tea quickly and continued the trip. From the cafeteria, in some thirty minutes, we reached my office.

Binil dropped me there and headed to the embassy. Sushmitha stepped out of the car. With her palms joined, she thanked me. She said that she would never forget us. She felt that her woes were finally ending.

I smiled at her and walked into my office.

As per the agreement, Sushmitha was to be dropped off at the embassy, from where, the embassy would move her to the shelter. In thirty minutes, Binil called me to inform that Sushmitha had been dropped off at the embassy.

And so, that chapter was closed. Sushmitha stayed in the embassy shelter for a few weeks and then was repatriated to India. On the day she left Oman, Sushmitha called to thank me once again. I told her to call Binil. She said she already had done so. She asked if we would come to the airport on the day she was flying out. We did not go to see her off. We usually don't.

We didn't take her Indian number. So, we are no longer in touch with her.

Binil and I talk about Sushmitha sometimes. She was a very innocent woman. She came with tiny dreams, but left the Gulf with her dreams shattered and empty-handed. Sushmitha's is not an isolated case. In my ten-year-long Gulf life, I understood that only the name and the place changes, while trafficking continues unabatedly.

While writing this chapter, I got yet another case from Sohar. It was the same story. Only the face and the voice change each time. If Sushmitha was from Bihar, the new woman is from Kerala.

Yes, even though I am in India, I still receive many cases. This particular case was of a Keralite woman being abused in an Arab employer's house. I have forwarded it to Saaed in Sohar. I have talked to him. He will take care of her. She will be rescued . . . I am sure . . .

6

Even a Pakistani Can Speak Malayalam

'Even a Pakistani can speak Malayalam . . . So, how can we verify that this undocumented child who speaks Malayalam is an Indian?'

This was the unanticipated question raised by a junior official at the Indian Embassy in Oman, when Binil and I approached them with Praseedha Aslam, a forty-five-year-old Indian woman from Kerala, and her six-year-old mentally-challenged boy—both undocumented overstayers during 2013.

Praseedha draped her dupatta over her head once again and stared at us with despair and pain. I understood why she gave us that despairing look. She had already concluded that their return to India was not going to happen. She was not at ease even in the luxurious atmosphere of the embassy meeting hall infused with the aroma of the jasmine room freshener.

After hearing what the official had to say, she sat on a steel chair nearby, holding her son's hand even though he tried to pull his hand away. We were sure that the boy did not understand what we were saying; however, it seemed that he understood something was wrong from his mother's gloomy face.

He had grown up isolated in his walled-home in Samail, so the Friday Open House crowd at the embassy was disturbing him. He didn't have any friends nor had he seen this many people before.

Praseedha had come from Samail to the embassy, hoping that we could help her out by getting their repatriation papers. But the embassy official's question disappointed her deeply. Wiping her tears, she told us, 'Sir, we will die here from starvation. That's what is going to happen in the end . . .'

'I don't have any papers to prove that I gave birth to my boy. Even the hospital couldn't give me the papers of his birth, because I was undocumented when I delivered him. When I begged in the name of the Almighty for help while I was suffering from labour pains in front of the hospital, they took me in and carried out the delivery. That's it,' Praseedha spoke about what had happened to her in front of the embassy official once again, in the hope that he may listen.

Yes, the official was listening. He was compassionate, too. But he was not in a position to give her a positive response. He looked at me and said, 'Tell them to wait. There are others who need to share their grievances at the Open House in the embassy as well.'

The boy, however, was not comfortable. He was repeatedly telling his mother he wanted to return home, a makeshift house in Samail at a tiny village 95 km away from Muscat, in Oman. Praseedha's home was about 150 m away from the tomb of Mazin bin Gadhuba Al Tayy and the mosque he had built in Samail.[1]

Mazin bin Gadhuba, who belonged to the Azd tribe, is recorded as the first Omani who embraced Islam in Oman during the seventh century. Mazin was from Samail. Before that, the Omani were pagans who worshipped idols. While making a sacrifice, Mazin heard a voice telling him to denounce his faith in idol worship and join Islam. Mazin heard the voice again. After that, he met a traveller from western Arabia who persuaded Mazin to convert to Islam. This was around the time Prophet Muhammed had moved to Makkah to expand his religious base. Mazin travelled to Madinah and converted to Islam.

Meanwhile, a merchant from Prophet Muhammed's tribe, Quarish, travelled with letters to the joint leaders at that time—the brothers Abd and Jaifar Al Julanda—to petition them to join their cause. Oman then became a Muslim-dominated country.

I had visited the tomb many times to do stories for our feature pages, and also to enjoy the pleasant climate in the location, which is watered by some 200 falaj channels. A falaj is a channel that is dug in the earth, through which water runs. It is an ancient irrigation system that has existed in Oman since 500 AD.

Binil and I met Praseedha during one such visit. We were doing a location shoot in that area when Praseedha saw us. Binil and I have features common to Keralites, so Praseedha had no doubts that we were from her homeland. Binil drives a big car. He is a pot-bellied person, and therefore, doesn't fit in small cars. '*Malayali aano*? (are you Malayali?)' she asked. Keralites are locally called Malayalis as they speak the Malayalam language.

Binil sometimes pretended to be harsh with people, even though he is a kind-hearted person. So, he asked '*Aanenkil . . . entho venam*? (If so, what do you want?)'

Praseedha went still for a moment. She pulled her son closer to her before responding, '*Veruthe chodhichu enne ullu,* sir. (Just enquiring, sir.).' She then walked away. I felt bad for her, but I was a little curious as well. An Indian woman, probably in her late thirties, with a mentally-challenged boy in a village-like Samail was an oddity. I had noticed that they both dressed untidily, in torn clothes. I know that other than a few bachelors, not many Indians or Indian families lived in that town. Only tourists came to the tomb of Mazin. So, seeing them there made me curious. I walked a little closer to them and smiled. She smiled back at me. But the boy was not ready to greet me. He was also a little reluctant to look at Binil, as he had raised his voice at his mother.

I could also sense that Praseedha had something to tell us. Soon, she was putting forth her request.

'Sir, we are in trouble. We would like to go home. Would you be able to help us . . . We don't know any Keralites here . . . So . . .' Praseedha said.

I told Binil that we can listen to what she had to say for a few minutes.

Binil was ready. Again, he raised his voice and said, 'Yes, tell us.'

I sat on a falaj stone. But Binil didn't. It is a bit difficult for him to sit on a low seat like a falaj stone because of his weight. Praseedha also didn't sit. Holding her son close, she started to tell her story.

Praseedha had come to work as a domestic worker in Oman in 2006, through irregular ways. She had experience working in Saudi Arabia from 2002 to 2005. Then she moved back to Kerala and divorced her husband who was abusive and an alcoholic.

'He was a carpenter. But he never used to work. He was addicted to alcohol and playing cards. I had an aged mother to look after. So, he used to stay with us. But in a few months, he became a nuisance. He used to beat me . . . I adjusted to that as well. But one day, he pushed my mother who came to save me from being beaten . . . and she fell. She got hurt . . . our neighbours took her to the hospital . . . I didn't have a single penny on me . . . and as I was beaten up badly with a plastic chair, I had bruises on my face as well . . .' Praseedha narrated her story.

Praseedha's mother was rushed to a government hospital. The hospital authorities informed the police, and following that, her husband was summoned. 'I did not want to live with him any more. So, we separated. There was no legal procedure, but he was moved out of my house by the police. So, that chapter was closed forever . . .' she said.

'I started to look for a job in the Gulf. As I had gone to Saudi Arabia once before marriage, I was an experienced applicant to employers. So, it was easy to find an agent and a job,' Praseedha continued.

Praseedha had approached a travel agent in a town nearby and given him her passport. He had assured her that the moment an opportunity came, she would be called. After a four-month wait, the travel agent called her and told her about a vacancy in Oman.

She agreed to go. Meanwhile, one of her cousin sisters, a divorcee, had come to stay in her house to look after Praseedha's mother. She was the same cousin who had looked after Praseedha's mother when Praseedha had gone to Saudi Arabia for work. 'She was a tailor. She was good at her work. She was able to find a job and earn a decent income,' Praseedha added.

A week after Praseedha was contacted by the travel agent, her visa came. She had to pay around Rs 65,000 for her ticket and visa, which was more than it should have cost her. 'When I went to Saudi Arabia, I had paid only Rs 35,000. I worked there for nearly two years. I was promised about Rs 15,000 as salary, but was given only Rs 10,000. So, I was not happy there. Luckily, the employer was a good person. When I put in my resignation, he asked me to stay for three more months and then leave. He did not pay on time but he never missed a payment. Even if it was delayed, he would pay me,' Praseedha said.

Praseedha left that employer after working for him for twenty months and then returned to India. Back home, she got married. 'I was not happy with the marriage. He was an abusive person,' she told us. And after the separation, she thought about migrating, and that's how she came to Oman.

Reaching Oman was not difficult. She was taken to Dubai and then to Oman. She was sold to the employer, but was not abused by him like many others. The house she worked in was in the Sohar area. That's all she knew. But she shared a few other details. The house was made with white marble. There were twelve people living in the gated villa,

including three women, six men and three boys, one Keralite
Muslim driver, a Bangladeshi gardener, and one Sri Lankan
maid; there were also six cars, two bikes, five Persian cats, and
eight goats.

The workload did not worry her. She was happy and
her salary was Rs 15,000 per month. She was saving money.
After a few months, she fell in love with the driver. 'Sharing
my happiness, woes, and everything else, made me feel that
I am not alone,' Praseedha said, while talking about her
relationship with the Keralite driver.

His name was Abdul Rasheed; he was a Muslim from
Kozhikode—a northern Keralite town—and he was working
as a driver for the last five years in the same house. When
Praseedha and Abdul realized that they won't be able to lead a
happy life together where they were employed, they ran away
from the gated villa.

Praseedha moved to Muscat with Abdul. Abdul had
found a shared accommodation in Ruwi, a small town
populated mostly with Asian migrants, mainly Keralites and
Bangladeshis. The town is centred around a police station. It
has one three-star hotel, a couple of Indian jewel shops, Indian
and Filipino restaurants, dry fruit shops, a few hypermarkets
for Asian migrants, photo studios, apartments, and a few low-
price item shops.

The readers may be surprised when I say that the
hypermarkets were for Asian migrants. The Arabs do not
patronize such hypermarkets, for they do not have goods
that are attractive to them. The Arabs usually like to go to
hypermarkets run by the French retailer Carrefour and other
Dubai-based and American-based retailer shops.

As I had mentioned earlier, Ruwi is where all the Indian blue-collar workers come to make their annual leave purchases. Good companies give a month's paid leave and airfare for their migrant workers after eleven months' work. But a few extend it to two months after twenty-two months' work. This is the time when Indian and other Asian workers make their annual leave purchases.

Whether it is required or not, they will buy at least two kilos of NIDO milk powder, a few big-sized bars of foreign chocolates, then hazelnuts, Emirati and Saudi dates, which are sweeter than Omani ones, Chinese-made electronic items like DVD players and emergency lamps, which will not last for more than six months, Chinese blankets that will occupy most of the luggage, Chinese-made fake cosmetics, Imperial bath soaps, which are a must for a Gulf family in Kerala, a duplicate gold-plated Rado watch that will lose its shine in a few weeks, and of course, a few Arab perfume bottles, too.

The maximum an airline would allow as check-in baggage would be 30 kilograms. However, most of the time, the luggage of the poor blue-collar worker would exceed the permissible limit, and he will have to pay extra money at the airline's check-in counter. In addition to his own packages, the blue-collar worker will also be carrying his friends' gift items, which will be either collected or delivered upon arrival.

While some airline officials are benevolent and turn a blind eye on a few kilos of extra luggage, others are quite strict, which often hurts the workers. The strict officials will make the worried and panicked workers open up the well-packed and wrapped boxes at the check-in counters and force them to remove the extra items.

Unpacking the boxes is a big part of the celebration when blue-collar workers reach home.

Some experts will tie the knots of the luggage in a way that even if a bad handler mishandles the luggage, it won't get damaged or open up. But for the experts to come and do this for you, a bottle of whiskey, beef fry, and Kerala parotta must be offered.

Most often, flights timings are early in the morning. So, the packing of the boxes and unpacking of bottles will start by the afternoon itself. And by 10 p.m., the boxes will be packed. Typically, the flights to India, especially to Kerala, are after 1 a.m., so that by 6 a.m., the flights land in Kerala. This is convenient for the Keralites, their faithful customers.

Praseedha was happy in Ruwi. She became pregnant, too. But that happiness didn't last for long. Abdul was jobless. However, he got a car and started to run it as a private taxi. Even though this is illegal, there are many private taxis in Oman. Although they are more convenient, one has to pay extra to use them. As I didn't have a driving licence in Oman, I used to depend on private taxis.

I used to call for private taxis only when Binil was not available or if I had to travel with my family. Otherwise, I depended only on shared taxis. I used to walk the three kilometres to the office. Those walks have got me several stories. I have read that journalists who know the fine art of loitering get great stories. Walking to the office was a sort of loitering for me.

I used to loiter under the flyover in Ruwi where workers would rest. Greeting them, sitting with them, sharing tea and cigarettes, talking to them, listening to them . . . this was my everyday routine. While some used to tell me about their workplace stories, others would tell me stories about their families. We would discuss movies, religion, exploitation, and of course, the politics of Kerala or India. But one thing we never missed to do was blame the Indian Embassy. Yes, it is very common for Indians to blame Indian embassies, based on the stories they have heard from their friends or from their personal experiences. Such stories may or may not be true, but I have witnessed workers being neglected at Indian embassies. Workers who come to the embassy in torn and untidy clothes will be stopped at the gate by a local security person.

Once, I had gone with two workers to register their complaint, wearing a t-shirt, torn blue jeans, and sandals. I was also looking tired. The workers were waiting for me in front of the embassy. I told them to join me, but while trying to rush into the embassy, we were stopped. Finally, I had to text the Indian Embassy's first secretary about the situation at the gate, and he had to ring the gatekeeper to allow us in.

Usually, the gates would be manned by local guards. They would speak Arabic and Hindi only. Most of them would be Balochis. Balochis are people who had migrated from Balochistan, an arid desert and mountainous region in south-western Asia, mainly Pakistan, Iran, and Afghanistan, during the early days of Islam around 1,400 years ago.[2]

Europeans who had visited during the sixteenth and seventeenth centuries had noted the presence of the Balochi community that settled in Oman centuries ago. According to historians, even though there were ties between the two communities throughout early history, there was no political association between Oman and Balochistan until the era of the

Yaruba and Al Busaid Dynasties in Oman. The Yaruba Dynasty ruled Oman from 1624 to 1744, and the Al Busaid Dynasty has ruled since 1744. It was the Yarubas who established a naval force with which they defeated and expelled the Portuguese from Oman, India, and east Africa. During this time, a large number of Balochi men joined the then Omani army.

It has been recorded in history that when the Omani Imamate dynasty preceded the (present) Al Busaidi Sultanate, Imam Seif bin Sultan employed hundreds of Balochis to displace enemies throughout the Persian Gulf and the Indian Ocean, considering them 'brave and well-armed with matchlocks'. They were used to protect and defend Omani ports and cities, and were instrumental in fighting the Portuguese alongside the Omanis.

The Balochi participated in several civil wars that took place in Oman as a result of the disputes among the sons of Imam Sultan bin Saif. When Sultan Taimur bin Faisal (1913–1932) ruled Oman, he continued with a policy similar to that of his predecessors, to combat the internal revolts that continually plagued the country. During the rule of Sultan Said bin Taimur (1932–1970), Makran in Pakistan continued to provide soldiers loyal to the Sultan for the Omani Army, many of whom served as his bodyguards.

'The first modern organized army unit in Oman was entirely [Baloch] in composition,' writes J.E. Peterson, a scholar of Oman's history.

The Muscat Levy Corps, as it was called, was created in 1921 and they became the genesis of the Sultan's Armed Forces.[3]

This unit, along with the Trucial Oman Levies, was integral to the British-backed Sultan's victory over the Imam of the interior Omanis, in the Jebel Akhdar War of the 1950s. British officers were tasked with training 'boatloads of recruits from Gwadar' brought to camps at the foot of Jebel Akhdar, or the 'green mountain', the Imam's last stronghold.

In 1964, the Sultan's Armed Forces were over 60 per cent Balochi, and there was an increase in recruitment, leading up to and during the Dhofar War in Oman's southern province, which stretched throughout the 1960s and 70s. After the war, Balochis who fought for the Sultan remained and settled in Oman, blending into Omani society like so many merchants, traders, slaves, and soldiers before them. Today, Balochi–Omanis maintain a strong presence in the security industry as soldiers, policemen, Ministry of Defence employees, and security guards.

Even though I have read and been told that many Balochis are rich and prominent traders in Oman, I have seen many a petty trader Balochi in Muscat and the Muttrah area, especially in the Muttrah coastal souq.

The Gazetteer of the Persian Gulf, Omàn, and Central Arabia, compiled by J.G. Lorimer for the then India at the beginning of the twentieth century, noted that the Balochis in Muscat and Matrah constituted half or more of the population and served as soldiers, sailors, porters, servants, and petty traders.

The tough Balochi guard, therefore, looks intimidating to the ordinary person. When a worried migrant worker reaches the embassy gate, he loses his confidence facing the Balochi soldier. As it is, he may be coming to an embassy for the first time. He may not know which gate to enter from, which way to walk, where to sit, what to do, and whom to meet.

In addition to the Balochi 'soldiers', every official, and even temporary staff, like translators, interpreters, clerks, and counter staff who are mostly Indians, will act as ambassadors. A distraught migrant worker may not be given the right response always.

There is no surprise in this. An embassy officer probably hears fifty cases every day. And all he can do is tell the migrant worker to write a complaint and tell him '*Dekh lenge yaar* (Let us see)' or '*Das din ke baad aana* (Come after ten days)'.

The procedure ends there. Only if the migrant worker goes with a social worker or a regular visitor to the embassy, would he be able to move a step further. Or else, the migrant worker will have to wait for ten or twenty days to hear from the embassy. And that update, most of the time, would be '*Kar rahe hein* (We are working on it)'. The embassy would call the employer and plead for a settlement, and if that doesn't work, then a letter with the complaint will be given back to the worker to be submitted at the local government's labour department.

And there, the complaint will be held back for some forty-five days. If the employer doesn't turn up there, too, then the complaint will automatically go to court. In the court, it takes time. Most of the time, the Indian embassy will provide legal support through their empaneled lawyers, but the winnability of the case depends on the interest of the lawyers.

The Indian lawyers who are empaneled in the Indian Embassy not only see it as a matter of pride but also as an invitation to enter any office, talk to the community, talk to companies, and take up cases, and are basically fully authorized to work on behalf of the migrant worker.[4]

I have noticed myself and from the information I received from senior officials that even though empanelled lawyers are supposed to take up all kind of cases, some of them prefer to handle only road traffic accident cases. Road traffic cases are usually settled in Arab countries without much delay. The compensation for the victim is paid with 'blood money'—an illegal practice in the Arab countries. The lawyer who takes up such a case will receive a certain per cent of the blood money from the victim's family. However, in labour cases, the compensation may not be as high as it would be in road accident cases; besides, they always take longer. Hence, some lawyers prefer road accident cases to labour cases.

My days spent enjoying the street food at teashops and drinking Amstel beers with bowls of popcorn at bars in and around Ruwi, have led me to many stories. Most often, when I hung out in a teashop near the Ruwi police station, I would bump into Bangladeshis who would stand around and ask us, in a very quiet voice, '*Ladkhi chahiye*? (do you want girls?)' when we cross them.

One day, while walking to the office, I was a bit troubled about not having a good front-page story in hand. My editor was a very strict person. At the 11 a.m. meeting, I had to give him a list of stories for the day. So, I decided to do the '*Ladkhi chahiye*?' story. It was only around 8.30 a.m. then. I still had time.

I easily found the agents at the teashop. And for company, I called my friend and cameraman Suresh P who was staying in Ruwi. By the time I had tea and a Dunhill Red cigarette, Suresh joined me.

I had noticed one such man in a brown t-shirt and blue jeans, glancing at me repeatedly. I was sure that he was an agent. I took one more cigarette and moved towards him. He was a little surprised to see me approach him. But I was confident. I asked him for a lighter for my cigarette. I had the spy cam of my iPhone on. After lighting the cigarette, I asked him, '*Ladki milenga*? (Will I get a girl?)' Without any change in expression, he said, '*Ji saab* (Yes, sir).' Hearing this, I became more confident, even though I could sense that Suresh was panicking.

Still, I continued my investigation. In five minutes, the Bangladeshi opened up completely.

He had with him girls from Malayali, Filipino, African, and Arab descent. It would cost me Rs 1,600 for thirty minutes with the girls. And if I needed a 'fresh' girl, then the rate was around Rs 3,000. When I told him that I needed a Keralite girl, he started to speak in Malayalam. Meantime, the spy cam was recording everything.

'It is just nearby. The place is safe. The girls are good. There are no issues. If you want to go now, we can, or whenever you like,' the pimp said. 'The girls are aged twenty-one and twenty-two . . . Keralite girls are also available.' On Fridays, Ruwi would be flooded with workers from camps arriving at the locality, reportedly looking for agents while the agents hunt for potential customers.

Thus, it was on Saturday that the news about the police raids in Ruwi to rescue twenty-one Thai girls from the sex trade broke out. A police squad from Thailand had flown down to Oman and liaised with the Royal Oman Police officers before the raids. The women had entered Oman on tourist visas. They were lured into Oman through fake job offers.

The raid came after the Thai authorities were tipped off by three Thai women, who had escaped from the sex trade in Muscat, and had returned to Thailand with the help of the Thai Embassy. The three had lodged police complaints against the five suspects.

So, I was excited about getting a hot story; one that was also timely. I paid the pimp Rs 500, took his number, and told him that I would call him in the evening for the Keralite girl. Suresh was looking frightened. I told him not to panic and to leave. I walked to the office. As soon as I got in, I emailed S the pitch.

By 10 a.m., S was in. He was also excited about the pitch. He called me as he entered his cabin. He watched the sting video I had just taken, emailed it to the newspaper chairman, and was waiting for the approval. It is a sensitive topic to report on in an Arab country. However, he told me that we would work on it.

Hussain Al Lawati, our Omani reporter, was told to contact the police and get their comment on the story. This sale of girls was happening a stone's throw away from the Ruwi Police Station. Interestingly, the police spokesperson told Hassan that soliciting is not a crime, and that action would not be taken against the perpetrators; they also told us to go ahead with the story. By then, the chairman had texted me telling me that the story could be printed but that he would like to see the front page.

While I was filing the story, I called an Arab parliamentarian to get his comment on it, too. He told me that such things happened because the government was not serious about enforcing the rules for tourist visas. Most trafficked women travel into Oman on tourist visas.

We printed the story. For the first time, a story talking about prostitution in Oman had been published. The story was well-received by the public. And I was advised by my editor to avoid loitering in that area at least for a week. I agreed. I had heard from my sources in Ruwi that the Bangladeshi agents were angry with me.

Praseedha and her partner were living in one of the apartments in the alleys in Ruwi. Praseedha's partner had become a liquor peddler. He used to 'purchase' liquor from shops and distribute the same for the 'needy' with a good margin.

It was illegal to sell or purchase liquor like Abdul did. In Oman, Arabs cannot purchase liquor from liquor shops. Only foreigners can do that. And to facilitate that, a card-based system was in place. If you earned 1,000 USD a month, you were be eligible to own a card with which you can buy liquor for 100 USD a month.

Both Arabs and migrants can drink in bars. However, Arabs don't come to bars often. They don't drink much. So, the majority of the tipplers are migrants. While white-collar migrants depend on expensive bars and own liquor quota cards, blue-collar migrants depend on people like Abdul for liquor.

Abdul not only bought liquor using his own cards but also procured them directly from liquor makers, which is not known to many. Most migrants in mid-level jobs owned a liquor card. But instead of purchasing liquor, they would sell their card quota off for double or triple the price.

I have come across stories and news reports that spurious liquor is made in fishing boats on the Oman coast, bottled, and sold as Indian-made spurious liquor. I knew a few Keralites in the coastal area of Oman, especially in Sur and the Salalah coast, who used to brew liquor in boats, bottle it, and sell it to peddlers as Indian-made foreign liquor. There was a story of a Keralite who was mistakenly shot dead by the Oman coastal police. The man was apparently brewing liquor in an anchored boat, when the coastal police arrived. He and his friends tried to escape by jumping into the water when he was shot dead.

I couldn't cross-check the story as it was told to me by one of the social workers. He had come to the Indian Embassy, with what he told me was the dead Keralite's post-mortem report, when I met him.

Peddling liquor is a serious crime in Arab countries. You can be jailed and deported. People in India believe that it is quite hard to get liquor in an Islamic country. However, the fact is, it is easier than in India. If you have the peddler's phone number, you will get liquor at your doorstep within thirty minutes of sending out an SMS or a WhatsApp message.

Abdul was one of the several liquor peddlers in Ruwi. Many liquor peddlers make money easily. In the Arab country, they may roam in a cheap car. However, back in Kerala, they own a big house. Their family members in Kerala have learned not to ask what kind of jobs they do in the Arab Gulf.

Like anywhere else in the world, in the Arab Gulf, too, money can be made easily from liquor sales and brothels.

'Abdul's business was doing well, even though I didn't like the business he was doing,' Praseedha had told me once. Prasedha was afraid of Abdul indulging in illegal business.

And as she had feared, Abdul was caught by the police and jailed.

'I was pregnant. There was no other revenue. Abdul was in jail and I was stranded. I moved to a smaller accommodation. I struggled for food,' Praseedha told me. She couldn't go to jail and meet Abdul. She was pregnant, without any money, and she didn't know how to meet Abdul.

She also discovered that her visa had expired. If she had to renew it, she would need her original passport, which was still with her previous employer. She would need a new sponsor, and also have to pay the renewal fee.

She couldn't do it alone. The visa renewal is done by the immigration department, which is run by the police. It's the same as going to a police station. So, she was afraid. She remained an undocumented migrant in Oman. It is easy to remain an undocumented person in Ruwi, especially for women. The police raid only certain areas where there are a large number of undocumented men. Usually, the women's living spaces are avoided.

In Ruwi, it is in the Hamariya area where the raids happen the most, to arrest undocumented workers. They are typically on free visas, about which I had written about earlier in the book. The majority of them would be undocumented and overstaying.

In reality, there is no such thing as a 'free visa'. It is an arrangement by which if the employers are paid a fee, they allow the migrant workers to work for any other employer. Although migrant workers are allowed to work for their employer only, if you pay additional money to enjoy the freedom to work anywhere, then the employer will allow the same. This is locally called a free visa. The worker will be compelled to pay approximately $60 per month to be on a free visa. If you work for a single employer, you may earn $350 per month. The kafala system keeps you bonded to your employer. It is illegal to work for a different employer who is not your visa provider.

But if you manage to have a free visa and work for different employers, you will be able to earn perhaps $600. The worker may be using a 'driver visa' or even an 'engineering visa', but will do car washing, carpentry, or other semi-skilled or low-skilled jobs to augment his income.

Additionally, you decide whether to work or not. You are your own master. But you are at risk of violating the local labour law by working for a different employer and doing different jobs other than what's mentioned in the visa. If caught, you will be arrested, jailed, and deported. In addition, the risk of becoming an undocumented worker while being on a free visa is very high. The moment you stop paying the monthly freedom fee, the employer will file a case with the local police claiming that you have absconded. He will file the case declaring that you are missing and that he won't be responsible for your subsequent actions. Only if he does so, will he be able to get a clearance for a new visa for an employee from the ministry.

Many mid-level-earning Arabs see the free visa sale as an income-generating source. All Arabs are not wealthy. There are grocery shop owners and taxi drivers, too. For them, being a kafeel (employer in Arabic) is an income-generating job.

Even as a taxi driver, if you manage to get six visas from the ministry through a small project, then you can sell those visas and get a monthly freedom fee from the visa holders. For example, if you have to pay Rs 40,000 including ticket fare to get a work visa, you may have to pay around Rs 1,00,000 or a little more than that to get a free visa. The employer/kafeel will sell the visa to a middleman, often a Keralite, who will find the potential migrant and sell the visa. If the kafeel gets only 20 to 30 per cent in addition to the visa fee he pays the government, the middlemen will profit from the rest.

Though the visa fee is around Rs 30,000, the worker will be forced to pay around Rs 1,00,000. The difference of Rs 70,000 will be pocketed by the middlemen. Additionally, let us assume that the employer has sold about six free visas. He will earn around $360 every month without any effort.

And when that doesn't happen, the kafeel will file an 'absconding case' so that he gets rid of the worker and stands eligible to get a new visa cleared from the government. Even though being on a free visa is lucrative, it has its risks, too. You won't be able to find jobs that easily. There is an off-season for jobs as well. So, to be employed regularly is very rare. Moreover, competition in the market is high.

If a worker from India can be hired to work for $10, a worker from Bangladesh can be hired to do the same work for $8. More often than not, due to a lack of work and less pay, they will fail to pay the monthly freedom fee. And when it accumulates and becomes a large amount, the worker will not meet the employer or pick his calls.

Interestingly, the worker's passport will be with the employer. And eventually, the worker will become undocumented and an overstayer after his visa expires. If the worker has to fix his irregular condition, then he has to first clear the absconding case penalty and the overstaying fine. Unfortunately, both will come up to around Rs 1,50,000 or more, which will force the worker to continue undocumented, go into hiding, and wait for an amnesty to be announced.

Workers in the Hamariya area sleep in turns in their shared accommodations. Often, two or three will stay awake at the small entry points, guarding the rest and staying alert for a police raid. Police raids often happen late in the night or early in the morning. It is not just police who are deployed to catch the undocumented workers. There are also black-clad police officers, who come with handcuffs and electric batons. Workers are arrested from their shelters and workplaces. As I described in the 'Appunni' chapter, free visa workers were arrested at the Muscat Airport construction site.

One afternoon, Praseedha suddenly started experiencing labour pain. She managed to go to a nearby hospital. But as she didn't have a valid resident card, she was denied admission. I knew one of the promoters of the hospital she mentioned. He was a friend. What began as a polyclinic is now a chain of hospitals in the GCC.

The hospital was just a stone's throw away from where she was staying. 'I only had 12 Omani rials (about Rs 1,200 then). I took that money, tied it in my dupatta, and somehow reached the hospital. It was summer. In my room, the AC was not working properly. I was struggling a lot. So, when I entered the hospital, I found it a relaxing environment,' Praseedha told me.

She waited for her turn. But before that, she was approached by a hospital assistant asking her if she needed any help. When she explained to him that she was suffering from labour pain, he called the nurses and made arrangements to admit her. At the same time, he collected her resident card and rushed to the counter.

The male nursing staff who was assisting her found out from the counter that her card was invalid and that she possessed neither money nor an insurance card. Baffled, he ran to his manager. On the way, he saw that the other nursing staff were moving Praseedha to the gynaecology department. His manager shouted at him and asked him to deny her admission, and the nurses were told to stop taking her to the gynaecology department.

'I could see that they were feeling bad about the situation. One of them turned the wheelchair and started to head towards the reception. The floor staff came and told me that I could not be admitted as I had neither a valid resident card nor money. They told me they were helpless,' Praseedha added.

Praseedha was clueless about what to do. When she tried to stand up from the wheelchair, she fell unconscious. The floor staff and nurses ran to her aid and put her on a stretcher She was admitted in 2007.

Her story was told to me by the hospital senior manager in 2013 when I approached them for help with Praseedha's case. 'When Praseedha fell unconscious, we moved her to the gynaecology department and treated her. We didn't think of money. It was a normal delivery. After two days of post-delivery care, we requested her to leave the hospital. She left. And the chapter was closed,' the manager told me.

On humanitarian grounds, a person must have or receive health access, but when the law stands in between, then it's a problem. In Arab Gulf countries, undocumented workers are denied health access, even now. When the COVID-19 pandemic happened, thousands of undocumented and penniless migrant workers struggled to get hospital admission.

Many had to take shelter in kitchens and terraces. I will write about them in the next and last chapter.

The hospitals that are humane enough to provide health access to undocumented and penniless workers, have to do it by violating the rules. The private hospital also violated rules by admitting Praseedha to help her give birth to her baby.

'It was a boy. I still remember that day. After two or three days, we had to discharge her. We didn't know where she was going. We didn't bother to note down her address either,' the manager told me. He was surprised that I knew about Praseedha.

Praseedha had delivered the boy in 2007. After six years, in 2013, I was enquiring about her at the hospital, with the manager.

When Praseedha approached me when we met for the first time near the Mazin bin Gadhuba Al Tayy tomb, she didn't tell me the entire story. At that time, she wanted me to help her to go back to India. She wanted somebody to talk about her case in the Indian Embassy. She was not opening up much either.

The third Friday Open House was about twenty days away, giving me enough time to listen to the rest of her story, although I already knew that her drunkard husband was in Kerala, and that she migrated to the Gulf and had fallen in love with Abdul. She told me how they fled to Ruwi and about their Ruwi days—about Abdul getting caught by the police and her delivering the baby in the hospital in Ruwi. She also shared the story of how she started a new life in Samail.

After delivering the baby, she couldn't survive in Ruwi. She couldn't leave the newborn baby alone in the room and go out looking for a job. Even the food was provided by the neighbours.

'I couldn't buy any kind of protein milk powder for my boy. Rice, dal, and Arab bread was the only food we got. As I was weak, I couldn't breastfeed my boy. I knew that my baby wouldn't be healthy. But I was not courageous enough to give him up and run away again. So, I held him close to my heart,' Praseedha told me.

For three months, Praseedha was able to continue living in Ruwi. But since she couldn't raise the money for rent and food was becoming a problem, she decided to leave Ruwi. One Friday, she left Ruwi with a 100-day-old baby.

A friend had told Praseedha that there was a domestic worker job in an Arab house in Samail. 'She had talked to the Arab. She said I would be provided with food, a stay, and a small salary. So, I decided to move to Samail,' Praseedha said.

Life was calm and quiet in Samail. She and her baby were given a bed space in a storeroom with old furniture. 'A bed was given, an old one. It was placed near a window. I could see the Arab mansion through that. There were a few broken chairs, a torn sofa, an old refrigerator, two broken western toilets, a few old dresses for kids, and some copper wire,' Praseedha described her 'home' to me.

'It was scary for me on the first day. But at the same time, I was happy, too. On the second day, I found some children's clothes. Only a few were torn. I washed them on the third day and used them for my baby. There was not much work there. The house had eight people, including three children. Once in a while, a few guests would come. The Arab's wife was a nice lady. She never harassed or overburdened me with work,' Praseedha said.

Praseedha was not paid well, however. She was paid only Rs 5,000. They had promised that she would be paid when she returned home. After a week, she was gifted an old phone.

'I didn't need much money then. I didn't have to remit money to anyone. I didn't have to save for anyone. So, whatever money I would get was put in my old bag,' Praseedha said.

'Time flew by. My boy was growing. I was buying new clothes for him. The household had a driver. I would give him money and he would buy what I wanted for my boy. But now, I felt like I should go back to India,' Praseedha had told me.

Only then did she find out that she and her son needed passports to fly back. The only document she had was a wrinkled photocopy of her passport. Her boy did not have any documentation. Praseedha had left the hospital without collecting even a birth certificate.

'They didn't charge me for the delivery. So, isn't it unfair to ask them for documents? And at that time, I was not thinking of collecting the documents either,' Praseedha told me.

So, when she wanted to go back after six years, she realized the need for a passport and found out from her friends that the embassy would be able to issue her one. She was looking

for someone who could help her get a passport. And that's
how she bumped into me in Samail.

At that time, all I could tell her was, 'I will call you. I will
ask for help at the embassy. Don't worry. We will get you help.'

The next day, after we returned from Samail, I called
Praseedha and started to talk to her. Most of the time, it was
during the breaks. She started to tell me of her struggles in
Kerala, her happy days with Abdul, the pain she suffered
while being pregnant, and the peace she experienced in
Samail. Now, her greatest worry was being undocumented.

Days before the Open House, I talked to the officials in
the Indian Embassy. They were very receptive. They told me
to bring her to the embassy. I was confident that the issue
would be resolved. But I never thought that the Indian
Embassy official would tell us, 'Even a Pakistani can speak
Malayalam.'

When the officer, looking at Praseedha's son, said that
even a Pakistani could speak Malayalam, I was dumbfounded.
I could not reply. The officer's point was that claiming and
proving that a person can speak an Indian language does not
make him an Indian.

Praseedha was uncomfortable waiting in the embassy hall.
She decided to give up and go back to Samail. However, I was
not ready to drop the case. I was confident about finding a
solution.

The officer walked back to his room in a hurry to attend
to other cases. I was clueless as to what I could do. But I ran
after him. 'Sir, give me a solution,' I pleaded.

'Let me think. Let's talk tomorrow. Tell her to go back.
We will find a solution,' the embassy official told me.

I had to send Praseedha and her son back, disappointed. She did not have the money to go back. Binil had a few rials with him. He gave them to her and sent her to Samail. I told Praseedha not to worry.

The next day, I got a call from the Indian Embassy official. 'Come, Reji. We have a solution,' the official said.

I was excited. I asked for a two-hour break from my office and rushed to the Indian Embassy. The officer was waiting for me.

'Okay, Reji. She gave birth to the boy in a hospital, right? So, go to the hospital and get the birth certificate or the file from there. With that, we will be able to get the boy his documents,' the officer told me.

I was happy to learn that. I called Praseedha right then, from the officer's room. 'Where did you deliver the baby?' I asked.

She gave me the hospital's name. I was greatly relieved. I knew the hospital and its founder. He will listen to me. I told the embassy official that I would be able to get the document. While going back to the office, I was feeling better thinking of how Praseedha's son will soon be documented. Praseedha had told me that she would go to Kerala with her son. I felt happy and relieved.

The next morning, I called the hospital manager and fixed an appointment to meet him, but I didn't tell him why. When I finally met him, he asked me why I was asking for the details of Praseedha's case. I had to tell him the entire story. The manager was a good person. Many a time, when low-paid workers were admitted to the hospital and nobody was there to pay their bills, the manager would help reduce the bill, sometimes by even 50 per cent.

However, when I told him the story of Praseedha and her urgent need for a document, he was reluctant. He told me that he would have to talk to the founder. I told him it would be better if I spoke to his boss, since I felt that I would be better at convincing the founder than the manager himself.

So, I sent the founder a text message requesting him to call me back when he was free. That evening, he called me. I told him about Praseedha and my request. He was not entirely convinced, but didn't say no. He told me, 'I trust you. I will tell the manager to help you.'

The next day was a Friday. It's a holiday in the Arab Gulf countries. So, I didn't call the manager. But on Saturday, at around 10 a.m., the manager called me to ask what kind of letter I needed to help Praseedha.

I told him exactly what I needed. He said the letter and the documents would be ready by the evening. I could collect them on Sunday, the first working day in the Arab countries.

In between, Praseedha called me. 'Be positive, seems like your son will get documented soon,' I tried to reassure her. I could make out that she did not really believe me. After talking to the manager on Sunday, I went and collected the document. It was in a sealed cover. I didn't open it. My job was to hand it over to the Indian Embassy official.

'We trust you. This should not get leaked. If that happens, it would impact our reputation,' the manager told me.

I assured him that the document would not be leaked and that I was not going to do a story about Praseedha any time soon. The next day, Binil and I went to the Indian Embassy and handed over the document to the official. He opened it, read it, looked at us, and said, 'Yes, this would help us make a document for the boy.'

'Tell her to come to the embassy next week,' he added.

I felt relieved. On the way back, I called Praseedha and told her to collect her Malayalam-speaking 'Pakistani' boy's passport from the embassy. I could hear her weeping on the phone. 'For almost seven years, my son and I had no identity. Now, we are going to have one again,' she said, while thanking us. A week later, she went to the Indian Embassy and did the paperwork required to collect the passport . . .

A few weeks later, she called me and said, 'We have got our passports. We will be flying home very soon.'

That was her last call to us. She would send messages to us regularly after that, but eventually, that too stopped.

7

All Returned Empty-Handed

On 25 June 2020, at around 5 p.m., Valsala PK, a Keralite domestic worker from Kozhikode, called me from the Bandar Abbas port in Iran. It was a WhatsApp call.

'Reji, I am boarding the ship. I am the only woman on board. But I am not afraid. After this, I may not be able to call you. When the ship leaves the port, I will text you again. I am boarding a ship for the first time in my life,' Valsala said.

I wished her a safe journey and hung up.

After being stranded on Kish Island in Iran, she was returning to India on an Indian Navy ship with 700 south Indian fishermen. It was a big relief for me. Valsala's case was my second COVID-19-related stranded migrant case. She was finally returning.

In thirty minutes, I received a WhatsApp notification. It was from Valsala. We had been communicating mostly through WhatsApp voice notes since the first week of March 2020.

I have not heard all her messages. I listen only to the first few seconds. If she is crying, then I listen to the entire message.

Or else, I would ignore it. I also forward the same to either Mini Mohan, a psychologist in Kerala, or Mahalakshmi S, a social worker in Oman. We had formed a WhatsApp group to manage Valsala's case. Whoever was free would attend to the message and respond, so that even if I missed her messages, someone else could attend to it.

I was getting exhausted, as from the last week of February 2020 till the end of July, I was flooded with SOS messages from the Arab Gulf.

When the COVID-19 outbreak happened in the Arab Gulf during the first week of March, I had become a regular debater on television channels telling viewers, policymakers, legislators, and parliamentarians that a delay in action would end in the death of our people. It would happen not only due to COVID-19, but also due to other illnesses and mental stress.

Yes, the mental stress of being alone in an Arab country, with friends becoming COVID-19 patients, the fear of being infected by the coronavirus, and also the hassles associated with returning home, had led to quite a few suicides.

Since March 2020, for the first time in Kerala's history, Keralite migrant workers' issues in the Arab Gulf were getting slots on prime time, that too on all the premier channels. They had to give this coverage, because there are 28 lakh Keralites in the Arab Gulf sweating under harsh and exploitative conditions, so that they may provide better lives for their families back in Kerala.

The Centre of Development Studies (CDS) in Kerala says that every fifth house in Kerala has a migrant.[1]

As was narrated in the first chapter, Keralites began migrating to the Arab Gulf in the 60s. But it had never been like this. During the COVID-19 times, their stories were told and debated on news channels on prime time. On some days, I would even attend three debates on three different channels, running from one to the other. My learnings about the Arab Gulf labour migration situation helped me state facts and predict what was going to happen. My statements earned me their respect.

However, being committed to the cause of migrant workers and informing the public about their plight openly on television during the outbreak of COVID-19 pandemic, was pushing me into a situation, which I never expected. After every debate, when I left the television studio, I would get between ten to twenty calls and fifty messages from the Arab Gulf, as my mobile number was on Facebook.

Most of these messages or calls would be from stranded Indian migrants in the Arab Gulf during the pandemic. They were different people with different issues.

I will tell those stories a little later.

As said in the previous chapters, by 2011, my stories on migration got me a spot at the Migrant Forum in Asia, a regional network of migrant rights organizations in the Asia and the Middle East. Working with them sensitized me further to issues related to migration. They enabled me to be part of regional and global meetings on migration. Every meeting helped me understand migration in a more detailed way.

With their help, I was able to do two fellowships with the International Labour Organisation (ILO) on forced labour and labour migration, and one fellowship with the Thomson Reuters Foundation on forced labour in the Arab

Gulf. I became a trainer as well, for the Thomson Reuters Foundation on Arab Gulf labour migrations.

What I learnt there helped me speak lucidly on migration. So, on television debates, I went right to the point. I was able to portray the real picture of the suffering faced by the migrants when the pandemic broke out. As I was not working in any Arab Gulf country and not tied to any office, I was free to tell the truth.

My co-debaters were either from the government, or were Keralite social workers or entrepreneurs from the Arab Gulf countries. The government and politicians from the ruling party did not want to focus on the issue. They were not keen to show that people were dying in the Arab Gulf, from COVID-19. I could see that they were uncomfortable with my narrating the real stories about laid-off Keralite migrant workers begging on the streets following the outbreak, committing suicide, and living in kitchens and abandoned cars, as they were not getting isolation wards to admit themselves into.

The Keralite social workers and entrepreneurs didn't want me to tell the real stories either. For them, everything was 'Kullu Thamam ("All is well" in Arabic)' because they had to protect their business interests.

An ambitious Keralite who earns decent money through business in the Arab Gulf, will never speak the truth about the Arab Gulf. He will never say that the Arab Gulf rulers and sheikhs are ignoring and exploiting Indian workers. To them, business comes first, and then comes the workers' welfare, if that's possible.

Even the wealthy Keralites in the Arab Gulf won't tell the truth. Small businessmen have small interests; however, wealthy Keralites in the Arab Gulf have bigger interests to be protected.

The first case I got during the COVID-19 outbreak before it was declared a pandemic by the World Health Organization on 11 March was from the Catholic Bishop House in Thiruvananthapuram.

The call came at around 10 p.m. It was from a nun who worked as a focal person of the coastal communities in Thiruvananthapuram. She called me asking whether there was any way to help some Indians stranded along the Iranian coast. I told her to pass my number on to them. In about five minutes, I got a WhatsApp call from an Indian number.

It was from a Wilson R, a Keralite fisherman from Chiruyeh at the Hormozgan province in Iran. After telling me his name, he began to cry. He and his friends were frightened, as they were hearing about COVID-19 spreading to Tehran and other Iranian cities.

In Iran, at that time, COVID-19 had claimed 43 lives, and around 600 were infected. Iran had shut down schools, universities, and other education centres. They had also cancelled all public gatherings like concerts and sports events to help curb the spread of the disease.

Around then, Iran had the highest number of deaths from the coronavirus outside of China. Globally, the coronavirus, which was reported first in the Wuhan province of China on 31 December 2019, had claimed around 3,000 lives; and there were around 90,000 people reported to be infected from all over the world.

The news was spreading like wildfire, instilling panic in everybody. When the Iranian cities were on an unofficial lockdown following the spread, the Indian fishermen along the Iranian coast were not infected. But they had a different problem to tackle: hunger. Their employers in the cities failed to send food supplies.

When Wilson called me, it was their third continuous day without food. '*Chetta*, (brother) we have nothing to eat. We will die here. We want to go home. Please help us. There are 600 people here. And in other areas, there are 300,' Wilson told me.[2]

The next morning, I wrote a story and shared it with Dr Shashi Tharoor, seeking his help.[3] He got in touch with Javed Zarif, the Iranian foreign minister and his former UN colleague, and Gaddam Dharmendra, the Indian ambassador in Iran. Zarif's office must have taken action. The Indian Embassy responded quickly, and soon, food and other essentials were sent to the Indian fishermen. Everything happened within a day.[4]

The fishermen called and thanked me. This was my first success story during the COVID-19 pandemic. After the food issue was resolved, the fishermen wanted to return home. Unfortunately, that couldn't happen. In a few days, on 24 March, India announced a lockdown by closing its land, sea, and air borders.[5]

I had no clue as to when the fishermen could return. Interestingly, Shia pilgrims who got stuck in the Iranian cities were evacuated. Kashmiri students who had gone to study medicine in Iran were brought back, but even after repeated pleas, emails, and phone calls, the issue of the fishermen was ignored.

By then, we came to know that there were more than 1,000 Indian fishermen on different Iranian coast and islands. A majority of them were from Gujarat and Tamil Nadu.

Mini started to talk to them and prepare a list. She managed to infer that there were 700 south Indian fishermen stranded there, and sent her findings to the Indian Ministry of External Affairs. Many of them didn't have their passports with them. They were recruited by employers from the UAE, Kuwait, Bahrain, and Saudi Arabia. They were then sent to these subsidiary Arab companies for fishing in Iran.

Most fishermen did not have their passports with them. This was a major difficulty that deterred the Indian Embassy in Iran from processing their repatriation. The south Indians, especially those from Kanyakumari and Thiruvananthapuram, had migrated to the Arab Gulf to work as fishermen. Interestingly, in most Arab countries, fishing is a localized profession, and only nationals can go fishing. However, as Arabs are reluctant to go fishing, they recruit Indian fishermen on different visas and send them to Yemen.

In November 2019, forty-one-year-old Noushad Ibrahim Kutty from Kerala and his eight other friends, fled Yemen's Ash-Shihr, a coastal town in southern Yemen. They travelled in a wooden fishing boat from Yemen to Kerala, as their Arab employer in the UAE was not providing them regular food, a salary, or even fuel to go fishing. They had to cross 1600 nautical miles—nearly 3000 km. But they took the risk and fled because, as they later said, they did not want to die as slaves in Yemen.

They were employed in 2018 by an Emirati, for fishing in the UAE waters. They had gone on a tourist visa to the UAE with high hopes. They were told that they would be moved to Oman, the neighbouring Arab country, to work on a boat soon. However, they were led to the Yemeni coast instead of Oman and told to anchor there, where they were forced to work under a Yemeni national.

While boarding the flight to Sharjah, Noushad was told that he would be given a salary of around AED 1000 (approximately Rs 18,000) per month, as well as a commission for working as a fisherman. But things changed when they reached their destination. While in Ajman, they were sent to catch fish only for a few days. They were paid a meagre wage even though they were promised a good salary. And soon, they were sent to Yemen.

The Yemeni employers would provide them with food only on the days they went fishing and AED 100 (around Rs 1,900) for fifteen days of work.

'We were like his slaves,' Noushad told me after he arrived in Kerala.

As they did not have the residency papers to continue staying in Yemen, they were not able to leave the harbour and find new jobs or demand proper wages. When Noushad and his friends were in the port, they were told to surrender their passports to the Yemeni police and warned from leaving. Even if they left the port, they were supposed to come back within the hour. For eleven months, till they sailed back on 11 November, they were in a fix.

As conditions worsened, Noushad and his friends contacted the Arab employer in Sharjah. But he didn't help. On the days when Noushad and the others were not going out to sea, they would work as loaders and mechanics in the harbour.

As they could no longer continue with the work physically, they fled. On the tenth day after their escape, Noushad and his friends arrived at the Lakshadweep islands. They had a satellite phone with them. But to save the battery, they did not switch it on till they were next to the Lakshadweep coast; once they were near, they called some of their friends, who then contacted the Church and the government. When the Church contacted the government, the Indian Coast Guard jumped into action.

The Coast Guard initiated an air–sea coordinated search-and-rescue operation, for which a Maritime Surveillance Dornier aircraft was launched at 3.30 p.m. on 28 November, from Kochi. The aircraft spotted the fishing boat about 100 nautical miles west of Kochi.

The Coast Guard ship *Aryaman* sailed from Kochi to assist the fishing boat. The boat was found 75 nautical miles off the Kochi coast. Noushad and his friends were brought to Kochi and handed over to the Coastal Police Station. They were lucky that they reached the Indian coast. Many a time, when Indian fishermen get trapped in the troubled waters of the Gulf, they won't be given much help.

For example, an Indian fisherman doing work fishing for his Arab employer might be there on a mason visa. If he is caught by the coastal police or meets with any accident, the first question he would face is, 'What is a mason doing in a fishing boat?' He could get arrested, jailed, and deported.

Additionally, many Indian-Gulf fishermen who go fishing in the Persian Gulf may stray into Iranian waters and get arrested by the Iranian coastal police. Rescuing them and bringing them back takes months. In 2017 and 2018, I had worked on a similar rescue case and it had taken a long time to repatriate the stranded workers.

In Wilson's case, they were officially sent to the Iranian coast, so, they wouldn't get arrested. But they were worried about their return. I relentlessly pleaded with the Indian Ministry of External Affairs but to no avail. In between, I even managed to air their videos on prime-time news debates; the videos were shared in between debates by the anchor.

When food supplies were depleting, I was able to push the embassy to supply them with food again. But other than that, nothing was happening.

At this time, things were getting out of hand in the Arab Gulf. During the first week of March, none of the Arab Gulf countries had officially reported that Indian migrant workers had tested positive for coronavirus, or were being quarantined. However, as the number of infected cases began to rise in the six Arab Gulf countries, Indian blue-collar workers who toil under exploitative working conditions began to feel the stress.

I remember how during the spread of the Middle East Respiratory Syndrome (MERS) and H1N1, the migrant workers were not given protection. They were forced to work without masks and hand sanitizers. If migrant workers fell sick due to any illness, they would not get leave, let alone protection from the virus. This being the situation, the workers did not believe they'd get masks and treatment on time if they became infected. I was not particularly optimistic about the Arab Gulf countries handling the situation and giving the migrant workers proper care.

I knew the reality of the Arab Gulf countries that were formed at the end of the 1960s. They lack experience in handling such pandemics, and there always tends to be a shortage of supplies in the government-run medical institutions. I knew that if there was an outbreak, it would be a disaster.

In the Arab Gulf countries, blue-collar workers largely live in camps, with ten people occupying a four-bed space room. The common washrooms are usually kept in unhygienic conditions. Even the kitchens are dirty. A medium-sized camp would be home to at least 1,000 workers in any Arab Gulf country.

The WHO EMRO Regional Director Dr Ahmed Al Mandhari had said that the areas with high-risk factors, such as camps and cities hosting mass gatherings, are of key concern.

I said this during the prime-time debates, but nobody heard me. Or they pretended not to. By the second week of March, COVID-19 was spreading silently in the Arab Gulf countries. If someone showed a symptom, then he or she had to go to a government testing centre and undergo the swab test.

After forty-eight hours, the results would be sent online. If the result was positive, the patient had to call a government hospital and seek admission. The hospital would send an ambulance and pick him up.

However, Indian migrant workers in the Arab Gulf were desperately looking for vacant flats during that time, as they wanted to house their COVID-19 positive friends and those with symptoms. As the number of COVID-19 patients was going up, a shortage of beds in government hospitals was reported in all the Arab Gulf countries. The Arab governments were telling migrant workers who had tested positive and those who had symptoms to remain in their flats where they lived with so many others.

In Dubai, a Keralite worker who tested positive was locked up in a kitchen by his roommates for twenty-eight days. Suresh Kumar S, the Keralite who had tested positive, agreed with his friends to stay locked up in the kitchen as he was neither getting a hospital bed nor had he the money to get a hotel room.

'I am a cleaner in a company. I get around Rs 20,000 per month. We had not been paid since January 2020. Even finding food was becoming difficult for me. I was living with the support of my roommates. In that condition, how could I afford a hotel room? So, I agreed to stay in the kitchen,' Suresh had told me then.

'The kitchen was small. I slept on the floor. My friends moved out to the hall. They cooked there and kept food for me outside the kitchen door. I thought I would die in there. After taking the medicine the government sent, my temperature would come down. But after a few hours, it would soar again. Those twenty days were like hell for me. I didn't inform my family either,' Suresh told me.

Suresh recovered and re-joined his job in the third week of July.

'I can't go back home, Reji. I have taken a loan of 3 lakhs for my daughter's marriage. I have to repay it. I can do it only if I am here,' he had told me then.

If Suresh stayed in a kitchen in Saudi Arabia, another Keralite migrant worker had to take shelter in an abandoned company car as he was not able to get an isolation ward in the hospital.

He was living in a shared accommodation, with ten people in a room. Unfortunately, he too did not have enough money to afford a hotel room.

So, for twenty-eight days, he lived and slept in the abandoned car. His friends would bring him food. Talking to me while he was unwell and living in the car, he told me that other than praying to the Almighty, he could do nothing.

'I don't want to die here. But as there are no flights back to home, I can't fly either. My four-months' salary is pending. How can I forget that and fly home?' he asked me.

He requested that nobody in India should know his name.

'My children are grown up. They will worry about my situation. I don't want them to panic. They will be ashamed to learn that I had to sleep in a car when I was sick. Let's see . . .' he told me.

I am not naming him here. He recovered from COVID-19. He resigned from the job and flew back to his hometown in June.

Meanwhile, by the end of June, the media in Kerala and the social workers in the Arab Gulf discovered that 300 Keralites had died due to COVID-19 in the six Arab Gulf countries. Keralites are a very closely connected community in any Arab Gulf country. So, if somebody fell sick or died due to COVID-19, the word would spread very quickly. And that's how the number of COVID-19 deaths of Keralites abroad was made public. At that time, the number of Keralites who died in Kerala was just twenty.

A Malayalam newspaper that published pictures of Keralites who had died in the Gulf countries due to COVID-19, faced the ire of Kerala Chief Minister Pinarayi Vijayan. Pictures of the deceased were not published in the Gulf edition, but only in the Kerala edition.

Unfortunately, no official data was collected about the number of Keralites who had been infected or died in the Arab Gulf. Interestingly, on 21 September, V Muraleedharan, Minister of State at the Ministry of External Affairs, stated in the Indian Parliament that only 373 Indians died due to COVID-19 in foreign countries.

Muraleedharan did not get his facts right.

The minister had said in parliament that, ' . . . as per details available with the Indian Missions, the total number of Indian citizens abroad infected with coronavirus stood at 11,616, as on 10 September 2020. Of these, 373 Indians lost their lives due to COVID-19'.[6]

The document placed in the Parliament reports that there were no COVID-19 deaths in Kuwait, and that only four Indians died due to COVID-19 in the UAE. But an RTI reply revealed that between 1 February and 30 June, in the UAE, 175 Indians had died due to COVID-19. And in Kuwait, between 1 February and 30 May, sixty-eight Indians had died due to COVID-19.

Surprisingly, to a question asked in the RTI on whether the UAE local government was keeping the Indian Embassy informed of Indians' deaths due to COVID-19, the embassy replied that 'usually, local authorities do not share such information.'

'However, the Consulate has received one such information from the local authorities of an Indian's death due to COVID-19, when the body was lying in the mortuary,' the RTI reply adds.

When Indians die due to COVID-19 in Arab Gulf countries, as per the pandemic protocol, their mortal remains are buried there. Only the bodies of those who died of other causes are transported to India.

In a reply to the Parliament on the details of the measures taken by the Indian Missions in extending necessary help to the COVID-19 affected Indians abroad, V Muraleedharan said that, 'Indian Missions arranged for the welfare of Indian nationals, where required, including through Indian community associations.'

'In some cases, arrangements were also made for boarding, lodging, and providing emergency medical assistance. The total expenditure incurred by the Missions in assisting Indian nationals in distress from the Indian Community Welfare Fund (ICWF) was close to Rs 22.5 crores,' the response stated.

Commenting on the expense, Lateefh Thechy, a social activist in Saudi Arabia, said that ' . . . although the MEA says that the Missions have spent around Rs 22.5 crores for Indians, we have experienced that the help was little.'

'We didn't even get ambulance services to transport COVID-19 patients. We struggled a lot. We know the cases of people who took shelter in abandoned cars and kitchens as they were not getting isolation wards. Any help provided by the Mission houses was very little,' Thechy added.

Meanwhile, the crisis at the workplace, the looming financial insecurity, fear of getting infected, lack of on-time medical assistance, and uncertainty over returning home, had put many Keralites in the Arab Gulf under mental stress, too, pushing them to think of committing suicide.

In the Arab Gulf, three Keralite suicides were reported from the last week of March 2020 till 1 May 2020. A friend of a Keralite who committed suicide told me that the now-deceased had been worried over the delay in his COVID-19 test result. He had been worried about whether he would test positive or not.

According to the National Crime Records Bureau, the all-India rate of suicides was 10.2 during the year 2018. The Andaman & Nicobar Islands reported the highest rate of suicide (41) followed by Puducherry (33.8), Sikkim (30.2), Chhattisgarh (24.7), and Kerala (23.5).

The rate of Malayali suicides in the Gulf countries during the pandemic period reveals that their suicide rates were double the national average.

The COVID-19 test result of the victim who had feared a positive result came out negative. He hailed from Kollam district in Kerala. However, he ended his life in the UAE before he got the results of his test.

Lateefh Thechy, a Keralite social worker in Saudi Arabia for the last thirty years, told me that when someone tested positive, they were told to stay in their rooms, due to the lack of available beds in hospitals.

'Without proper medication and care, these patients struggle. And finally, if some social workers rush them to hospitals when the beds are available, the patient would be in a critical condition and die,' Lateefh had told me.

Even a shortage of medicines for other ailments was claiming lives. Usually, Indians get medicines through their friends and relatives when they travel back to the Gulf countries from India. Another way is to have the medicines couriered. Unfortunately, as India closed its land, sea, and air borders, travel came to a standstill. Courier services had come to a halt as well.

Medicines are very costly in the Arab Gulf, and many compositions prescribed by Indian medics are not available there either. So, when there was a lack of medication, many who were suffering from heart ailments and other diseases began to suffer, which added to the burden. Eventually, their diseases worsened and they died.

From the newspapers, I recorded nine cardiac deaths in the UAE, two in Kuwait, and five in Saudi Arabia since the last week of March 2020, when the COVID-19 crisis started to worsen. During the second last week of March, the Kerala government had arranged for a courier service to send medicines for the needy.

However, delays in shipments were worrying the patients. According to a Lancet study, the mental health effects of the COVID-19 pandemic might be profound and there were suggestions that suicide rates would rise, although this was not inevitable.

'Suicide is likely to become a more pressing concern as the pandemic spreads and has longer-term effects on the general population, the economy, and vulnerable groups. Preventing suicide therefore needs urgent consideration. The response must capitalize on, but extend beyond general mental health policies and practices,' the study had said.

The study added that there was some evidence that deaths by suicide increased in the USA during the 1918–19 influenza pandemic and among older people in Hong Kong during the 2003 Severe Acute Respiratory Syndrome (SARS) epidemic.

'The current context is different and evolving. A wide-ranging interdisciplinary response that recognizes how the pandemic might heighten risk and applies knowledge about effective suicide prevention approaches is key,' the study proposed.

Even though medicines and medics were promised to be sent to the UAE in the last week of April 2020, it did not happen. Unfortunately, it was not only migrant workers whose situation was bleak. Migrant healthcare workers employed in many private and government sector hospitals in the Arab Gulf countries faced a tough time as well, being overworked.

The healthcare sector in the Arab Gulf countries is dominated by private hospitals. And most of these private hospitals are run by wealthy Indians. When the government hospitals became stressed with more and more patients, the Arab governments allowed private hospitals to admit COVID-19 patients.

Unfortunately, this was a risky move. The migrant nurses working in the private hospitals were forced by the migrant management to work overtime.

In private hospitals, the majority of migrant nurses would be from Kerala. In India, especially in Kerala, private hospitals don't pay much for nurses. A majority of the nurses would be paid only Rs 10,000 or sometimes, even less than that, even though they signed Rs 20,000 salary slips.

So, to earn a little more, Keralite nurses migrate to the Arab Gulf only to be enslaved by the migrant management. The migrant nurses who were on the frontlines treating

COVID-19 patients continuously for fifteen hours, were not given leave either.

Additionally, many were not getting PPE kits as well. And in some cases, the migrant nurses on the frontline tested positive and were forced to continue to work. As they had handed over their original educational qualification certificates and passports at the time of joining itself, they could not quit the job and return. By holding back their certificates and travel documents, the migrant nurses were enslaved.

In Kerala, the majority of nurses come from middle-class or poor families, who take bank loans to complete the nursing courses. With low wages and a contract employment, most of them struggle to repay these loans.

For many, at least five continuous years on the job are required to repay the loans. As a result, most would not dare question the employer or refuse a job.

'We have to continue to work. But nobody is thankful for the risks we take. People praise us in the media but if you hear our inside stories, you would agree that slavery still exists in this world. We are slaves in white dresses,' Josephine J, a Keralite nurse in Oman, said. Josephine also added that while doing this risky job, citing economic conditions, their salaries were cut by around 30 per cent.

'The condition was that either we should agree to the slashed salary and continue, or quit and return,' she had told me.

Interestingly, when there was a shortage of nurses in the Arab Gulf countries, Indian-run hospitals in the Arab Gulf started to take nurses from their Indian branches. Many saw it as a laudable move. The nurses were seen as angels. There were media photoshoots at the airport. Migrant nurses were seen waving Indian flags and posing for pictures. But the truth is that many were forced to take up jobs in Arab countries as they needed the salary.

'If we didn't agree, we would be terminated from the job. As we had no other options, we had to take up the job,' a nurse texted me, requesting me not to reveal her name.

In April 2020, the World Health Organization (WHO) said that nurses were on the frontline fighting COVID-19, but that there was 'an alarming failure' in the global supply of protective clothing and new coronavirus test kits, along with 'unprecedented' overwork linked to global staff shortages—a statement that highlighted how vulnerable they are.[7]

The International Council of Nurses (ICN) had released a statement in June 2020 claiming that more than 600 nurses had died from COVID-19 worldwide.[8]

Founded in 1899, the International Council of Nurses is a federation of more than 130 national nurses' associations. Worldwide, there is no systematic and standardized record of the number of nurses and healthcare workers (HCWs) who have contracted the virus or died from it.

But the ICN's analysis, based on data from national nursing associations, official figures, and media reports from a limited number of countries, indicates that more than 2,30,000 HCWs had contracted the disease, and more than 600 nurses have now died from the virus.

By the third week of March 2020, almost all the Arab Gulf countries were halting their operations and locking down their borders. The entire Arab Gulf came to a standstill, as did other parts of the world. All the Arab Gulf countries had announced that if businesses were hit by the coronavirus, they could implement a remote work system for their employees, send them on paid or unpaid leave, and temporarily or permanently reduce their salaries.

The countries also said that business houses could reduce their staff strength, but that surplus staff must be registered in the ministry's virtual job market so that they could be hired by other companies. However, the decision states that it is mandatory for companies to provide employees with accommodation and other dues, but not salaries, when they are made redundant.

In the UAE, business solutions provider Transguard Group announced in March 2020 that it would be reducing management staff salaries for April 2020 for the purpose of covering the cost of housing and feeding its more than 12,000 site-based employees who were temporarily idle due to the changing market conditions forced by the coronavirus.[9]

According to the S&P Ratings report in March 2020, coronavirus weighed on the economies of the Gulf Cooperation Council (GCC) region, as weakening global demand dragged down oil prices and hampered important industries such as tourism and real estate.

'As global financing conditions deteriorate, funding costs for more-leveraged borrowers are rising, the investor appetite for less-creditworthy issuers could fade, and the high level of uncertainty regarding the duration and eventual severity of the crisis will increase downside risks,' the S&P Ratings stated.

The rating agency said that that in the GCC, in the hospitality industry, which includes sectors like airlines, hotels, and retail, would see lower revenue because of decreased tourism and business flows, as travel aversion and restrictions affect the peak tourism season.

The S&P Global Ratings had also said that it expected the Arab Gulf countries' government debt to increase by a record high of about $100 billion in 2020, as funding needs a spike due to the COVID-19 crisis and low oil prices.

The ratings agency estimated that Gulf Cooperation Council (GCC) countries would register an aggregate central government deficit of about $180 billion, to be financed with $100 billion of debt and $80 billion draw-down in government assets.

It based forecasts on an average Brent oil price of $30 per barrel for the rest of 2020, $50 in 2021, and $55 from 2022.[10] What do these figures suggest? It points to the fact that migrant workers' jobs are at risk in the Arab Gulf countries, where a majority of overseas Keralites work.

The International Labour Organisation (ILO)'s 5th edition of *COVID-19 and the World of Work* published in June 2020, said that the loss of working hours in the second quarter of 2020 relative to the last quarter of 2019 are estimated to reach 14.0 per cent worldwide, equivalent to 400 million full-time jobs, with the largest reduction.[11] They predicted that in the Arab region alone, an estimated 6 million jobs will be lost, as already mentioned in their May report. The fact is that a majority of the jobs in the Arab region are held by migrant workers.

And during the COVID-19 pandemic, workers were repatriated or were forced to fly home by their employers.

Unfortunately, the workers were repatriated hurriedly, and this was done without proper controls in place.

Employers took advantage of the mass repatriation programmes to terminate and return workers who had not been paid their due compensation, wages, and benefits citing a pandemic-led economic crisis. Workers in distress had accepted it as their fate and refrained from complaining lest they lost their jobs, or worse still, remained back under the fear of being made undocumented.

Is it that migrant workers were left in the lurch by employers only during the COVID-19 crisis? No. Social workers in every GCC country confirmed to me that there were thousands of migrant workers stranded on the roads, laid off by their employers, much before the COVID-19 pandemic outbreak happened.

The majority of the workers who had been laid-off much before the COVID-19 crisis, were undocumented as well. According to data from the Solidarity Centre, a non-profit aligned with the US-based labour federation AFL-CIO, there were six million undocumented workers between 2015 and 2018 in all the six Arab Gulf countries.[12]

Shameer U, an Indian migrant worker in Oman, was laid off by his employer in January 2020 along with some 400 workers, much before the COVID-19 outbreak happened in Oman. He had become undocumented in December 2019 as his employer failed to renew his work permit. And when his pay was stopped in January 2020, everyday food also became a challenge eventually.

When the Indian government arranged a repatriation mission in May 2020 to bring back Indians stranded abroad due to the COVID-19 outbreak, Shameer had also registered with the Indian Embassy in Muscat to return back home.[13] He got a call from the Indian Embassy confirming that a seat was available on the repatriation flight. But he had two challenges. One, he had to clear the overstaying fine, which was around USD 1,200, and two, purchase a ticket with his own money.

Social workers in Muscat raised money, bought Shameer the air ticket, and also cleared his fine. He then flew back to India. But he had to give up his unpaid wages and it marked the end of his service benefits as well.

There were many Shameers and there continue to be many, in big numbers, left in the lurch before the COVID-19 outbreak happened, still languishing in the Arab Gulf countries. Unfortunately, the review of an Indian repatriation form, an online Google document form put up by the Indian Missions in the Arab Gulf reveals that, out of the nine checkboxes listed asking why the person is seeking repatriation to India, there is only one checkbox asking whether the migrant worker is being laid off or not.[14]

The option reads, 'Migrant worker/labourer who has been laid off.'

This gives no space for an Indian migrant worker to detail his grievances if he needs to. Indian embassies were not entertaining in-person visits by the aggrieved workers, due to COVID-19 protocol. The in-person visits were restricted through the token system.

'We are recording only the reason for Indians leaving the country. We are neither addressing the workers' rights violations, nor are we taking any power of attorney,' a senior

Indian Embassy official in Kuwait told me. A senior official at the Indian Ministry of External Affairs in New Delhi told me that they were only recording the information asked in the repatriation form.

And courts in the countries of destinations are not functioning at full strength due to the COVID-19 lockdown. Their labour ministries are not exercising due diligence concerning wage theft and other grievances that migrant workers may have before repatriating them.

Dr Shashi Tharoor, Indian parliamentarian and former Minister of State at the Indian Ministry of External Affairs, said that Indian Missions in the Arab Gulf countries should record wage grievances of Indian workers who are leaving due to the COVID-19 outbreak, as documentation is vital in addressing the wage theft issue. Tharoor also suggested a system where an escrow fund be set up, in which six months' worth of wages could be deposited by the employer until the visa is approved for the worker.

'This escrow fund can help pay the worker when pay default happens, especially during a COVID-19 crisis,' Tharoor said, adding that the pandemic had become an excuse for employers in the Arab Gulf to remove migrant workers without clearing their unpaid wages and end-of-service benefits.[15]

Interestingly, in 2015, in a bid to safeguard Indian domestic workers recruited in the Arab Gulf, the Indian government had made it mandatory that the employer should deposit a bond worth of 2,500 USD in the Indian Embassy if he has to hire an Indian domestic worker.[16]

The bond system was seen as similar to an escrow fund to protect worker's salaries and meet any medical emergency.

However, in 2017, the Indian government eased the bond norms and now every employer doesn't need to deposit money to hire an Indian domestic worker.[17]

According to the Migrant Forum in Asia (MFA), a regional network that stands up for the rights of migrant workers, wage theft will account for millions of dollars to the detriment of workers, and many countries of origin do not have transitional justice mechanisms at their mission houses in countries of destination, to address the grievances of workers who are leaving the country in a hurry.

MFA says, ' . . . millions will suffer if this crime goes unnoticed. We cannot see this as collateral damage brought by the pandemic.' They also said that it should be a priority to guarantee that all repatriated workers with legitimate claims can access justice and some kind of compensation.

On 1 June 2020, led by the MFA, a coalition of civil society organizations and trade unions, had launched an appeal for an 'Urgent Justice Mechanism', to address the plight of millions of migrant workers who have been repatriated or are awaiting repatriation as a result of pandemic-related job loss.

The appeal had called on governments to establish a transitional justice mechanism that would specifically address the huge volume of cases of wage theft and other outstanding claims heightened during the course of the pandemic, ensuring migrant workers can access justice and receive their due compensation.

Realizing that large scale returns had become a reality, the MFA and its partners renewed their call in July 2020 for the implementation of the justice mechanism and urged governments and the United Nations agencies to take immediate actions like setting up an international claims commission and a compensation fund, and the reforming of national justice systems.

According to the coalition, an international claims commission must be set up as a specialized international quasi-legal body of expedited justice, to adjudicate on claims of migrant workers on an expedited basis, in cases related to wage theft and other outstanding claims and to provide equitable remedies.

'Cases could be received directly from migrants themselves or through entities providing support or legal representation to migrants. All pre-existing case documentation should be referred to the claims commissions for resolution,' the MFA said, adding that the International Claims Commission could be administered jointly by the International Labour Organization (ILO) and the International Organization for Migration (IOM) together with other relevant stakeholders.

ILO has the technical expertise and experience with an international compensation mechanism in the United Nations Compensation Commission. Also, its work in Qatar on the workers' support and insurance fund, provides a model in which the remedy is expedited by having judges, independent lawyers, legal experts, migration experts, and academia among others.

The MFA says that it would be desirable if sub-commissions are also set up regionally and nationally, where capacities exist to address the huge volume of emerging cases. They added that claims commissions could look into all cases of wage theft and other outstanding claims, like non-payment of wages for work before the onset of the pandemic, after which it became impossible to pursue claims due to pandemic-related lockdowns, repatriations, etc.

It could also look into non-payment of wages or reductions in wage payments for work as the pandemic and associated economic effects started taking hold, and the non-payment of other contractually owed benefits (allowances, end-of-service benefits, housing benefits, leave benefits, unpaid overtime, medical costs, costs of travel to the country of origin, etc.)

The MFA adds that the loss of expected wages due to layoff, reduction in hours, or reduction in hourly wage, and the non-payment of wages for more work than what is required or contractually agreed upon should also be considered in the Claims Commission.

On the procedures for filing claims, the MFA says that it should be affordable, simplified, publicized, and made available in different languages. Additionally, the MFA adds that the International Organization for Migration's significant experience in administering land and property claims programmes, which while being different from non-payment of wages, is highly relevant and can be used in the International Claims Commission.

'A compensation fund can be set up at the global and national level and it can accompany the work of the Claims Commission and act as its executive branch, dispensing appropriate compensation in cases determined as wage theft,' says the MFA.

'Funds must be set up at the national level, and contributions to them could be ensured by the government, along with private contributions, business, and philanthropic foundations,' the MFA says, adding that funds advanced by the government could be later recouped from employers and businesses who were involved in wage-theft.

This approach would ensure that migrant workers are paid their dues without delay and that cases are resolved swiftly. It would also ensure that employers and businesses that have not respected their contractual obligations face accountability for their actions.

Additionally, a global solidarity fund also needs to be established for those workers whose cases have been determined as genuine wage theft but are unable to access compensation from national funds. However, the MFA says that national and global claims commissions and compensation funds are no substitutes to fair and functioning justice systems at the national level.

'Availing of remedies under the transitional justice mechanism is not exclusive and without prejudice to the availing of more favourable legal remedies available under the existing national justice systems,' they state.

So far, national justice systems have largely failed migrant workers; this failure should no longer be accepted or normalized.

Even in the best of times, migrant workers like Shameer face insurmountable obstacles while accessing justice and seeking legal redress. Challenges in accessing justice for wage theft at the national level cuts across various areas. Access to courts and police stations, documentation and proof of violations, cost, and duration of litigation, language barriers, status dependency on employers, and requirements for in-person testimony are among the chief challenges to justice in the context of migration.

Unfortunately, domestic workers are frequent victims of wage theft and face additional barriers to access to justice, which are not limited to restrictions on the freedom of mobility alone.

The MFA says that the lack of political will and weak enforcement mechanisms are also obstacles to justice for the migrant workers.

Meanwhile, it is evident that the COVID-19-induced economy crisis, which has led to mass layoffs of migrant workers, is going to affect remittances badly.

The World Bank estimates the global slump will wipe 19.7 per cent—or $109 billion—from the portion of money that flows to the Low and Middle-Income Countries (LMICs) that need it most. This has been the sharpest decline in recent history.

The World Bank's June report says that, in 2020, remittance flows to low- and middle-income countries are expected to drop by around 20 per cent, to $445 billion, from $554 billion in 2019.[18]

Interestingly, the responsibility of this doesn't fall on a decline in the stock of international migrants, but largely due to a fall in wages and the employment of migrant workers in host nations due to COVID-19.

The World Bank says that the decline in remittance flows is expected to be sharpest in Europe and central Asia, south Asia, and sub-Saharan Africa.

In India, remittances are projected to fall by about 23 per cent in 2020, to $64 billion—a striking contrast with the growth of 5.5 per cent and receipts of $83 billion seen in 2019.

In Pakistan, the projected decline is also about 23 per cent, totalling about $17 billion, as compared to a total of $22.5 billion in 2019, when remittances grew by 6.2 per cent. In Bangladesh, remittances are projected at $14 billion for 2020, a likely fall of about 22 per cent. Remittances to Nepal and Sri Lanka are expected to decline by 14 per cent and 19 per cent, respectively, in 2020.

The World Bank also adds that the Coronavirus-related global slowdown and travel restrictions will also affect migratory movements, and this is likely to keep remittances subdued even in 2021. The projected remittance growth of 5.8 per cent in 2021 will keep total regional flows at about $115 billion.

The World Bank also says that falling oil prices will affect remittance outflows from the GCC countries and Malaysia.[19]

Many migrant workers have reconciled to the situation of wage theft in the form of unfair or unpaid wages for months and years before the COVID-19 pandemic. They have accepted it as their fate and refrained from complaining lest they lose their jobs, or, worse still, live under the fear of their status being made undocumented.

Without proper controls, employers might take advantage of mass repatriation programs to terminate and return workers who have not been paid their due compensation, wages, and benefits. Millions will be repatriated to situations of debt bondage as they will be forced to pay off recruitment fees and costs, despite returning empty-handed.

Without ensuring that companies and employers are doing their due diligence to protect the human and labour rights of repatriated migrant workers, states across the migration corridor become complicit in overseeing procedures where millions of workers will be returning without their earned wages or workplace grievances being heard, nor seeing justice in their situation.

'Extraordinary times call for extraordinary measures,' said William Gois, Regional Coordinator of Migrant Forum in Asia, 'millions will suffer if this crime goes unnoticed. We cannot see this as collateral damage brought by the pandemic.' According to Gois, it should be a priority to guarantee that all repatriated workers with legitimate claims can access justice and some kind of compensation.

The appeal, which civil organizations and trade unions have launched together, calls on governments to urgently establish a transitional justice mechanism to address grievances, claims, and labour disputes of repatriated workers who have lost their jobs as a result of the pandemic.

'The pandemic must not stifle our will, our spirit, and commitment for justice,' Gois said.

'If we are to "Build Back Better", we cannot continue to turn a blind eye to the issue of wage theft that has been persistent across migration corridors for years, and will be unprecedented in the case of repatriated migrant workers in the COVID-19 pandemic,' Gois added.

On 7 May 2020, the Indian government initiated a massive repatriation operation titled Vande Bharat Mission to bring back stranded Indians in different parts of the world in the wake of the coronavirus crisis. According to a document placed in the Indian parliament, as of 11 September 2020, more than 13,85,670 Indians have returned to India under the Vande Bharat Mission from various countries.

In a different document placed in the Parliament, India has stated that of the 13 lakh who had returned, 3,08,099 were workers and that not all of them had lost their jobs, but had returned on account of the COVID-19 situation.

However, the arrival of stranded and shattered Keralites from the Arab Gulf was leading to an unexpected situation. They were discriminated against, as unfortunately, the Kerala government was releasing disintegrated data of COVID-19 cases daily, which had the number of incoming COVID-19 positive migrants.

In those days, 90 per cent of the positive cases reported in Kerala were from the incoming Keralite migrant workers from the Arab Gulf. Slowly, Keralites began to see their brothers and sisters from the Arab Gulf as super-spreaders. Many Keralite migrants from the Arab Gulf had to get police support to get into their homes as neighbours and villagers would throw stones at them.

'Around 1.65 lakh Keralites have returned from COVID-19-hit foreign countries between 7 May and 18 August 2020,' reveals data shared by the Non-Resident Keralites Affairs (NORKA). NORKA is the Kerala government agency set up for the welfare of non-resident Keralites.

According to their data, 3,00,021 Keralites have arrived since 7 May 2020 by sea and air from COVID-19-hit countries, and of that 1,65,891 have returned due to job loss, which is more than 50 per cent.

On 1 July, the Kerala government rolled out a 'Dream Kerala Project' to tap the potential and experience of those returning from abroad and other states after losing their jobs due to the COVID-19 pandemic.

Kerala Chief Minister Pinarayi Vijayan said, while announcing the cabinet decision on 1 July, that the state government would work in a time-bound manner to get the project rolling by 15 November. The chief minister had said then that a timeline had been fixed for the implementation of the Dream Kerala project.[20]

The chief minister added that the general public would be given opportunities to provide ideas and recommendations for this project on Kerala's future development and needs. The government would then conduct a hackathon with a special focus on how to implement the selected ideas.

'The "Ideathon" will be held between 15 July and 30 July. And between 1 to 10 August, a hackathon will be conducted and a presentation of the selected project will be held in the virtual assembly on 14 August,' he said, adding that projects would be implemented in 100 days. Unfortunately, the virtual assembly, which was scheduled to be held on 14 August to select projects did not happen.

Even though Keralites had started migration from the 1960s and are remitting around Rs 2 lakh crore annually, there are no credible plans on the ground, which can help the reintegration of returnees. Many Keralite migrants who came back home disappointed, wanted to return. Anish P, who returned from Oman empty-handed in June, said that he is ready to go back and has already started to look for a job. Anish was working as a steel fabricator in Oman. Due to COVID-19, the company was forced to stop its operations in March. When the work was stopped, his salary was not paid. This was in addition to the non-payment of the salary of January and February in 2020. And finally, when Anish travelled back in June last week, he had to forget about the five months' worth of salary. Anish's monthly salary was around Rs 24,000.

'Even food was a problem. We had to depend on a charity group. We slept hungry for a few days. Finally, with the help of a few good people, we returned. But I will go back again,' Anish said.

'There is no use staying here. Getting a job is very difficult in Kerala. And I don't have any other sources of income. Additionally, I have a bank loan of Rs 5 lakh pending, too. I have two children studying in school. If I don't go back, then we won't be able to live,' Anish added.

Anish knows that the COVID-19 crisis won't end soon. But as the Arab Gulf countries are restarting their business activities, he is confident that he will soon get a new job.

'There are no Gulf-returnee rehabilitation plans here in Kerala. Even if we succeed in taking loans to start small-scale projects, we will get trapped in the red tape of it all. And eventually, we will run into loss and shut down operations. I don't want to do that. It is safer to return to Gulf and work, even if it is for a smaller salary,' Anish added.

If Anish is planning to return, Nikhil Antony, a mechanical engineer, who returned from Kuwait due to job loss, is clueless about his future. Since 2010, Nikhil has been travelling to the Arab Gulf countries to work. He had worked in Qatar and the UAE. In Qatar, he managed to work for four years. After returning, he migrated to the UAE. But, due to the economic crisis of 2016, he was forced to quit.

'I decided not to migrate. But getting a job with decent pay here was quite difficult. So, I was looking for a job again in the Gulf. I found one in Kuwait and migrated in September 2019,' Nikhil said.

In Kuwait, Nikhil was deployed in a US army base camp for work. For the first two months, he was not paid as his company claimed that his work visa had not been issued. Nikhil agreed to that half-heartedly. And finally, in February 2020, the project got cancelled and Nikhil lost his job.

While Nikhil was looking for a fresh job, Kuwait locked down its borders with the onslaught of COVID-19. He was stranded without a job and food. Even shelter was a problem for him. However, finally, with the help of a few good friends, he reached back home in Kerala. Talking to the writer from the quarantine centre, he said that he didn't know what to do next.

'My father is an AC mechanic. I would like to join him and start a small business. But I won't get a loan since we don't have a deed for our house. I have younger sisters to marry off as well. I have to care for their futures,' Nikhil said.

When Indians return from the Arab Gulf and other foreign countries after losing their jobs, does India or Kerala offer them reintegration plans? The answer is simple. It is a no.

Many south Asian migrant-sending countries have migration policies and a few have reintegration policies as well. Interestingly, a few also have tailored reintegration policies as COVID-19 has impacted their workers abroad. Nepal has a migration policy but not a reintegration policy. However, Nepal has initiated a few plans following COVID-19.

Talking to this writer, over the phone in Kathmandu, Nilambar Badal, a migrant rights activist, said that their government has formed a task force to study the returns and chalk out plans for reintegration.

'There is no specific financial assistance declared or provided to the returning migrant workers upon arrival. However, the government has announced to link the returnee workers to the PM Employment Programme, which will provide them with job opportunities,' Nilambar said.

According to Nilambar, the government is trying to create special, sector-specific economic areas, where the returning migrant workers' skills, knowledge, and capital will be pooled and utilized.

Annually, Nepal has received remittances, which totalled $8.1 billion last year, or more than a quarter of Nepal's gross domestic product. More than 56 per cent of Nepal's estimated 5.4 million households receive remittances that are a vital lifeline for families that have no other source of income.[21]

Bangladesh too has a migration policy with international standards to protect their citizens working abroad and has tailored a special plan to support returnee migrants following the COVID-19 outbreak.

'The government has formed a working committee with representatives of all the ministries concerned to help our returnee migrant workers, as well as those who are stuck in foreign countries,' Marina Sultana of the Refugee and Migratory Movements Research Unit, a migrants' rights group in Dhaka, said. Marina said that the government had given $2.3 million to migrant workers through 32 foreign missions so that workers do not go hungry. 'And around $60 was given to each worker who returned between 31 March and May as their conveyance allowance,' she added.

Additionally, Marina confirmed that the government has also created a fund worth $23.4 million from the Wage Earners Welfare Board and deposited it to the Probashi Kallyan Bank. International remittances normally represent around 7 per cent of Bangladesh's GDP. A total of 10 million migrants from Bangladesh had sent close to $18 billion in 2019.

The Philippines already has reintegration services, which are a package of interventions and mechanisms developed and implemented by social partners to facilitate the productive return of the Overseas Filipino Workers (OFWs) to their families and communities upon their completion of overseas employment.

The Philippine government announced that job opportunities in the business process outsourcing (BPO) industry will be made available to overseas Filipino worker (OFW) returnees, especially those with a background in the fields of information technology and healthcare.[22]

Already, the government has announced welfare assistance for returnees, primarily through immediate financial assistance and transportation to home communities.

Sri Lanka also has a migration policy, which includes provisions to ensure fair reintegration practices, too.

Following the COVID-19 outbreak, to help its overseas migrant workers deal with the coronavirus, Sri Lanka's Ministry of Foreign Relations launched an online portal where citizens can voice their concerns.

According to Sujeewa Lal Dahanayake, a migrant rights activist in Lanka, the Sri Lanka Bureau of Foreign Employment (SLBFE) is currently in the process of preparing an action plan for returnees post-COVID-19 with the International Labour Organization and the International Organization for Migration (IOM).

'And Lanka had also exempted remittance flows from abroad from some regulations and taxes,' Sujeewa added saying that more welfare plans are expected from the government for the returnee migrants.

On 24 June, the International Labour Organization said that policies need to be put in place to protect stranded migrant workers and to ensure the reintegration of those who return to their home countries.[23]

'This is a potential crisis within a crisis,' said Manuela Tomei, Director of the ILO's Conditions of Work and Equality Department.

'We know that many millions of migrant workers, who were under lockdown in their countries of work, have lost their jobs and are now expected to return home to countries that are already grappling with weak economies and rising unemployment. Cooperation and planning are key to avert a further crisis,' the ILO official added.

Michelle Leighton, chief of the ILO's Labour Migration Department, said that with the right policies, the return of these workers can be converted into a resource for recovery.

'These migrants will bring with them talents and new skills, and in some cases capital, that can support efforts in their home countries to build back better. We must help these countries grasp the opportunity,' the ILO official added.

Unfortunately, India neither has a migration policy nor a reintegration policy.

Professor Irudaya Rajan of Centre for Development Studies told this writer that at least 15 lakh will be returning to India empty-handed and without a job.

'They are going to add more stress to the unemployment situation here, which is already in a bad shape,' he added.

Let me go back to Valsala and those fishermen. I won't be able to close this chapter and end this book without sharing their story. As I said, after the fishermen's case, Valsala's case was the second COVID-19-related stranded migrant case I got in the first week of March 2020.

Valsala didn't know Persian or Arabic. She could speak only Malayalam and a little Hindi. So, the only five people she had spoken to for 121 days was me, Thayyil Habeeb, a Kerala Lok Sabha member in Oman, Mahalakshmi, the charity worker in Oman, Mini, the psychologist in Kerala, and Manu Mohan, a Keralite engineer working in Kish Island. It was Habeeb who introduced Valsala to me during the first week of March, over the phone. His wanted to know whether I could do something for Valsala.

Valsala had gone to Oman to find a domestic worker job on a tourist visa. But as she had to be on a work visa, she was sent to Kish by her employer as soon as she found a job. The only way to convert your visitor visa to a job visa is to exit the country and re-enter on a job visa. People who have money to spend, fly to Dubai and return to Oman on a job visa. But those who look for cheaper options, fly to Kish Island.

Valsala was sent to Kish by her employer in Oman. She had a ticket to return on 26 February, in a late-night flight to Oman. But when COVID-19 started to take lives in Iran from the second week of February 2020, Oman banned flights to and from Iran on 27 February. Eventually, Valsala got stuck on the island, with nowhere to go and nobody to call.

Habeeb had called me seeking help for Valsala as her Omani sponsor was finding it difficult to support her.

All I could say was, 'Yes, let me try.'

Habeeb shared Valsala's number. I called her. Valsala had spent two weeks in the hotel by then. Valsala hailed from Kozhikode in Kerala. She had gone to the Gulf to find work to look after her family back home. Even though she had not migrated through the official channels, she was lucky to find a good employer. Unfortunately, she got stuck in Kish.

By the time I called her, India had not gone into a lockdown and the coronavirus was spreading in Iran. The World Health Organization had declared COVID-19 as a global pandemic. India was mulling over locking down its borders. Indian evacuation flights were airlifting Indians from Europe and south-east Asia. India was also operating emergency flights from Iran. Even during the last week of March, India had brought back students and pilgrims from Tehran.

But as there were no domestic flights from Kish, which was 1000 km from Tehran, Valsala could stuck there. Moreover, she was confused as to whether she should go to Oman to work or return to India halfway, giving up the job.

'I presumed that COVID-19 would end soon. But it didn't. Both in India and Oman, the situation was going from bad to worse. I read WhatsApp forwards stating that India was going into lockdown on 23 March and Oman had

declared COVID-19 a community spread. I was losing hope,'
Valsala told me then.

I drafted a complaint and tweeted it to the Indian
government, tagging ministers. I told Valsala that I would get
her help. I was expecting a positive response in Valsala's case,
but it didn't happen. We waited for four days. Even though
many retweeted the tweet, we didn't receive any help.

By then, Habeeb called again and told me that Valsala's
Arab employer was running short of money and we needed
to support him by finding money for Valsala's hotel bill and
food. I said, yes, we will find it.

Valsala had told me that she had not eaten food for two
days.

'The hotel manager wasn't there. I didn't know the
language. The staff didn't know what to do either. Even
though I was starving, they refused to give me food without
money. At least they were kind enough to not throw me out
of the hotel,' Valsala said.

I didn't know what to do to help a person stuck in Kish.
All I knew was that Valsala needed money. So, I called up
Mahalakshmi, who has helped me several times before,
while I was a reporter in Muscat. Whenever I did stories on
workers in distress, Mahalakshmi and her team would help.
In this instance, too, she was ready to raise the money. She
managed to raise some Rs 15,000 within hours and remitted
it to Valsala's hotel account. Rekha Prem, another Keralite
in Oman, also chipped in. With the money they raised, they
managed to pay the hotel bill.

But the problems didn't end there. Valsala was growing
depressed. I was also getting tired. Apart from Valsala's case,

I was receiving ten cases a day. As I was participating in TV debates, people started to call me to find solutions for their problems.

Valsala, who didn't know that I was handling other cases, would call me and break down in tears. The isolation was beginning to overwhelm her. So, I got Mini Mohan, a psychologist in Thiruvananthapuram, to talk to Valsala. Mini did her job perfectly. She helped Valsala stay strong.

By then, the month of Ramadan had begun, and food was becoming a problem again. In the Arab countries, it is very difficult to get food during Ramadan. Even though she was a Hindu, Valsala had started fasting. But to break the fast, she was not able to adjust to just fruits and dates.

I was worried about her. But as I was telling Valsala's story on social media, Nishant Jacob in Oman came forward. He introduced me to his cousin, Manu Mohan, the Keralite engineer in Kish. I called him and spoke to him. He was ready to help. On the same day, Manu went and met Valsala. Manu continued meeting Valsala every third day to reassure her that there was somebody for her and she wasn't alone.

Many a time, Manu had to rush to her with food, skipping his workday. Apart from her unsatiated hunger, we understood that she was losing hope. In between, I started to contact my sources in the MEA to get help for Valsala but to no avail.

An official from MEA told me, 'Only after the lockdown is lifted, can something be done.'

The same was repeated by the MEA in an official statement during the second week of April.

'Moving these people will heighten the risk of spreading COVID-19 in the country where they are, as well as in India,' a senior official in the Ministry of External Affairs (MEA) said, adding that these are 'difficult times'.

Meanwhile, my friends were constantly in touch with the Indian Embassy in Iran to include her in their repatriation list. Manu included Valsala's name on the list and sent it to the Indian Embassy.

By then, we had crossed April 2020. Valsala would call me. Mini would call her. Manu would meet her. We had settled into a routine.

Finally, in the first week of May, when I told Nisha Purushothaman, a Malayala Manorama TV News anchor about Valsala, she said that she would forward the case to V Muraleedharan, the Minister of State at Ministry of External Affairs.

Luckily, the minister did a FB Live on the Vande Bharat Mission initiatives and during the live, he mentioned Valsala. He assured us that she would be brought back.

The next morning, the minister called me. I was surprised, but I remained calm. I wanted to explain what was happening on the ground. We talked about the Indian fishermen stuck in Iran and also about Valsala. He reassured me that she would be brought back. And about the fishermen, he said that ships would be sent to evacuate the fishermen.

I was the first reporter who reported the plight of 1,000 Indian fishermen stranded in Iran and who arranged food for them. My friend Mini prepared the list of stranded fishermen, which was forwarded to the MEA.

When the food issue was solved, the fishermen were worried about their return back home. As Iran was fighting Covid-19, employers were not able to look after the fishermen. The fishermen would call me every day. The only question they would ask is, '*Chetta, njangalude kaaryam enthaayi* . . . (Brother, what happened to our matter . . .)'

Simultaneously, I appealed for the fishermen and shared it with Fr Eugene Pereira from Bishop House in Thiruvananthapuram. Fr Eugene was posted in New Delhi. He was in charge of workers' rights. He took the appeal and the list and shared it with Dr Tharoor and also with the MEA. Dr Tharoor shared the appeal with the MEA and requested for the repatriation of the fishermen.

However, everything got delayed. Both the fishermen and Valsala had been stranded since February 2020 in Iran. In Valsala's case, we eventually ran short of money to clear the hotel bills. But with the help of two of my friends in Oman, we raised some more money.

In between, Valsala's visa expired. It was Manu who got it renewed for her. On the day of departure, he bought her new clothes, shoes, and handed over some gifts, too. We worked as a team with focus and consistency, and thankfully, they were returned home.

Those 700 fishermen and Valsala came back together in the last week of June 2020. They came to Thoothukudi, a coastal town in Tamil Nadu. From there, they came in buses to Thiruvananthapuram. While the fishermen went into COVID-19 protocol quarantine, Valsala headed to Kozhikode, her hometown.

The rest of the fishermen, about 300 of them, returned in the following weeks.

Both the fishermen and Valsala called me when they landed in Thoothukudi and and later Thiruvananthapuram.

All they could say to me was: 'thank you'.

Dr Tharoor had retweeted Valsala's story from my page, with a quote.

It read, 'Who says journalists are just observers and reporters of injustice or suffering? Here's a heartwarming story by a journalist who intervened to help a person in distress. Do read!'

Yes, I always fail to see that thin line separating a journalist from an activist. I listen to people in distress and tell their stories to the world.

Acknowledgements

I couldn't have written this book, if those thousands of stranded, enslaved, and exploited undocumented migrants who I met during my ten years in Oman, had been reluctant to express their sufferings and tell their stories. So, if there is someone whom I have to thank first, it's those undocumented migrant workers who trusted and talked to me.

I would like to thank one of my close friends in Oman, whose anonymity I must maintain for his own protection. When we both were on early morning missions to rescue locked-up women domestic workers from Arab mansions, he was my protector, guide, interpreter and transporter. Those rescue missions were unique and were the source of many of my stories.

Next, I have to express my gratitude to an Indian tailor who migrated to Oman in the early 1970s, well before I was born, for helping me learn the ground realities of migration. For around five years, I was his petition writer for the hundreds of stranded migrant workers cases he brought every week to the Indian embassy. I cannot name him either, but I cannot miss thanking him here.

Next in line is my wife Karthika Reji. In April 2017, I was summoned by the Oman Ministry of Information and ordered to quit the country, because I had exposed the human trafficking of Asian domestic workers in a front-page news story. It was a shock for us but we agreed to leave. When we boarded the flight to India, we were clueless about what was next, as I was the only earning member of my family. But she told me, 'We are leaving Oman after exposing human trafficking. It has resulted in the rescue of a few women, hasn't it? That is enough. We will find a new job in India, don't worry, everything will be fine.' Even now, I don't have a regular job. But Karthika isn't worried. She knows how to run the show with whatever I earn.

Then comes Rafeek Ravuther, an India-based migrant rights activist with around twenty-five years of experience. It was he who introduced me to the world of migrants. We have been good comrades since 2012.

I cannot forget to thank my mentor, William Gois, the regional advisor of the migrant forum in Asia. I first met him in Oman in 2012 when he came for a meeting, and he has been my mentor ever since. If he hadn't trained and guided me, I wouldn't have understood migration issues with this clarity.

Sandhya Sridhar, my publishing agent, was the one who secured this writing deal with Penguin Random House India. She has put in a lot of time and effort right from the beginning, from teaching me how to make a digital signature to reviewing my manuscript at least half a dozen times. These stories would have remained untold if I hadn't met her. I am lucky and thankful to have her as my agent.

I also want to express my gratitude to Manasi Subramanian, Executive Editor and Head of Literary Rights, for accepting my proposal for a book about undocumented migrants, offering me a contract to write it, edit it, and publish it.

I want to thank Ray Jureidini—a global migration professor, scholar, researcher, consultant and author—who reviewed my book pitch first, and encouraged me to begin writing.

I also owe a debt of gratitude to Mini Mohan, an Indian migration expert, who inspired me to write this book and assisted me in overcoming obstacles when I was stuck.

I cannot miss thanking my late father PG Kuttappan and my mother Remani KK. The values they taught me helped me to understand the woes of the less fortunate. If they had not inculcated those values in me, perhaps I would not have listened to the stories of those undocumented migrants.

I would like to thank my sister, Rekha K too. It was, she who encouraged me to migrate to Oman when I got a chance, towards the end of 2006. She wanted me to explore new places and meet new people. If she hadn't pushed me then, I would not have had the experiences that I did in the Arab Gulf.

I thank my boys Rishikesh Reji, 11, and Kasinath Reji, 9, who have read a few chapters of the manuscript and told me that it is excellent.

I also want to thank VS Pramod, my close friend, who has always showed patience in listening to these stories while I was writing them.

Finally, I would like to thank all the experts who have taught me the nuances of migration.

References

Chapter 1: On a Persian Uru

1. 'East Indies: February 1615'. *British History Online*. https://www.british-history.ac.uk/cal-state-papers/colonial/east-indies-china-japan/vol2/pp376-389
2. 'British Era'. *National Archives UAE*, https://www.na.ae/en/archives/historicalperiods/britishprince.aspx
3. 'History of the UAE—The Official Portal of the UAE Government'. *UAE*, https://u.ae/en/more/history-of-the-uae
4. Al-Otabi, Mubarak. *The Qawasim and British Control of the Arabian Gulf* (1989). London. University of Salford International Studies Unit, http://usir.salford.ac.uk/id/eprint/14700/1/D091406.pdf

Chapter 2: This White Car Will be My Coffin . . .

1. 'What is forced labour, modern slavery and human trafficking (Forced labour, modern slavery and human trafficking)'. International Labour Organization, https://www.ilo.org/global/topics/forced-labour/definition/lang--en/index.htm

2. 'Oman Ministry Bans Companies from Keeping Employee Passports'. *Khaleej Times* (2018), https://www.khaleejtimes.com/region/oman/oman-ministry-bans-companies-from-keeping-employee-passports--#:~:text=Mohammed%20Ibrahim%20Al%20Zadjali%2C%20chairman,the%20interest%20of%20fair%20labour.%22

3. Bhatia, Neha. '1,000 Workers Arrested at Muscat Airport Project'. *Construction Week* (2015), https://www.constructionweekonline.com/article-33834-1000-workers-arrested-at-muscat-airport-project

4. https://www.unhcr.org/cy/wp-content/uploads/sites/41/2018/09/TerminologyLeaflet_EN_PICUM.pdf

5. 'WHY 'UNDOCUMENTED' OR 'IRREGULAR'?' *PICUM*. https://www.unhcr.org/cy/wp-content/uploads/sites/41/2018/09/TerminologyLeaflet_EN_PICUM.pdf

6. 'UN Expert to Europe—'Migrants Are Human Beings'—International Detention Coalition'. *International Detention Coalition – Human Rights for Detained Refugees, Asylum Seekers and Migrants*, https://idcoalition.org/news/un-expert-to-europe-migrants-are-human-beings/

7. https://www.unhcr.org/cy/wp-content/uploads/sites/41/2018/09/TerminologyLeaflet_EN_PICUM.pdf

Chapter 3: Pakistani Bhais Smuggled Majeed Out of Oman . . .

1. https://www.mea.gov.in/transfer-of-mortal-remains.htm

2. 'Question no.654 transportation of mortal remains from abroad'. *Ministry of External Affairs, Government of India* (2019), https://mea.gov.in/rajya-sabha.htm?dtl/31508/QUESTION_NO654_TRANSPORTATION_OF_MORTAL_REMAINS_FROM_ABROAD

3. 'Hardline kerala communists losing out, but party still opposes civ-nuke deal'. *WikiLeaks* (2008), Public Library of US Diplomacy, https://wikileaks.org/plusd/cables/08CHENNAI36_a.html

4. Shamshiri-Fard, Marral. 'Why Oman's Sultan Qaboos Loved Iran'. *Foreign Policy* (2020), https://foreignpolicy.com/2020/01/16/sultan-qaboos-oman-loves-iran-shah/

5. 'Cable: 09MUSCAT1067_a'. *WikiLeaks*, https://wikileaks.org/plusd/cables/09MUSCAT1067_a.html

6. Solomon, Jay. 'Secret Dealings With Iran Led to Nuclear Talks'. *WSJ* (2015). The Wall Street Journal, https://www.wsj.com/articles/iran-wish-list-led-to-u-s-talks-1435537004

7. Quinton, Sophie. 'Oman Foots $1 Million Bail to Free U.S. Hikers'. *Atlantic* (2011), https://www.theatlantic.com/international/archive/2011/09/oman-foots-1-million-bail-to-free-us-hikers/245480/

8. Makovsky, David, and Matthew Levitt. 'Keeping Iran's Feet to the Fire'. *Foreign Policy* (2015), https://foreignpolicy.com/2015/07/14/the-nuclear-deal-doesnt-mean-the-end-of-sanctions-iran

9. 'Understanding Trafficking in Persons in the MENA Region: The Causes, the Forms, the Routes, and the Measures to Combat a Serious Violation of Human Rights'. *The Protection Project*, (2013), http://www.protectionproject.org/wp-content/uploads/2012/04/Understanding-Trafficking-in-Persons-in-the-MENA-Region_Oct-2013.pdf

10. 'UAE-Oman Porous Border Contributor to Human Trafficking'. *Americans for Democracy & Human Rights in Bahrain* (2016), https://www.adhrb.org/2016/10/uae-oman-porous-border-contributor-human-trafficking

Chapter 4: My Son Is My Arabab

1. 'Oman'. *RSF*, https://rsf.org/en/oman

2. 'Oman: Freedom in the World 2018 Country Report'. *Freedom House* (2018), https://freedomhouse.org/country/oman/freedom-world/2018#:~:text=Freedom%20of%20expression%20is%20limited,if%20they%20cross%20political%20redlines

3.   OCHR-Oman, 'Press Freedom in Oman: Almost Non-Existent'.
     The Omani Centre for Human Rights (2020), http://Facebook.com/
     ochromanorg, https://ochroman.org/eng/2020/04/press-freedom/

4.   'Pranchiyettan and the Saint (2010)'. IMDb: Ratings, Reviews,
     and Where to Watch the Best Movies & TV Shows (2010),
     https://www.imdb.com/title/tt1695800/

5.   PressReader.Com, https://www.pressreader.com/oman/times-of-
     oman/20110509/281483567955730

Chapter 5: We Kidnapped Sushmitha

1.   Shaibany, Saleh. 'Lulu Supermarket Set Ablaze by Oman
     Protesters'. *The National* (2011), https://www.thenationalnews.
     com/world/mena/lulu-supermarket-set-ablaze-by-oman-
     protesters-1.566581#:~:text=SOHAR%20%2F%2F%20
     Demonstrators%20set%20a,%2C%20demanding%20
     jobs%2C%20witnesses%20said

2.   Schade, A., 'Counterinsurgency Strategy in the Dhofar Rebellion'.
     Small Wars Journal (2017), https://smallwarsjournal.com/jrnl/
     art/counterinsurgency-strategy-in-the-dhofar-rebellion

3.   'Arab world's longest serving leader leaves Oman to his cousin
     in sealed letter opened after his death'. *The Telegraph*, (2020),
     https://www.telegraph.co.uk/news/2020/01/11/sultan-qaboos-
     oman-key-western-ally-middle-east-dies-aged-79/

4.   'Little Food, No Basic Amenities In Indian Embassies' Shelters'.
     The Lede, https://www.thelede.in/inclusion/2020/01/09/little-
     food-no-basic-amenities-in-indian-embassies-shelters

5.   'Big Sums Spent on Indian Embassy Shelters but Women
     migrants Don't Get Food'. *The Lede*, https://www.thelede.
     in/inclusion/2020/04/05/big-sums-spent-on-indian-embassy-
     shelters-but-women-migrants-dont-get-food

6.   QUESTION NO.2659 COMPLAINTS FROM EMIGRANTS.
     Ministry of External Affairs (2019), https://meacms.mea.gov.in/

lok-sabha.htm?dtl/32148/QUESTION+NO2659+
COMPLAINTS+FROM+EMIGRANTS

7. QUESTION NO.2411 ILLEGAL RECRUITING AGENTS.
Ministry of External Affairs (2018) https://mea.gov.in/lok-
sabha.htm?dtl/30283/QUESTION_NO2411_ILLEGAL_
RECRUITING_AGENTS

8. The Indian Penal Code, https://www.iitk.ac.in/wc/data/IPC_
186045.pdf

9. Times News Service. 'Housemaids from Asian and African
countries 'for sale' in Oman' (2016), https://www.timesofoman.
com/article/95079/Oman/Expat-housemaids-from-Asian-and-
African-countries-%27for-sale%27-in-Oman

10. Thesiger, Wilfred. *Arabian Sands* (1959). N.p.: Penguin Classics.
1959.

11. Shackelton, Lord. 'Slavery in Africa and Arabia'. *Hansard.
parliament.uk*, 14 July 1960, https://hansard.parliament.
uk/lords/1960-07-14/debates/a3b95646-466d-487a-89b4-
4f7385d84664/SlaveryInAfricaAndArabia

Chapter 6: Even a Pakistani Can Speak Malayalam

1. Pike, John. 'Oman From the Dawn of Islam'. Globalsecurity.
org. https://www.globalsecurity.org/military/world/gulf/oman-
history-4.htm

2. Pillalamarri, Akhilesh. 'A Brief History of Balochistan'. *The
Diplomat*. 17 February 2016. Accessed https://thediplomat.
com/2016/02/a-brief-history-of-balochistan/

3. 'Soldiers and Sultans between Balochistan and Oman'. Institute
of Current World Affairs. 8 November 2017. https://www.icwa.
org/soldiers-and-sultans-between-balochistan-and-oman/

4. https://www.thelede.in/inclusion/2019/11/21/everyday-
52-indian-migrant-workers-lodge-complaints-from-gulf-
countries

Chapter 7: All Returned Empty-Handed

1. 'Migration From Kerala Declined 11% In 5 Years: Study'. 2021. *Business Standard*, https://www.business-standard.com/article/news-ians/migration-from-kerala-declined-11-in-5-years-study-118091700486_1.html
2. https://www.thelede.in/kerala/2020/03/02/1000-indian-fishermen-stranded-in-coronavirus-hit-iran
3. https://twitter.com/shashitharoor/status/1234420531929088001
4. https://www.thelede.in/kerala/2020/03/03/the-lede-impact-1000-fishermen-in-iran-get-food
5. Hebbar, Nistula. 'PM Modi Announces 21-Day Lockdown As COVID-19 Toll Touches 12'. *The Hindu* (2020), https://www.thehindu.com/news/national/pm-announces-21-day-lockdown-as-covid-19-toll-touches-10/article31156691.ece
6. 'QUESTION NO.475 INDIAN DEAD IN GULF COUNTRIES.' Ministry of External Affairs, Government of India, https://www.mea.gov.in/lok-sabha.htm?dtl/32974/QUESTION_NO475_INDIAN_DEAD_IN_GULF_COUNTRIES
7. 'COVID-19 Highlights Nurses' Vulnerability as Backbone to Health Services Worldwide'. *UN News* (2020), https://news.un.org/en/story/2020/04/1061232
8. 'Protecting Nurses from COVID-19 a Top Priority: A Survey of ICN's National Nursing Associations'. International Council of Nurses (2020), https://www.icn.ch/system/files/documents/2020-09/Analysis_COVID-19%20survey%20feedback_14.09.2020%20EMBARGOED%20VERSION_0.pdf
9. 'Coronavirus in UAE: Dubai Firm Diverts Senior Staff Salary to Feed 12,000 Workers'. *Khaleej Times* (2020), https://www.khaleejtimes.com/coronavirus-pandemic/coronavirus-in-uae-dubai-firm-cuts-management-staff-salary-to-feed-shelter-12000-employees

10. 'Prolonged COVID-19 Disruption Could Expose The GCC's Weaker Borrowers'. Accelerating Progress, S&P Global, https://www.spglobal.com/ratings/en/research/articles/200311-prolonged-covid-19-disruption-could-expose-the-gcc-s-weaker-borrowers-11382803

11. 'ILO Monitor: COVID-19 and the World of Work. Fifth Edition'. International Labour Organization (2020), https://www.ilo.org/wcmsp5/groups/public/@dgreports/@dcomm/documents/briefingnote/wcms_749399.pdf

12. https://www.thelede.in/governance/2020/03/28/undocument-migrants-at-greatest-peril-as-they-are-denied-access-to-healthcare

13. 'Vande Bharat Mission—List of Flights'. Ministry of External Affairs, Government of India, https://mea.gov.in/vande-bharat-mission-list-of-flights.htm

14. 'Embassy of India Information Collection Sheet'. Google Docs, https://docs.google.com/forms/d/e/1FAIpQLSe5f6iMNMfovllq_6q0BRao8MAXKzcnzCfCnWc9ZVLtvBLfKA/closedform

15. 'Mission Houses in Gulf Nations Should Record Indian Workers' Wage Grievances before Repatriation, Says Tharoor'. *CNN-News18* (2020), https://www.news18.com/news/india/mission-houses-in-gulf-nations-should-record-indian-workers-wage-grievances-before-repatriation-says-tharoor-2732261.html

16. 'Guidelines for Emigration Clearance System'. Ministry of External Affairs, Government of India, https://www.mea.gov.in/emigration-clearance-system.htm

17. Kuttappan, Rejimon. 'Migrant Maids in Oman at Risk as India Scraps Rescue Scheme'. *Reuters* U.S. (2017), https://www.reuters.com/article/us-india-oman-maids/migrant-maids-in-oman-at-risk-as-india-scraps-rescue-scheme-idUSKCN1BU299

18. 'World Bank Predicts Sharpest Decline of Remittances in Recent History'. World Bank, https://www.worldbank.org/en/news/press-release/2020/04/22/world-bank-predicts-sharpest-decline-of-remittances-in-recent-history

19. 'COVID-19 Crisis Through a Migration Lens: Migration and Development Brief 32'. World Bank Group, KNOMAD (2020), https://documents1.worldbank.org/curated/en/989721587512418006/pdf/COVID-19-Crisis-Through-a-Migration-Lens.pdf

20. Krishnakumar, R. 'Kerala Announces Special Project for Expatriates Who Lost Jobs in COVID Crisis'. *Frontline* (2020), https://frontline.thehindu.com/dispatches/article31964965.ece

21. Thomson Reuters Foundation. 'Nepal Families Face Hunger, Skip Meals as Pandemic Hits Remittance'. *News.Trust.Org*, https://news.trust.org/item/20200630001455-xx653

22. Patinio, Ferdinand. 'BPO Jobs Available to OFW Returnees: DOLE'. Philippine News Agency (2020), https://www.pna.gov.ph/articles/1107016

23. 'COVID-19: Protecting Workers in the Workplace: ILO Warns of COVID-19 Migrant "Crisis within a Crisis"'. International Labour Organization (2020), https://www.ilo.org/global/about-the-ilo/newsroom/news/WCMS_748992/lang--en/index.